Tales of a Catskill
Mountain Plumber

Tales of a Catskill Mountain Plumber

Allen J. Frishman

ISBN: 1523632178
ISBN 13: 9781523632176

Explanation of the Cover

The cover of the book was photographed at a bungalow colony in Woodridge, previously known as the Care Free Colony. I was looking for a unit that showed some real Catskill flavor, and I think I found it. The signs are part of my Catskill memorabilia collection.

My family's bungalow colony Hemlock Grove, became an estate after my cousins bought their own units and formed a co-op.

Route 42 is one of the main arteries through Fallsburg. This style sign is the old metal pressing that was common in the 50's.

The small sign below that is from the Sullivan County Bungalow and Rooming Association from 1952. I was lucky to find a stack of them in what I believe was the President of the organization's basement in Mountaindale. If you'd like one of these classic porcelain signs, e-mail me. I have a few left.

I would like to mention to the reader that the spelling of Mountaindale had two variations. It was written as one word and sometimes two. It was recently spelled Mountain Dale as per the 911 system. I chose what I thought was the more popular spelling from years past. This way you don't have to write me that I misspelled the word throughout the book.

Next to that is my grandfather Irving's Licensed Plumber sign that hung on his shop for many years. Yes, there was a time when a license was required to work in the Mountains. What happened was that one old-timer just couldn't pass the plumbing test, so instead of grandfathering him in, they dropped the whole thing. Plumbing then turned into the wild, wild West.

In years past, there were so many people that walked on the main roads in the concentrated areas of some of the hotels, that a sign was needed to slow down traffic. I found this rare sign in the woods near Sadownick's along the Old Liberty Road.

Swimming pool signs let prospective tenants know that they wouldn't have to swim in a lake or the cold water of a creek.

The Inter-City Bus Line was one of the popular bus companies used by many travelers in the 40's and 50's to get to the Mountains. Someone was throwing out this historic sign in Mountain Dale: one of the many stops along the way.

Kutcher's is forever gone, but I'm glad I was able to acquire this Catskill relic.

Bungalows for Rent and Now Renting are two examples of signs used to grab the prospective tenants' attention. Once the colony owners reached their goal, the sign was removed with relief letting people know they were fully rented for the season.

The last sign, which is partially worn away, is my grandfather's first companies plumbing sign. On top, but hard to read, is his name Irving, followed by Plumbing and Heating Contractor, Glen Spey, N.Y. and below that Port Jervis.

Of course, I'm the guy holding the plunger ready to do my job in my Frishman Brother's work shirt. Can you believe it's over 30 years old. That's a collectable and it still fits!

Dedication

This book is dedicated to my family, the Frishmans and the Bailins, but there are two family members in particular who were very special. The first was my grandfather Sam, who taught me so much about life. For example, if he noticed my sad face on a rainy day he'd say, "You know Allen, the umbrella man has to make money too." The second was my amazing mother, Irene, who recently passed. She nurtured my creativity and loved every project that I worked on. Goodnight Irene. You will forever be missed.

The Parts List

The Instruction Manual

When I hear someone mention the "Catskill Mountains," it triggers memories of great times growing up in the summer: first loves, first kisses, first Ruby's knishes. These memories are the common thread for all who stayed or worked here. You might be at a conference in California, or at a friend's house having dinner, when the conversation strays to the Borscht Belt. At that point, someone will mention staying in a bungalow colony one summer as a kid. You hear that person reminiscing and you remember your own experiences in the "Magical Catskills."

If you never stayed here, these were not the Catskills where Rip Van Winkle *schloft* for all those years. He didn't have Map Quest when he *plotzed* next to a tree. Otherwise he would have made it to the "Jewish Alps," where people vacationed in places like Cutlers in South Fallsburg, Breezy Corners in Monticello, or maybe Grossinger's in Liberty.

The conversation continues as you compare hangouts like the Playland Arcade, or Kaplan's on Broadway in Monticello. These were definitely the good old days. I attended a conference at Kutcher's about twelve years ago, or maybe it was thirteen. Who can remember anything at sixty four? It was sponsored by the Catskill Institute, an organization dedicated to preserving the Catskills. What an experience listening to owners of a hotel or a professional who worked in the Catskills relating their tales. That's when it hit me. "Allen," I said to myself, "You have so many funny family stories, and you know so much about the area's history. Why don't you write a book?"

I started jotting down all my family's classic tales. When I told them about the project, there was a new story told to me at every family function. Our get-togethers were like a family intervention with lots of crying, but that was from laughing so hard.

Also, my family on both sides owned bungalow colonies. This gave me what I think were added credentials in writing the book. Having lived in the Catskill's my whole life makes me a true "local yokel". I've witnessed both the hey-days and the death of The Mountains, giving me even more reason and inspiration to put together all these tales.

For me, it all began in 1951 at the Monticello Hospital. Just like all the other Baby Boomers of my generation, we were a welcome group after what had been the biggest World War in history. For the New York City folks, the Catskills, or the "Mountains" as it's sometimes referred to, became the place to go to escape the city's summer heat and cramped up life. If your family had a few coins, your parents made the trip on Decoration Day, the original name of Memorial Day, to begin the search for a bungalow to rent for the season. Once they found their summer paradise they staked their claim with a deposit. When the month of June almost ended it was time to *schlep* the whole family up to the Catskills.

Your mom and dad would be packing the car with some bare essentials as you were saying goodbye to your friends. Always included were your mother's favorite pot, some simple clothes and your baseball glove, but never a bicycle, because there wasn't any room left in or on the car. Besides, there were so many great things to do in The Mountains: lakes for swimming and boating, streams for catching frogs, trees to climb or for building tree houses, and the country roads where it was okay to sit behind the wheel in your father's lap and steer the car.

You said your final goodbye's when your mom shouted," Everyone in the car. Your dad's ready to go." Oh, I almost forgot. Your grandmother on your mother's side squeezed in the back seat along with your sister. Just before leaving, your mom would say, "Did you *pish* Leon? It's gonna be a while."

Finally, you were on the road traveling up Route 17 with its winding curves as you left the city further and further behind. After driving for a while, you could see the oasis in the distance. You could almost smell it. As you pulled in, you saw the biggest piece of fruit that mankind had ever made. Welcome to the Red Apple Rest, the official half-way point to the country. It was time to grab a burger and some fries. Oh, and of course Leon's mom saying, "Leon we're not stopping till we get to the bungalow. Make sure you *pish* again, even a little bit. It will make your mother happy."

The excitement grew knowing you were going to be in the country for two whole months. But your father wished he could have left his mother-in-law at the Red Apple for the two months. Like that was going to happen.

Eventually, after traveling another two hours, you arrived at your destination in Monticello, Liberty, Swan Lake, South Fallsburg, or Loch Sheldrake. You jumped out of the car with great excitement as you were greeted by your summer friends that were joining you for the party, and what a party it was going to be with no school. Well, maybe you had to do a little reading so you wouldn't forget how. But, even that was a joy since you got to read comic books like the latest Superman or Detective that you traded with your friends.

Let's go back to Decoration Day. The Catskills had been sleeping all winter. You couldn't just flip a switch and it all started working again. Someone had to "shake out the blankets" and plug in the Frigidaire's. That's where my family came in. It was the tradesmen like the electricians, carpenters, painters, and especially the plumbers, protectors of the throne, who got things moving again. Now, let's face it, you could deal with a leaky roof by putting a *schisel* under the drip until the owner would come with a can of tar. If the single electrical outlet in the bedroom didn't work, that was no big deal. You could run to Sabloff's in Liberty and buy an extension cord. However, when the double-basin cast iron sink got clogged, and your grandmother couldn't wash the dishes, THAT became a problem. Who used paper plates back then? And, God forbid your toilet was stopped up and your plunger didn't work. ("Leon, I told you a million times. This is the country. There's hardly any water pressure. Stop using so much paper!") This was worse than getting a speeding ticket on Route 17 during the "bull run", (the name coined by women describing their husbands' return to the Mountains on a Friday night).

My dad and his father-in-law had been plumbers in the area for nearly 50 years. My employment in The Mountains began as a plumber's helper for my dad when I was about ten years old. You see, if I wanted to be with him during the summer months, "the season" as it was referred to, I had to work with him. Besides teaching me the plumbing trade, he also taught me how to repair coin-operated washing machines that he installed in many bungalow colonies.

We were among the year-rounder's who worked behind the scenes; the people who were responsible for getting the water to flow out of the old, rusty pipes. I was fortunate that my grandparents owned two very different bungalow colonies. Sadownick's was owned by my mother's parents, Irving and Shirley Sadownick, located in Monticello on the Old Liberty Road just down from the Delano Hotel. The other was Hemlock Grove on Church Road in Mountaindale, owned by my dad's parents, Sam and Celia Frishman. It was across the road from the Hey Ru Trout Fishing Preserve.

Having two bungalow colonies in one family was unusual. Incredibly both colonies were still standing until just a few months ago. They were true monuments in the history of the Catskills. Thousands of structures had been abandoned, or succumbed to "Jewish Lightning" which is a Catskill Mountain phenomenon that I've devoted a whole chapter too. As Building Inspector for the Town of Fallsburg, I was able to enter many establishments before their removal, and saved some valuable Catskill memorabilia. Nowadays, only the occasional driveway markers or foundations are left to serve as proof of their existence.

In addition to my service work, I had performed in hotels and bungalow colonies with my teen band, "The New Generation." Perhaps you saw us perform somewhere, like in the Teen Room at Kutchers Country Club or the convention hall in the Pines? I also belonged to a comedy jug band called "Chicken Lips," which used to perform regularly in the late 70's. We gigged in such places as the Asprei Ski Chalet at the Concord Hotel, the Joker's Tavern in Mountaindale and The Loft in Liberty which was condemned years ago. They all closed. There was even a time that we played on the sidewalk in front of Murray Snyder's music store on Broadway, Monticello. Murray passed away a few years later. So you might say, wherever the Lips played, we left our mark.

I'm going to tell you that all of the stories you are about to read are pure fact. Nobody could make this stuff up. Many of the characters will be referred to as "the tenants," which was the typical reference to the seasonal dwellers. You may even know some of them like the woman from Lewinter's Bungalow Colony in Monticello who was always complaining about losing money in the coin-op washer machines. Or maybe the kids from the White Rock Bungalow Colony in South Woods, or Louie Slamowitz who owned the Ideal Bungalow Colony in Monticello. You may recognize some of the landmark locations in the stories like Lefty's, or the Lantern Chinese Restaurant in Monticello.

I need to thank the tenants and summer customers who broke all those old faucets or stuffed those toilets. Without you, this book wouldn't be possible. After setting up for the season, which began as soon as the winter weather ended, we had a "test period" which took place during the first two weeks of summer. We always had to tell the tenants, "If you sat still in an old stinky room for ten months, you wouldn't work well either for a while." The concept always made sense to the tenants, but it didn't lessen their frustration.

So with this wealth of stories, I came up with *Tales of a Catskill Mountain Plumber*. Now, sit back in your Adirondack chair (they now make them in plastic, *feh*), with a Reingold beer, a Kaplan's Hebrew-National hot dog with mustard and sauerkraut, and let's throw in a Mom's Knish. Isn't that what it's all about?

How We Got Here

How We Got to Monticello

In the late 1930's my grandfather, Irving Sadownick, was working for the owner of the International Paper Company in New York City as a plumber. The owner of the company bought the Bel-Air Hotel in Glen Spey as a summer retreat for his rather large family and his friends. Since my grandfather was so knowledgeable in a variety of different trades and also had a strong work ethic, he was asked by the owner if he would relocate for the summer and work as the Bel-Air's plumber. Irving thought that this was a great opportunity since it would allow him to take his family out of the hot city to enjoy all the amenities of the country, especially the fresh air. After working his first summer at the Bel-Air and being the enterprising young man that he was, he decided to buy his own summer home in Glen Spey. It reminded him so much of the area in Russia where he had grown up. The house that he purchased was located next to the Glen Spey Inn. It's still there, and looks just like it did back in the late 30's. But before my grandfather could purchase the building, he was given an ultimatum by my grandmother, Shirley. She would not move up to the Mountains unless he renovated the building into three apartments: one for her, and two for my grandmother's sisters', Minnie and Jennie to visit for the summers.

By this time, Irving was becoming a well-respected plumber in the Glen Spey area, but he feared that if the locals found out that he was a Jew, they would never hire him again. He never used his last name Sadownick, and was only known as Mr. Irving. Glen Spey, or "Bund Country," as it was sometimes called, actually had a Nazi training camp in a remote location deep in the woods. Because of the anti-Semitism that existed there, it was not considered a true part of the Jewish Borscht Belt. Out of ignorance, some of the *goyim* in those days actually believed that Jews had horns growing out of their heads.

On the left is Grandpa Sadownick with one of his plumbing apprentices'. His Polish helper ate black bread and raw garlic for lunch every day and never got sick. Of course he didn't have many friends either!

After he served in the Navy during WWII, a bronze plaque was placed in front of the Glen Spey Town Hall honoring the Armed Forces veterans. My grandfather's true identity was revealed after his full name appeared on the plaque with the other area veterans. The cat was let out of the bag. When some of the locals realized that Mr. Irving was a Jew, they actually tried to scratch his name off. A Jew amongst all the *goyim*... how could that have happened? After that, things started getting nasty in Glen Spey as the locals turned against him. He had already met some of the Monticello crew, like Maxie Feldman, Joe Sommers, Meyer Schachnovsky, and Harold Alport, who all suggested that he move to Monticello. The Bel-Air Hotel, where he was still doing some work, was going to be closing soon, but the final decision to move was made after one of the neighbors contaminated his water by throwing a dead animal in his well. Irving knew it was time to leave and made the move to the "big city" of Monticello. He built a brick house on Smith Street, right behind the County Courthouse, and just as in Glen Spey, because of his hard working attitude he became well known and highly sought after in Monticello. People knew that they would get their money's worth if they hired Irving.

After several years of hard work, Grandpa started to explore other businesses and considered investing in his own bungalow colony. He felt that this was where he could make some real money. My parents had recently married and settled in Monticello, and his plan was that they would share in the running of the business. He wouldn't have to hire other tradesmen for most of the work, like many of the other owners, because of the expertise in the construction field that both he and my dad had. During his search for the perfect place, he found the Spring Lake Lodge, which was an operating hotel on the Old Liberty Road, right outside of Monticello. The purchase was made, and the Spring Lake Lodge became Sadownick's in 1951, the same year that I was born.

Arrangements were made with the prior owner to leave everything behind. Right after the official closing the family went to their new property and found that half the linens, blankets, kitchen equipment, and all sorts of other items were gone. This was not uncommon in those days as often, the prior owner would try to squeeze that last dollar out of the property. Most likely, the past owner sold all the missing items for additional profit, which is what my grandfather had planned on doing. (Another common source of last minute income was having a property logged of its valuable timber leaving a huge mess behind in the once pristine woods).

There had to have been a huge, and I mean huge, inventory to begin with, because for years and years after that initial purchase there were always extra sheets, blankets and hotel dishes that circulated throughout my family. Even today, my mom will pull out an old blanket or sheet and say, "This is from the bungalow colony. Can you believe it?" Knowing how much she saved, I always answer, "I believe it. I really do!"

It was now time for Irving to roll up his sleeves and transform the hotel into a bungalow colony. This meant converting the single rooms to apartments by adding kitchens and bathrooms. He had to remove the hotel's existing kitchen and dining room to create more rental space, and convert all of the out-buildings to newly renovated bungalows. Old staff quarters were not necessary any longer. Despite the extensive project, Irving still plumbed with my dad to make sure that the steady cash flow didn't dry up. After one exhausting year, it was finally time to hang up the "Now Renting" sign.

The large "modern" steel pool was still under construction when the first couple arrived inquiring about a rental. They asked if the pool was going to be heated, which was unheard of in an outdoor pool in those days. My grandfather was extremely offended that they didn't even bother to look at the bungalows or the apartments which he had spent so much time and effort renovating. He was so upset that he asked them to leave. My grandmother Shirley said, "Irving, what did you do? We need customers." "Not like them. They'd be a pain in my *tuchas*," my grandfather firmly replied.

The following day, the Paul family came looking for a bungalow and were quite impressed by all the work that had been done. They rented a unit and remained loyal tenants up until the day my grandfather sold the property.

Interestingly enough, a few years after my grandmother Shirley passed away, Irving married Katzy Paul, a cousin of the Paul family. It's funny how things work out.

My grandmother Shirley also worked pretty hard at the colony. She could sometimes be seen single handedly *schlepping* mattresses down the three story metal fire escape by herself. She couldn't wait for someone to help her. It just needed to be done, so she did it herself. Like so many other bungalow colonies, Sadownick's had a small grocery store which my grandmother ran with help from her daughters, Rosalie and my mom, Irene. Having the grocery brought in extra income, and was a necessity for the tenants who couldn't get to town to go shopping. For my brother and me it always meant picking out something we liked to nosh on. Those bungalow groceries were the precursors of today's convenience stores.

So, together my grandparents and family ran Sadownick's Colony, just down the road from the Delano Hotel. Maybe you stayed there, or you remember seeing it while driving to Kutcher's?

How We Got to Mountaindale

Sam Frishman, my extraordinary grandfather, was working in New York City in a millinery factory on the lower East side, and just like so many other Jews in the 30's, he was dissatisfied with city life. As luck would have it, he bumped into a distant cousin, Mr. Kesten, who offered him the possibility of becoming a partner in the Chester Hill House, a small hotel on Park Hill Road in Mountaindale. The offer sounded like a wonderful financial opportunity, and a way to give the family respite from the over-crowded tenements of lower Manhattan in the summer. Grandpa knew that this was his ticket to a new and better life.

To get into this new venture, he had to invest three hundred dollars, which was not easy at the time, plus the will to work hard, which he was accustomed to. It was agreed that at the end of the season, all the profits were to be split 50-50 with the Kestens'. So, instead of making hats in the city that summer, he and my grandmother joined the ranks of Jews trying to make a buck in the Catskill Mountains.

Upon arriving at the Chester Hill, Pop became the all-around maintenance guy, being resourceful and good at fixing anything. My grandmother, Celia Frishman, was also no slouch. Being a fantastic cook landed her the job of running the kitchen. The guests and staff took an immediate liking to both of them, but particularly my grandfather. His graciousness and his willingness to help anyone at any time presented a problem for Mrs. Kesten, who grew extremely jealous of my grandfather's popularity.

Celia and Sam worked like dogs that first summer, and when it came to an end, they were disappointed that the profits were only a pittance compared to the amount that was projected. After the last guest left and they were closing for the season, Mr. Kesten said, "Sam, there's still lots of food left over in the coolers. Let's split it 50/50." It sounded like a good idea, especially since it was an expensive commodity in the late 30's. But there was one problem. Pop couldn't take his share just yet because he had to rush back to the city to marry off his daughter, Helen. He figured it would be there when he returned the following week, but when he got back to the hotel he was shocked to see that the coolers were totally emptied.

He couldn't believe his partner had the *chutzpah* to take all the remaining food. "How could he?" he thought to himself. Confused and in disbelief, he drove into town and happened to be speaking to some of the townsfolk. They told him that Kesten had asked if they wanted to buy some of the leftover food since he was having the electric turned off at the Chester Hill for the winter. They agreed, but had their suspicions of him, knowing some of his past practices. When Pop told them the real story, they felt so bad they gave him back his share of the food. The locals told him what a *gonif* Kesten could be, and that he should be careful of his shenanigans.

Sam met with his "partner" a few days later and told him that he found out what happened to the missing food. Kesten gave him some ridiculous excuse. My grandfather was about to wash his hands of Kesten once and for all, but somehow Mr. Kesten convinced him that there would be no further incidents like that ever again. He pleaded with Pop to help run the hotel, because he knew my grandparents worked hard and made the hotel a special place for the guest's. Because Pop couldn't hold a grudge and was always forgiving, he decided to take one more "chance of a lifetime" the next season.

Things were going rather smoothly at the Chester Hill, and by the third season my grandmother knew all of the regular guests quite well, especially their food requests. Maybe it was no salt or less butter in their particular dishes. But whatever it was, she made sure to accommodate their dietary needs in her kitchen.

There was one special gentleman, Mr. Schwartz, the owner of a large manufacturing business in New York City, who held a great affection for my grandmother throughout the times he spent at the hotel. Every time he came for a visit he would enter the kitchen and welcomed Mom in a loud, affectionate greeting using her Yiddish name.

"*Simca*," he would shout, which was always followed by a big hug and a kiss. This was always how his stays at the hotel began.

Unexpectedly, on the second night of one of his vacations, he was summoned back to the city due to an emergency in his factory. He quickly packed his things and immediately left the hotel. The next morning, with a saddened face, Mr. Kesten told my grandparents that Mr. Schwartz had passed away in the middle of the night. To avoid any *tummel* among the guests he had called Patty Michaels, the local policeman, and had his body properly taken away. In a rather convincing sad voice he told my grandparents that he was returning Mr. Schwartz's money to the family for the funeral. "It was the right thing to do," he explained. That would be the end of Mr. Schwartz's visits, as far as my grandparents knew.

They were truly touched by the whole event, especially my grandmother, who missed him dearly. In the early part of the next season, while my grandmother was cooking in the kitchen, she suddenly heard a voice say, "Hello, *Simca*." My grandmother nearly had a heart attack when she saw Mr. Schwartz standing there!

My grandparents couldn't believe what Kesten had told them about Mr. Schwartz passing away so unexpectedly, and the whole *schtick* about Patty Michaels plus the return of his money for the funeral. Mr. Kesten, the crook that he was, pocketed most of the money that Mr. Schwartz had to forfeit for the remainder of his vacation, and once again the truth came out. That was the final straw. It was the last season that they worked at the hotel since Kesten couldn't be trusted. After that, they started wondering just how much money he had REALLY pocketed in the past few seasons.

That winter, my grandmother bumped into Maxie Shabus' son, Pesach Shabus. (Do you think he was Jewish? He was named Pesach because he was born on Saturday during Passover). Anyway, she met Pesach outside the *Shul* where they both *dovaned* in New York City. His dad was a *launtsman* where he had known my grandmother's mother quite well. After my grandmother told Pesach about what had been going on at the Chester Hill, he immediately said, "Celia, we have to find you your own place".

The search was on. Pesach went with my grandparents to look at several old farms and small hotels that were for sale in the area. Then they found the Andrews farm on Church Road in Mountaindale. They fell in love with it immediately. I wish I could have seen Pop's face when he first saw the lake (It was actually a pond, but the lake sounds so much more impressive, doesn't it?) Understanding the value of water, even back then, he used to say, "Water is like gold." There were many other qualities of the property that he deeply appreciated, such as the grassy fields, the variety of trees and the huckleberry bushes.

It was 1941 when they found their paradise. The bank was foreclosing on the property, which helped to bring down the purchase price at about $4,000 for 77 acres. What a steal! But they still didn't have much money to their names even after working at the Chester Hill, their first "gold mine." So the arduous task began of asking all of the family members and their friends, of which there were many, if they could help them with the purchase of the property. They were loaned $10.00 from this one, or maybe it was $25.00 from that one. Finally, when it was pooled together, it enabled them to secure a big enough down payment to make their purchase of a lifetime.

Okay. Now that they bought the farm it was time to get their hands dirty. Remember Pesach Shabus? (How could you forget a name like that?) He told my grandparents to invest in raising chickens. He had become a big poultry dealer in the city, and could get them "stamps" for feed. You needed them to get anything during the war, and he was their connection. "They're easy to raise and you'll make some extra money," he professed. So, in addition to renting rooms, they purchased about 1000 chicks, a brooder and some feed. My uncle Jack Frishman, took on the responsibility of raising the chickens.

In the early years of owning the farm, my grandfather still had to make his living in the sweat-shops. Although my grandparents returned to the city for the winter, Pop and his two sons would come up quite often to check on things. Since my grandmother wasn't there, she had to make sure that all her boys had something to eat when they came up. Before leaving the Mountains, the chickens' were sold at a good profit, except for a few that were slaughtered and then "canned" in Ball jars for the winter. After the jars cooled they were stored in the cold cellar. My dad says to this day, "It wasn't the tastiest meal, but after a hard day's work, at least we had something to eat other than potatoes," which was the typical staple.

In addition to the wonderful lake that became the "swimming pool," the property had a gorgeous farm house with lots of rooms and a beautiful wrap-around porch. The building was eventually referred to as "The Main House". There were also a few out buildings like a chicken coop, a pig pen (which in later years became my bungalow, no pun intended), and the big barn. Unfortunately, after owning the property for just a few years, a huge bolt of lightning hit the barn, and it wasn't "Jewish Lightning" by any means! (Be patient, I'll explain it to you a little later on). The resulting blast was so strong that the electrical charge ran along the wiring to the main house and blew off the outside wall of a room where my dad was sleeping. Thankfully, nothing serious happened to him except for a temporary loss of hearing for a day or so. He still says that it was one of the scariest moments of his life.

While my dad was stationed in England towards the end of WW II, he had a photo of the main house in his wallet. He met a German P.O.W.'s who told him he was a painter. My dad acquired the materials he requested, and Mr. R. Bacci painted this amazing portrait of the place he loved so much. It proudly hangs in my living room.

The barn caught fire and was completely destroyed, but thank God none of the animals that were sleeping inside were injured. They all managed to get out in time which was an incredible miracle, especially since one of the horses, whose name was Nimbus, was blind. Even so, he worked really great next to the other horse in the fields, plowing with him side by side. He must have heard his buddy stirring, assumed he was leaving to get to work, had no idea that it was still the middle of the night, and followed closely behind to get out of the barn.

The fire was seen as a sign for the family, and the decision was made not to rebuild the barn. More and more guests had already been coming for a respite from the city and would stay for weekends. It was time to give up farming.

There were so many things that needed improvement: inside-plumbing, out-side-fences topside-roofing, outlets-inlets and toilets.

The original barn, like most, had been built into the slope of the land, so they were able to reuse the hand-laid stone foundation. A new winterized home with two additional apartments for rentals was constructed where the barn once stood. Now they could live comfortably in Mountaindale in the winter like *menschlachite.*

Located in the floor of the hallway of my grandparent's unit, was a trap door which led downstairs into the basement where my grandfather built a huge workshop. He could work there all thru the winter, and in the corner, on its concrete pedestal, in shiny white enamel, stood a modern wonder to all households, a Bendix washing machine. It was converted to one of my dad's first coin-operated washers that the tenants used when the bungalow days began.

On the deep side of the lake was a small wooden bridge that spanned the spillway of the man-made stone dam. After crossing the falls, the path led to the upper field that was farmed as a potato patch until the bungalow colony was introduced. Pop conveniently hired his new neighbors, the Lybolt brothers, to level-off the field with their bull-dozer. All it needed now was a simple backstop, and the old potato patch was easily transformed into a baseball field: a mandatory feature of recreation at all bungalow colonies.

When the time came to convert the farm into an official bungalow colony, the name Hemlock Grove was easily chosen because of the large stand of hemlock trees that were next to the lake. Everyone referred to this special spot as the "grove", and it became a focal point of the colony.

Under the hemlock's canopies, three hand-laid brick fire pits were constructed for use by the families for cooking their steaks or chicken. It was the customary job of the children to collect firewood for this typical weekend ritual. During the week there were more dairy meals eaten, but when the husbands came up from the city, it seemed almost mandatory to cook a few nice big steaks. It was a celebration to have reached the status of having a place for your family to enjoy in the summer, away from the city's heat. Cooking dinner outdoors also helped to keep the temperature down inside the bungalows, especially if you rented an apartment on the second story of the main house which was always hot to begin with. Remember, there was no insulation in these buildings, and who knew from air conditioning?

You could always tell when somebody had started cooking by the delicious smell of meat wafting through the premises. Typically, on a Saturday night, all three grills would be going at once with families waiting in line to take over someone else's fire. The next group of kids were already collecting branches and sticks for the fire pit to keep the "heat on" for their soon to be cooked dinner. On occasion, a branch would be brought over that was too long and it was the husband's job, after telling the kids to stand back, to smack the branch against one of the large hemlock trees. Some of the trees that are still standing in the grove today have permanent scars from breaking the firewood into those smaller pieces.

Nobody in my family was left without a job, and it became my Aunt Helen Harris's task to call prospective tenants in the winter from her apartment, and ask for deposits for the upcoming season. I guess you could say she ran the "central rental office" in Bensonhurst, Brooklyn. This of course saved lots of money because the phones calls were local. Remember, long distance calls were expensive, and every penny counted back then.

Having the natural resources of hemlock and oak trees allowed Pop to have rough cut lumber at hand for building new bungalows or any other project he was working on, but because it was war time other building supplies were hard to come by. He had a very good friend, Mr. Berman, who had connections with some of the heavies at Rockefeller Center, which was under construction at this same time that Pop was getting into the bungalow colony business. We all know that important lesson in life, "It's who you know, not what you know." Sam, along with my dad and my uncle Jack, drove into Manhattan to pick up all sorts of building materials and tools that Mr. Berman would salvage for my grandfather. One such item was a really big table saw and planner, which was used to build the entire bungalow colony. I mean this table saw was huge with an 18 inch blade. It had more than enough power to rip the biggest boards that he needed to work on. The planner allowed him to finish all the trim that was necessary to complete a window sash or maybe a door jamb on a unit.

He really appreciated all the items that he received, but Pop informed his friend, Mr. Berman, that he was experiencing a problem purchasing nails, at least at a reasonable price. Mr. Berman made arrangements with some of the main *schtockers* he knew at Rockefeller Center and told my grandfather to drive his truck to Manhattan and meet him at a certain time and location.

When Pop arrived, Mr. Berman said to him, "All the big shots are waiting for you." My grandfather had no idea what he meant by that comment. He drove down with the expectations of picking up some nails and maybe some other items thrown in, and wasn't dressed appropriately for any type of meeting. "It's a little more complicated this time Sam," Mr. Berman informed him.

They both entered a room where Pop was introduced to several well-dressed business men. The first gentleman was in charge of all the electricians working on "the Center," the second gentleman happened to be the head carpenter. You get the picture, I'm sure. Mr. Berman told the group about my grandfather struggling in the Catskill Mountains, trying to build a bungalow colony. He then asked what the group of gentlemen could do for his good friend.

The chief carpenter said that he could spare one barrel of new nails, along with a barrel of bent nails. Bent nails were saved and re-straightened by hammering them out, and then reused because of the scarcity of new nails due to the metal shortage. The head of the electricians followed suit by agreeing to give my grandfather a barrel or two of nails. By the meeting's end, he had enough nails to last him for the next twenty years. He walked into the room a poor country farmer, but walked out a king.

It was only recently that my dad told me this story, solving my age-old question of why there were so many bent nails in various cans and boxes all over Grandpa's basement shop. I could never figure out why such a good carpenter made that many hammering mistakes, and then kept the bent nails to boot! It finally made sense.

Hemlock Grove became my father's side of the family's summer retreat. It helped to keep the family together for the longest time, and was an immense source of enjoyment for all who stayed there. After I graduated from college it became my turn to get a piece of Hemlock Grove. One bungalow had been vacant for a number of years. It needed too much work for anyone to live in it, but it became a construction challenge for my brother and me. We planned to make this *facockta* unit into a year-round paradise. For starters, we gutted the structure and took part of the ceiling out to create a loft that became my room. Halfway up the stair/ladder was a platform just big enough for a small mattress that became my brother's personal space. We called it Barry's shelf. We had an antique wood cook stove that became our primary heat source. We were truly roughing it. Throughout the bungalow we hung an enormous amount of unique items from the open joist, natural wood ceiling. The walls also had on them a collage of various funky and different objects. There were so many unusual things throughout the bungalow that people called it the "Dale Museum".

Our converted unit became a popular hang-out, not only for my friends, but also for some of my relatives when they would return for their summer vacations. I was officially designated the colonies caretaker, and watched over the property all year round. (By this time my grandparents were spending their winters in Florida). As a result, vandalism was stopped, except for an occasional theft of some rhododendron branches cut in the woods without my knowledge.

The winter months were truly a fantasy with the waterfalls outside of my window providing a great source of visual stimulation. I didn't have a television, and besides, the reception was terrible. I can still remember walking into my grandparent's house and seeing them watching the TV. All they had were the few basic channels: 2, 4, 5, and 7, with a very "snowy" screen, but when my family assumed ownership of the colony as a co-op (which they now called the "Estate"), they installed a TV antenna on top of the main house. Finally there was improved reception. By this time everyone had a television and wanted a better picture. Still not being a fan of TV, I never bothered with acquiring one until I found a discarded "gutless" metal television cabinet from the Dumont Television Company lying around in back of my grandparent's house. I placed it strategically outside my window that faced the waterfalls. If a guest came to my house for a visit, and asked where the TV set was, I pointed out the window. "It's over there," I'd answer and usually got a strange look back. That was until they looked out the window and saw the TV cabinet with the waterfalls in the background. Not another word had to be spoken.

This was our bungalow in 1976 right after my brother and I installed our first woodstove. We set the stove in the basement, but we didn't have enough stove-pipe to properly run it straight up like it should have been. The chimney doesn't even come to being code compliance! We did straighten things out a few days later, and thank God we never burnt the place down.

During the late 1970's there appeared to be what may have been the rebirth of Mountaindale. Many of the vacant stores resold for ridiculously cheap prices. In most cases, the original owners had passed on, and their children had no interest in keeping their parents properties leaving Mountaindale virtually dead. This new group of spirited individuals bought many of the vacant buildings and became part of a group known as the Mountaindale Pioneers. We all did the best we could in renovating our building with the little money we had, but with help from my friend, Steve Proyect, the Building Inspector, we were allocated money from a Community Development HUD grant. This enabled us to get building supplies used to fix our newly purchased vacant buildings. The Pioneers held several annual block parties, which were huge successes. Unfortunately, there were a few old timers that wouldn't sell to other potential buyers, and that kept us from generating enough energy to create what we thought was going to be the next Woodstock.

My brother Barry is an exceptionally artistic, and was experimenting with large weavings at the time that led us into taking on the project of opening an art gallery in Mountaindale. Because we had to work our day jobs to maintain a cash flow, we usually worked through the night taking great care in restoring the vintage storefront of our new building.

I was carefully studying it's façade in the wee hours of the morning, when I fell asleep on the double yellow line in the middle of the street. Sydney Rosenthal, owner of the local dairy, was beginning to make his early morning rounds to some of the area colonies. He carefully drove up to this large item lying in the middle of the street, not knowing what it was until he got closer and leaned out the window of his old station wagon. What followed was, "Frishman, don't you have a bed to sleep on?" "Yeah, but I was checking out the building and fell asleep right here. Thanks for the wakeup call Syd," I said without hesitation. As if it was normal to fall asleep in the road.

We hadn't finished the second floor apartment when my brother took up part-time residence in what was a construction zone. I was still living with my first wife at Hemlock Grove when my grandfather Irving came to me one day and said, "You're married now and can't live like a hermit anymore in that shack. We'll finish the apartment and you'll move in so you can live like a *mensch*." Upon completion, we gave him an award which read, "Thanks for making miracles from *dreck*. It was truly well-deserved.

We left the bungalow colony as my brother moved on and we moved into downtown Mountaindale. What a huge change to be living right on Main Street. The building was five feet from the road, and our bedroom was on the second story. At night, the large trucks would come barreling down the road and we could feel the building shake under our feet, I mean under our bed. Things changed once again with the birth of my son, Chad. It became apparent that we needed to move back to the "country" for his protection by eliminating the possibility of him running into the street.

It seemed like a no brainer to buy some property from the family at Hemlock Grove. They agreed to sell me three acres along Fox Hill Road where we now lived on a quiet dirt road. There was hardly any traffic, and I was so glad we had moved back to the country.

My architectural model business was growing and I needed a larger workshop. The space that I was using in our building back on Main Street was too small, so it was time to construct a large workshop. The construction began for a new building using some of the lumber that was milled from the hemlock trees that I had cut down to provide a clearing for my new home. Dwight Baxter, a long-time resident of Mountaindale and old friend, helped me load the hemlock trees onto his trailer and transport them to a local sawmill in Forestburgh. While I was working with the hemlock boards I felt a strong closeness to my grandfather, since I was building my new shop using the same resourcefulness of the local wood just like he did.

I had the property, the materials, the skill, and the money. What I lacked was a simple piece of paper called a building permit. That's right. I was caught building a structure without a mandatory building permit from the Town of Fallsburg. Who would have thought? The funny thing was that I had just finished roughing out the building and had been laid off by my prior employer. I went down to the Town Hall to discuss my woes with the building inspector, Steve Proyect, my future boss. After a well-deserved chewing out, Steve asked if I wanted to go to work with him for the Town of Fallsburg. He knew I had an architectural education, contracting experience, and that I knew the area and its people. I was out of work and figured, "What the heck? I'll do it for a year or so."

It became twenty four years working for the Town as Code Enforcement Officer. I always say that it must have been truly *beshart* that I received that stop-work order, since it led me to where I am now.

So there you have it. I have the proud distinction of being the last remaining Frishman of the original Frishman family to still live in Mountaindale, or in Sullivan County for that matter.

Kids Just Wanna Have Fun

The Puke Machine

WARNING: THIS TALE IS GRAPHIC AND HAS EXPLICIT CONTENT WHICH
MAY CAUSE SIDE EFFECTS!

Every bungalow colony had to have playground equipment for the children. Actually, the whole place was a play area, but I am referring to the more conventional items like the shiny, metal slides with temperatures that rose to about one hundred and twenty degrees when located in the sun: real "Butt Burners". There were the swing sets with a leg that lifted out of the ground as the rider shot up in the air, and of course there was always the merry-go-round. At Hemlock Grove, the merry-go-round was no different from many others, except that in my wacky family we had a special competition. It wasn't how long you stayed on, or how fast you went, or even if you were able to climb to the center while it was spinning. No, it was who regurgitated first, and that's why it was dubbed "The Puke Machine."

Now don't get me wrong, it did have its regular hours of usage for general entertainment. But after dinner, when all the kids were hanging out, someone would suggest going on the puke machine, and that's when the evenings' excitement began. The question was who was going to be the first one to lose it tonight?

We'd all get on, except for the designated pushers, who were usually the kids who had a light dinner and were not that susceptible to the eventual outcome. The merry-go-round would start up with riders hanging on for dear life. There was no room at all for any more kids. Round and round it would spin, waiting for that first burst of dinner to repeat itself. To hasten things up a bit, the "pushers" would stop and reverse the merry-go-round in the other direction. After a few minutes, if no one gave in, or gave it up as the case may be, a chant would start: "Puke, Puke, Puke, Puke," over and over again. There had to be some psychological effect that the chant would signal the brain, because this always brought on our winner of the evening. You always had to keep an eye on your neighbor making sure to get out of the way if need be. On one momentous night, a young lady (and yes, this game was not reserved for the boys only), let loose a spew that left everyone gasping for air. We never found out what she ate for dinner that evening, but it was so bad that the merry-go-round had to have a wash down after that episode. The reason I went into such detail with the last event was not to gross you out, but to prepare you for the next tale. So if you're a brave reader, keep going. It gets better.

On the puke machine at Sadownick's. The riders L to R: Grandpa Irving holding my brother Barry, "Little" Irene Needleman behind him, me, and I don't know why or how I got away with sticking out my tongue, and Sheila Needleman holding her daughter Andrea.

Originally, the playground area at Hemlock Grove was next to the laundry room, but this spot was now needed for a new pool. Having a lake on the property, before there was air conditioning, was the big draw for beating the summer heat, but eventually swimming pools became a necessity with pressure from both the tenants and the Department Of Health. New signs were going up all over the mountains to announce the big attraction: modern swimming pool. Modern was put in to differentiate between a filtered pool or the earlier kind which were cement-wall-lined, creek fed, always ice-cold water, swimming holes. My grandfather had to find a new location for the playground. He obtained a second swing set and a higher slide *Hoo-Hah* (not a real Yiddish word but used by the tribe to mean 'Oy, such a big deal'), and moved the new equipment about thirty feet from its original site, putting the play area closer to the old cesspool.

That was the standard sewer system back then. Remember, I'm from a plumbing family so I know about this stuff. These early sanitary sewer systems were stone-lined hand-dug holes which were usually covered with big logs, or even better, discarded railroad ties. (The discarded ties were all along the abandon railroad beds from the closing of the O&W Railroad. It was easy for the locals to grab them for their needs). Wood planks were laid on top of them to help cover and seal the hole with a final earthen covering used to hide it all and to contain the smell. Houston, we may have a problem. While everyone was playing on the swings and running around the slide, one of my cousins ran a bit too far to the right, stepped in just the exact spot where some of the planking had begun to rot, and instantly dropped into the awaiting cesspool. This could have turned out to be really, really, serious. Thank God, he only went up to his waist because it wasn't that full yet of… Well, you know. The laughter that followed became hysterical as he climbed out of the pit. That baby was ripe and so was my cousin as he made his way back to his bungalow. Wow, was that a night and a smell to remember!

Sex Education 101

Now don't get all excited about the title because the event took place when I was about eleven years young. My parents were letting me stay for the weekend at Hemlock Grove, my favorite treat when I was growing up. I was going to be "vacationing" with my cousin Marty Fox. His bungalow was modest, with a tiny open porch, small kitchen/dining/living room, and one large bedroom that had three beds: one for his parents Harry and "Nurse Mary", his sister Arlene, and one for Marty that we were sharing that night.

The young kids planned a Friday night camp fire located next to the creek. Some of the mothers donated hot dogs, and some a loaf of wonder bread, while others provided us with marshmallows, a main ingredient at any campfire. Then there was the most important item needed, a pack of matches. They probably weren't given to us, but since so many of our parents smoked cigarettes, they were quite easily obtainable.

As nighttime was nearing, some of us gathered by the "Big Rock" which really wasn't so big, but became a land mark as the entryway into the woods. This was not going to be a boy's only night but a co-ed camp fire. A bunch of girls also met us at the designated location, and off we went on our adventure. Little did I know what lay ahead. We crossed the bridge over the creek, and we started smelling the distinct pungent odor of wood burning. Some of our friends had *schpelkis*, and left a little earlier to start the fire. We could see the glow of the flames in the distance through the trees as we walked ever closer to our final destination. We picked up fallen branches as we entered the camp circle and threw them on the fire, making the flames crackle and jump almost twelve feet high. Not the safest thing to do, but we honestly didn't know better. Hey, I wasn't a building inspector yet! As the flames started to die down we began cooking our incredibly nutritious dinner.

After getting full from the hotdogs, marshmallows, and a bottle of Orange Mission Soda, it was time for some storytelling and then game time. Now, I'm not referring to monopoly, which was the favorite board-game at Hemlock Grove. No, I'm talking about SEX games! You know, like spin the bottle or seven minutes in heaven. Well, it was my turn and I had to step up to the plate. I don't remember exactly which game we were playing at the moment, but I had to kiss Barbara E., which wasn't a bad thing, only I was REALLY quite shy. So we stepped off into the woods for a little privacy, and the kissing started.

But what kind of kiss was she giving me? She kept trying to push her tongue into my mouth. What the heck was that all about? "Don't you know how to kiss on the lips?" I kept thinking to myself. After a few more unsuccessful attempts of trying to open my mouth with her tongue, she gave up and that was it. We went back to join the rest of the group, some of whom had begun their own little rendezvous in the surrounding woods. A few hours passed and it was time to get back to the colony. I just kept thinking how weird it was how Barbara kept trying to push her tongue into my mouth.

When we got back to Marty's bungalow, my Aunt Mary asked us if we had fun, and we both blurted out in unison, "Of course!" It was time to hit the sack and after peeing in the toilet together (that was a cool thing for boys to do when we were young), and washing up, we crawled into his small bed while listening to the crickets and the cicadas singing outside. No one else was in the bedroom yet, so we quietly started whispering about the night's events. Naturally, I brought up the tongue thing that happened with Barbara. Marty proceeded to tell me how that was the way adults kissed with their tongues. I couldn't believe it! I was shocked. "Really? " I said. "Yep. That's what they do," he replied convincingly. "Hey, be quiet in there boys," was the next thing I heard. So I turned over and fell fast asleep.

At the next campfire, I was ready to take on the challenge. This time, when another young lady and I were chosen to kiss, I was quicker than she was to touch tongues. You know, it really felt good! I guess I paid attention during my first sex education class, since this young lady commented on how good a kisser I was! Thanks, Marty.

Mendel's Mansion & the Secret Secret

At every bungalow colony it was a young boy's responsibility to build a treehouse, more commonly referred to as the "fort." Even today, I see them being built and sometimes I wonder how they stay together. Thank God they're small enough that they don't require a building permit. The materials used to build these

Cousin's Ricky Harris, left, and Marty Fox after a successful
huckleberry picking expedition. (Huckleberries are wild blueberries).
We had a name for the really big ones, *bumbas*.

masterpieces came from the scrap wood that was left over from the owner's various construction projects. It was an unwritten rule to never throw anything away
that could be used in the future. A small piece of plywood or a cut off piece of 2X4
could come in handy for another job. Generally these left over pieces were simply
tossed under an adjoining bungalow, which became the norm at Hemlock Grove.

My earliest recollection of a fort was built by my older cousins Robby (who later
became the master architect of Mendel's Mansion), Freddy, and Gary along with
their close companions from the colony at Hemlock Grove. To reach it, one first had
to cross the creek over a new hand-made bridge, which in itself was an engineering
marvel. And there on the other side amidst the blooming rhododendron shrubs,
was the most incredible structure I had ever seen. It was built with white birch saplings nailed to the many hemlock trees that formed the outer perimeter. There were
scraps of plywood used for closing some of the bigger openings amongst the saplings, and hemlock branches were carefully laid on top to form a dense cover for the

roof. What a great *succa* this could have been! It was picture perfect as it stood out in the woods with its' white walls. They called it the Secret Secret.

It was off limits to girls and supposedly well-hidden, but the young ladies at the colony knew exactly where it was located! So along with my younger cousins, Ricky, Stevie, Mikey, Marty, and some of the tenants like Pauly Rosenblatt, (it seemed like almost everyone back then had their names followed with a Y except for me), decided that we needed our own fort since we were too young to hang with the older guys. So we found a location along the lake's edge that was heavily wooded and closer to the colony. It wasn't the greatest, but it did have one unique feature. It had a small walkway of earth held together by the large roots of a hemlock tree that hung over the lake. We could walk to the end of this earthen protrusion, hang on to a tree and easily pee into the lake. There was something about peeing in the lake that was just the coolest.

In the summer of 1957 there was a record breaking hurricane with torrential rains and wind, and the Secret Secret, that was located next to the creek, succumbed to this devastation. This great hideout washed away along with the bridge over the creek. So, it was back to the drawing board. It was now my younger cousins turn to build a new fort in the woods. But first on the agenda was reconstructing a higher and longer bridge. Cutting down the logs was the easy part. The more difficult challenge was getting the two main logs across the creek and setting them in place. We enlisted the services of our dads to help with this part of the project. After the bridge was constructed, we built a tree house to avoid the flooding issue. The fort had a metal bucket (remember, plastic buckets weren't made yet), with a pulley system to bring up provisions such as lunch. Typically we would have a Yoo-Hoo and tuna fish sandwiches made with Miracle Whip. It was easier than carrying things up the rickety ladder. This was the fort's uniqueness-the pulley system.

The older boys still wanted a new fort for themselves after the demise of the Secret Secret. The ultimate clubhouse (not a fort), was to be constructed at Hemlock Grove and it was named Mendel's Mansion. Nobody knows where the name came from since there was no one named Mendel in the family, but the clubhouse was definitely a tribute to the name! Do you remember seeing clubhouses on the "Little Rascals" episodes? That was the same caliber of construction. And don't forget, those were built by studio carpenters.

Now, taking on this endeavor was no easy task. There had to be construction materials made available, such as real wood planking rather than the abundant saplings, scrap plywood, or trees used in all the other forts for wall construction. There would also be a tremendous amount of nails needed to hold the new clubhouse together. And who would be the construction supervisor in charge of this mammoth project? They needed someone with vision, someone with construction knowledge, someone who could actually use a saw. My cousin Robby was nominated for this daunting task. Not only did he know how to pull planks off Grandpa's lumber pile without him noticing, he also knew how to sneak into the basement to borrow nails for the project. He hid in the bushes to see where Pop kept his specially made "key" so he could get past the iron vault door into the basement workshop where the nails were stored. (This was no ordinary locking device. It had to keep intruders out of the basement during the time my grandparents were in Florida. This device truly needs some explaining).

Pop was inventive and figured a standard lock could be smashed or shot off. He designed a steel bar with notches that could only be slid to the side with a special right angle hook that he made from a small diameter steel rod. It went into a small hole through the thick wooden door, grabbed the notched steel bar and when turned to the right, the steel bar slid and the door could be pushed open. Without the special hook, you couldn't open the door if your life depended on it since the steel bar acted like a cross bar, similar to the ones the knights would drop into place in the old castle doors. This was sort of a modern, mechanical version. Sorry to digress, but it was such a cool lock.

Remember those barrels of bent nails Pop had picked up in Rockefeller Center? Who knew their true purpose was to be used on Mendel's Mansion? Pop could never figure out why the nails kept disappearing. He kept the shop locked to keep the tenants and the rest of the family away from his tools and many other items, (but of course that didn't keep Robby out!)

The location of Mendel's Mansion was also critical. All the other forts were con-structed deep in the woods. But this time, someone said, "Let's build it close to Pop's wood pile and the basement shop". This way the construction crew, I mean my cousins, didn't have to *schelp* all the building materials through the woods. It was conveniently built about fifty feet away from my grandfather's wood pile, right at the edge of the woods. (Sam bartered his resource of timber with a local logger, and instead of getting paid, he received a nice pile of rough cut lumber of different sizes. When the boards were delivered, Pop would carefully stack the wood behind his workshop). He knew all along what the kids were doing, and approved of it knowing they were having a good time, which was paramount to his way of thinking.

Grandma Frishman looks like she's standing guard in front of the wood pile. I'm sure she's probably helping my grandfather stack the wood so it would air dry. These were freshly cut planks that were milled from the hemlock and oak trees on the property. It turned out to be great lumber if it was used within the first few years, but as it aged it became extremely hard to penetrate. Many years later, if I was working in someone's bungalow, I needed to use cement nails because the lumber was as hard as steel.

Mendel's had some surprisingly modern features, like running water which came from a large open six foot diameter tank that was somehow lifted on the roof. (Nobody can remember how it was done, so it will remain a mystery like the building of the pyramids). It collected rain water that was plumbed to a faucet into an old cast iron kitchen sink. Its height was designed low enough to be able to use it as a pissing trough. This was really convenient since you didn't have to go outside to take a leak. This was living large! There was also a small attic space into which you could crawl and look down at whoever was knocking on the front door. The roof was also made weather proof with old shingles and scrap tar paper. Mendel's Mansion was built so well that on more than one occasion, when the colony was over rented on a weekend, my grandmother shared a bed with her daughter Helen, and Pop would sleep in Mendel's on a cot. This was done so they could rent their own bedroom for a Saturday night. Remember, if you could make an extra buck renting your own bed for a weekend guest it had to be done. Mendel's lasted for many years until an old maple tree crushed and destroyed what was undeniably the most remarkable clubhouse built in the mountains!

So what was the second most important activity that we enjoyed as kids growing up in the mountains? Constructing go carts!

It was Passover, 1958, and the family was staying at Hemlock Grove in observance of the holiday. My younger cousins and I had just finished a grueling game of Monopoly. During this marathon, there was only one interruption: breakfast, which of course was Matzo Brie. At the conclusion of our game the command went out from our parents, "It's turning out to be a real nice day. You kids go outside and play." That meant one thing: go carts! Not the motorized kind, but the building of customized "street illegal" vehicles.

Our first step was to go to the old colony dump. Back then, every property owner just threw things out wherever they could, and left the items to rot. We had a plethora of junk to pick from. Damaged furniture occasionally yielded custom wood pieces that were used for detailing. A discarded tin can might wind up as "tail light". An old water pump part might be used for a steering component. Inevitably, the most valuable items in the junk pile were the baby carriages, because they supplied the wheels and axles. That particular morning we found two carriages with different sized wheel assemblies. The smaller set went on the rear of the cart giving it a "pumped up" look. The larger set was built into our steering bar. We were lucky enough to have found an old license plate that we put on the back of the cart for added authenticity. Now let's not forget the brakes which consisted of a wooden handle strategically located in line with the rear wheel. To slow down, you pulled back on the pivoted bar which put resistance against the wheel of our latest contraption.

After working on this baby for two hours it was time to go on a trial run. We started on the small hill located in the middle of the colony to make sure that our cart wouldn't fall apart. Several runs later it was time for the real deal.

We took the go-cart onto Church Road right in front of the bungalow colony. This would give us a much longer and smoother ride. It became my turn, along with my cousin Ricky, to take a shot. As we started our adventure on the road, a large truck came creeping up behind us. We steered towards the side of the road allowing the truck to pass. The only problem was the truck's contents. It was hauling a fresh load of chicken manure from Suchovolsky's egg farm on Taylor Road. In those days there was no code regarding the transporting of this waste product, so as the truck went by, the splish-splash of the manure in the rear of the dump truck flew out of the open hopper and landed on the two of us.

We pulled off on the side of the road and realized what had just hit us. Our run was cut short as we dragged the go-cart up the road, back to the rest of my cousins who had witnessed what had happened. All of them were appropriately holding their noses, and there was a heck of a lot of laughter and teasing. What was even worse was that we knew the poop was REALLY going to hit the fan when we saw our Moms. We slowly entered the main house expecting the worst, but instead the laughter continued, since they just happened to be outside when the truck drove by the colony. They knew exactly what had happened to us. It was time for a quick shower. (To save money, Pop constructed made them out of water proof asbestos panels, which is now considered a hazardous material, but we lived). We changed our clothes, and back outside. Of course the cart also needed a good washing to get rid it of its awful smell.

A few days later when I returned to the colony, everyone was talking about riding the go-cart down Snake Hill. This is a section of Church Road that has switch back curves as you go downhill. It's really a hell of a ride on a bike, but this would be a momentous experience on our go-cart. Which of my cousins was going to be the first to accept this challenge? After several rounds of, "Once, twice, three, shoot," guess who won? That's right, Ricky and I. Now that was luck.

We all walked slowly to the top of Snake Hill and looked down its menacing length. At that moment it looked pretty scary, but what could go wrong with my fearless co-pilot aboard? We hopped on and had no need for an extra push start, the usual operating procedure. Off we went, racing down towards the first curve. Everything was going smooth as silk. What a great run this was turning out to be. But wait, something was wrong, really wrong, as we entered the second turn!

There in the middle of the road was one of Adee Budd's cows. It had slipped under the barbed wire fence looking for that greener pasture on the other side of the road. The problem was she hadn't gotten there yet, so what were we going to do? In matters like this, your co-pilot is there for assistance. Ricky instantly pulled back on the brake stick, but he pulled so hard that the brake handle flew off the cart! I shouted, "Oh man we're dead!" We still had a short distance to go before our inevitable collision. "Shoe brakes"! Ricky yelled, and instinctively we both thrust out our legs and used our sneaker heels on the rough pavement to help slow us down. At that same moment the cow decided to resume walking across the road as we deftly swerved around the huge heifer. It was absolutely incredible. Our driving skills were unsurpassed. We finished our ride and looked up the hill to see everyone applauding us this time. Redemption is sweet, and we deserved it after the other days manure mishap!

We are getting ready to test drive our new go-cart at Hemlock Grove before considering Snake Hill. L to R: Cousins Mikey Frishman, me (I'm holding the Israeli flag), Stevie Frishman (brake man), and Ricky Harris (steering).

As we continued building these simple wooden vehicles, my older cousin, Robby Bailin was learning the workings of gasoline engines at Carnesi's Garage. They loved having him there, and after a while he had the run of the place. He was ready to build his own motorized go-cart but needed a starting point. He looked at several discarded lawnmowers behind grandpa's shop, and chose the one with the most potential. Somehow he pushed it by himself almost 900 feet to Carnesi's. He was about to put all his newly acquired knowledge to the test. He constructed a motorized single seat go cart from scratch using Pop's lawnmower as the foundation. What a thrill it was when he started riding it around the garage. He jumped off for a second to make an adjustment, left the cart running, pulled back a lever that disengaged the clutch, and ran inside to grab a tool. As it was idling, somehow the handle fell forward and the clutch re-engaged. The cart took off by itself and took a hard left turn. It was heading directly towards a vehicle that was being gassed up at the pumps. There was a loud smashing sound as Robby's contraption somehow got itself jammed under the front bumper of the customer's car. Thank God no one got hurt! Everyone came running out of the garage to see what had happened. The customer had no idea why his car shook, and immediately put the hose back in the pump and ran to front of his car. The guys in the shop couldn't help laughing, but the customer started screaming at Robby in English and Yiddish, "That's my lawnmower! You stole my lawnmower, Robertal!" The laughter was so contagious, and since there was no damage to the car, Pop just let it all go because he was so good natured.

Moving ahead, it's now 1963. Robby had moved into our home to work with my dad. His obsession for working on cars had continued to grow as he was in the process of customizing a 1953 Chevy that he had just bought. The body work was completed but now he had to find the right color. As my dad and Robby entered the supply house for some plumbing supplies, there was a display rack of industrial spray cans of this funky purple color that was on sale. "Looks like I found what I needed for my car Hy," Robby said to my dad. He bought a case of the spray cans and that evening, with lots of excitement and energy, he began the spraying process in our garage. After it was completed he came into the house and announced how great the car looked. We all checked it out and he was right. It was a really cool paint job that looked great. The following day when he pulled the car out of the garage for its first test drive, it all went downhill. The paint started cracking as the sunlight hit it. It must have been the first crackled paint job on a car in Sullivan County. Even with the custom paint job, he also wanted something really different in the interior too. In my dad's shop, he found an old brass bathroom faucet, and with all his plumbing knowledge, it made sense to have running water coming out of the dashboard. By hooking up an air tank in the trunk for pressure, the old brass faucet made a comeback. It looked outrageous and worked great until it started dripping, after which it was simply moved outside to the rear fender. What could say "Catskill Mountains" better than a cheap but acceptable paint job and a leaky faucet?

Helpful Tip #1- Make sure your wearing new sneakers before riding on a home-made go-cart. It could mean the difference between life and death.

The Curse of Abram Wood

A short distance from Hemlock Grove was the intersection of Church and New Road, which we affectionately referred to as the "four corners". Because of the increased summertime traffic, a yellow and red flashing light blinked religiously in years past. (I can't lie; the light was sometimes used as a target for stone throwing). On the other side of the property was a quiet dirt road called Fox Hill. If you didn't feel like crossing the bridge over the dam, you could use this path to get to the baseball field. Kicking stones and telling stories was part of the hike when we walked to the end of Fox Hill to visit the haunted house. There wasn't much left of this once happy home, but it made for interesting tales told by my cousins and friends.

Fox Hill Road separated our two small lakes with a seven foot steel pipe that we called the tunnel. The smaller of the two became our favorite spot for "skiffing". You know, that's how you skip flat stones across the water. If there was a group of us hanging out, and we were in competition mode someone would yell something like, "Did you see that '5z' go?" It took real skill to get multiple bounces.

We'd sometimes hang over the tunnel, and yelled into the pipe listening to the echoes that it created. And what could be better than to row the boat that was appropriately named the Hy-Jak, after my dad and Uncle Jack, through the tunnel. That was forever cool!

My Aunt Helen Harris with her two daughters, Barbara in her lap and Diane, seated in the HYJAK. Directly behind them is the bridge over the dam and waterfalls.

There was also the stream or some called it the creek, and all the surrounding woods which became my favorite places to play as a kid. It was a true paradise except for one spot that scared us to death, and always gave us the willies. That was the infamous Hillside Cemetery. It was just up the road from the bungalow colony and contained numerous old gravestones. It hadn't been maintained for years, so its abandoned appearance made it quite eerie. In fact, in my entire lifetime, or my cousin's, which was only about eleven years, we'd never once seen, or even heard of any burials there. I think this helped make the Hillside even creepier than most. It was about this time in our lives that we all had the occasion to meet Mr. Wood. Now, before I go into detail about him, I'd like to tell you how perfect the cemetery was for a scary movie backdrop.

My cousin Morris Bailin, who was very artistic, made a family film starring his two children, Freddy and Gary, and our cousin Marilyn using the Hillside as a prop for their ghost story. It was filmed several years prior to meeting Mr. Wood. So by now you might be asking yourself, "Who is this Mr. Wood?" He wasn't the cemetery's caretaker or a seasonal visitor, but a permanent resident of the Hillside Cemetery.

One grey day, a few of us decided to take a walk up Church Road and stopped in front of the Hillside for no special reason. We all started talking about nothing in particular, but soon the direction of our conversation was about how a person would be cursed for life if he pushed over a grave stone. Now, at this gullible young age, some of this conversation sounded very reasonable. Who knew? Now, before you could say, "Hemlock Grove", all of us slowly started climbing up the moss covered stone steps to the gravesites.

Standing on the grounds of the cemetery, that weird feeling began to sink in and there was dead silence. (Good one, right?) Finally, someone reopened the talk about the gravestone curse, and before long one of my cousins was put to a dare. He shall remain nameless since I am not sure if the statute of limitations has expired for this deed of vandalism. But after the relentless badgering by everyone present, and his reluctance to believe the other kids that there could be such a curse, he placed his two hands at the top of the gravestone, leaned against it, and with one mighty push he triumphed; it came tumbling over! Everyone jumped back as the gravestone hit the ground with a thud. A dust cloud ensued as we were all still in disbelief that he took us up on the dare. The owner of this sacred head stone belonged to a war hero named Abram Wood. Thankfully, nothing happened to my cousin after he pushed the gravestone over and we were all very relieved. Maybe the curse was just a *"bubba micea"* that someone had made up. What we didn't know was the power that even a pretend curse could hold! It was much, much more then we could have known.

The following morning, everyone woke up to gather on the front lawn to raise the American flag and enjoy another great day in paradise. Someone asked, "Where's Melvin?" He was nowhere to be found. So we went to his bungalow, knocked on the screen door, and asked his mom where he was. She said that he came down with a strange illness during the night and would have to stay in bed all day. It was at that moment that we all looked at each other and realized he had succumbed to the "Curse of Abram Wood." That really put the fear of God in us to ever enter the Hillside Cemetery again. Until this day, I do not think that any of us have ever gone back there.

Many years later, when a new home was being constructed on the lot adjacent to the cemetery, I had to perform an inspection for Paul Lucyk, the owner. While I was standing on his front stoop that overlooked the cemetery, I could feel the presence of Abram Wood lurking over my shoulder. Paul saw me looking into the cemetery and said," I have very quiet neighbors." I turned to him and replied," I don't know about that."

To Day Camp... We're Marching One by One

Most of the Catskill baby-boomers, like myself, attended day camp. It was a key amenity necessary for all the larger colonies and hotels, and was really the unofficial baby-sitting service. At the colonies, if there was a food concession, the kids could buy the campers' lunch of the day. That way the moms didn't have to prepare that meal, which gave them more free time to hang out with their Bungalow Bunny friends. What a relief! The husbands were in the city and the kids were being watched by the senior counselors, or maybe a C.I.T. (Counselor in Training).

One thing that all the resorts had in common was that they each had their own theme song which was passed down from season to season. Sometimes, the composers were a collective group of counselors who had to write a song for their camp play, or a tenant who had musical abilities and loved the place. The songs that were written were generally about the guest's wonderful experiences.

This first one was told to me by David Herskowitz who stayed at Lewinters' Bungalow Colony in Monticello, located right behind Lefty's Restaurant. By the way, David, it must have been a killer smelling that good food cooking all the time. Here goes:

We welcome you to Camp Lewinters'....... We're mighty glad you're here

We'll set the ground reverberating.............With a mighty cheer
We'll push you in...... We'll pull you out.....For you we'll give a mighty shout
Hail, hail, the gang's all here......................Welcome to camp Lewinter's

Hotels also had their share of tunes. When I told Ted Drew, attorney and friend, about the book, he shared this ditty that he remembered singing as a kid while staying at the Nasso Hotel in Mountaindale.

Come to the Nasso, the Mountains' best hotel........Come to the Nasso, where everything is swell
Take the pool, take the rooms, take the food...........We love every dish,
Especially Mrs. Hoenig's Gefilte Fish.........................Come to the Nasso,
Hear everybody tell, take a rest with the best at the Nasso Hotel

Several years ago I had the pleasure to speak at a meeting for the Seniors of South Fallburg. My topic was the Borscht Belt, what else? At my presentation's conclusion several people came to me with the songs they remembered at places where they had vacationed. Sally Israel Massarsky stayed at Zager's Farm in Mountaindale, and remembered this tune.

Come one Come all, Come along
Come to Zager's Farm, and hear our song
Take out your chewing gum, and stick it to the floor
And I'll tell you a story, you've never heard before.

Nobody ever said the songs had to make sense, they just had to rhyme. Mike Gastwirth, when he first met his wife at the Arcadia heard this song that all the guests were singing.

In the Arcadia Lake Hotel............ Where everything is swell
With a high di dill ho-ray............ Arcadia Lake Hotel

I recently met Eve Minson at a dinner party and the subject of the Catskills came up. She had worked at the Homowack Hotel in Spring Glen during the late 70's, and when I mentioned the book, she started singing:

Homowack, Homowack,.............. where happy people come, to have a lot of fun... ....Oh Homowack.

It was sung to the tune of Camelot. There's more, but like most of us that's all she could remember.

Another song that was sung to me by my Aunt Helen was written by Hemlock Grove's long time tenant, Florence Balch. There is a fabulous photo of her packing up for the summer in "Labor Day, It's All Over". This one was written to the tune of "Fernando's Hide-Away."

There is.... A place..... In Mountaindale, You go... there strong...and come home frail
We go.... There for.... A summer's stay, It's known...... as Frishman's Kuchalaine

Unfortunately, that's all that she could remember.
The popularity of the current movies and their theme songs was a great starting point for a day camp song. The counselors used the tune "Bridge Over the River Kwai," a huge hit in the late 50's, for a Sadownicks' camp song.

To day camp....we're marching one by one.... At Sadownick's...we're having so much fun
The counselors...... they make you happy........ You wish you never have to go home

And just like some of my friends, I too can't remember any more of the song.

This is the typical group shot that was taken at every large bungalow colony of
their day camps I am standing furthest right on the fourth row with that great
smile. My aunt, Rosalie (Sadownick) Cohen, is directly behind me. Directly in front
of me, third row, was my best friend Eugene Gorelick. My brother, Barry, is second
from the right on the second row sitting next to my cousin, Andrea Needelman.

Now the truth of the matter was that I wasn't always having fun. I didn't like
swimming in the pool and I wasn't into sports much since I wasn't that great
an athlete, but when it came to the camp's annual play or building the haunted
house for the camp carnival, I was there!

I had an advantage over my fellow campers since I lived in Monticello, and could
build things in my house for these extravaganzas. Remember, I wasn't "visiting" the
Mountains like all my summer friends. As my senior camper experience was coming
to a close, someone in the group suggested that we convert the day camp building

into a haunted house and charge admission for our efforts. And for one day, the most cheerful of all the structures at Sadownick's, with its multi-colored interior of campers' signatures and tempera painted hearts with lovers' names, became the most frightening exhibit of horror that the Catskill Mountains had ever seen. At least we thought so, and so did the little kids in the colony who were too scared to even enter. Just by blocking out the sunlight to darken the inside of the building, adding a few small fans to move the air, and attaching strings and fabrics that were hung from the open rafters, we created a creepy, crawly, haunted house.

Some of my friends were dressed like typical monster characters, made up to look scary with their moms' makeup. I needed something way more creative with action for my character, and since I had just finished reading some of Edgar Allen Poe's short stories in school that year, I chose "The Pit and the Pendulum." I built a simple device that consisted of a 2 x 4 bolted from the ceiling, and a nice shiny silver blade made from cardboard and aluminum foil. Let's face it. A real blade wasn't going to cut it, no pun intended. I made it look authentic with the tip covered in ketchup: the blood of choice. It looked great as it swung from side to side, especially the ketchup-I mean the blood that was dripping from the blade passing just above my belly. With my added sound effects, I could scare the bejezzes out of our guests!

Our host, Michael, I mean "Dracula", told our visitors how he got rid of bad campers by cutting them up into little pieces and then feeding them to the animals in the woods. All the while he was repeatedly swinging the blade and emitting a ghoulish laugh. Everything was going great for about the first hour until someone found out that it was ketchup and not real blood that we were using. It wasn't the parents or the kids in the colony. No, it was the flies. Of course there were always flies in the over-heated, non-air conditioned day camp building, with its dirty floors from kids dripping ice cream at break time that had never been mopped. What I didn't know was that day the flies were having a convention, and my stomach, with this ketchup treat, had become their smorgasbord. I couldn't take it any longer.

It was getting too intense. What were we going to do? Camp paint to the rescue! We used the same tempera paint that was all over the inside of the building. I quickly washed off the ketchup as Larry Kornbloom and Eugene Gorelick liberally applied the washable red paint to the blade and to my revived chest. The show went on without any more glitches.

At Sadownick's there was a structured day camp, like most of the other large bungalow colonies. Therefore, the camp events were expected. Maybe because Hemlock Grove didn't have such a formal day camp, they made up for it at their unsurpassed annual carnival. It truly was like no other that was held throughout the Mountains. Not only did the colony's tenants and family members look forward to this spectacular event, but all the surrounding colonies in the area made sure to attend this amazing festival.

Everyone in the family had their own specific job. For example, my uncle, Aaron Harris, who was a comedian at heart, would purchase all the prizes needed, which seemed like a truck load of toy store yo-yo's, paddle boards, dominoes, kids' tricks, magnets, jacks, you name it, in New York City. Cousins George and Dave Bailin belonged to the electrical union and would create some sort of mechanical gadget where the players needed skill to win a prize. One of those crazy devices was the mechanical hand. George acquired it from a department store when they were going to throw it out, but he saw its true potential. The hand, with its long delicate fingers, had its palm face-up, allowing you to place an item on it for display. When the motor was turned on, it would slowly lift up and down by the joint in the elbow and would catch your eye. To make this hand an integral part of the carnival, a plastic Crowley's sour cream container was attached to the hand's palm. The object of the game was to toss a ping pong ball, or a Spalding pink into the moving cup. Those of a slightly smaller physique were allowed to toss the ball from close range, resulting in becoming a prize winner. That was the real objective of the carnival; all the kids were winners!

Now, for the real gamblers we had a numbers wheel. Players put their pennies on a number, one thru sixty, on the table, and if it came up on the wheel, they took everyone else's pennies. It was the first real casino in the Mountains. (And would you believe I still have that wheel)?

You could always find my aunt, Mary Fox, and cousin, Ceil Bailin, behind the roaring propane gas burners that were boiling huge pots of water. One was filled with delicious hot corn and the other with hotdogs. My uncle, Jack Frishman, "hawked" people to try their skill at ringing the bell at the top of the post using a huge wooden mallet. The best part of the day was always the great shows and skits that the children performed, orchestrated by my aunt, Helen Harris. But the classic skit performed by some of the tenants, starring Manny Krupp, who was a natural, was "The Doctor and the Operation."

For that one day the parking lot was transformed into the carnival grounds. At the far end was the casino with its raised porch, making it a perfect stage for everyone to see. A large white sheet was hung between two posts and a bright light was strategically placed behind the sheet creating a shadow effect. Even on the brightest days, this worked well because there were two pine trees that had been planted by my grandfather years earlier. These helped to shade the stage area. Now, that's planning ahead! A long table was placed directly behind the curtain. When the light was turned on, not a sound was heard among the attentive crowd. The doctor and his nurse entered the stage and walked in front of the sheet followed by a thunderous applause. After being introduced over the loud speaker, the next person to appear on stage was the patient. As his hands were rubbing his belly, he informed the doctor that he was suffering from a very bad stomach ache. "Let's take a look. Come into my office," the doctor said very concerned. They all proceeded to walk behind the sheet into the "office" as the patient was laid down on the table. All that was seen by the audience from this point on were the performer's shadows. The nurse began comforting the patient, as the doctor carefully examined his stomach. You could hear, "Ah hum, ah hum." Suddenly, with a resonance that could be heard throughout the Mountains, the doctor shouted, "I found the problem! Nurse, please hand me my saw."

In one quick motion, the nurse bent down to reach under the patient's table, and handed the Doctor a large carpenter's saw that had been hidden from view. The doctor began cutting the patient open whose arms and legs went flailing in the air. He then leaned over and looked directly into the patient's seemingly open stomach. What happened next was even more amazing. Because of the shadow effect, it appeared that various items were being extracted from inside the patient's stomach. This apparently was the cause of all his discomfort.

First, the shadow of a small vase with flowers was clearly seen behind the illuminated sheet. That was soon followed by a frying pan. The stuff kept getting larger and larger. Next it was a car jack, then a tire, all of which were hidden below the table. One after another, the unimaginable articles seemed to come out of his stomach. The final items to be removed were a toilet seat accompanied by a plunger, which always brought on the most laughter from the audience. This was one of the funniest moments at the carnivals. It left such an impact on one of the children, Robert Supree, who was a distant cousin, that years later he wrote a children's book titled "The Doctor." It was written using the same shadow style, with the removal of many of those same outrageous items.

On occasion, there were guests who came to enjoy the day, but instead became very involved. This was the case of Alwin Nikolais and Murray Louis. My cousin, Gladys Bailin, was performing with the famous dance troupe, the Alwin Nikolais Dancers, in New York City. Alwin and Murray's careers were just taking off when Gladys suggested to both of them to take a short respite from their work and come up to Hemlock Grove for a week's vacation. They accepted her offer and it happened to be the same week that the family was preparing for the annual event. They couldn't resist joining the colony's excitement and jumped right in with their expertise, designing some of the sets for the children's plays and skits. One of the standard features at all the carnivals was a huge maypole in the center of the carnival grounds, under which many of the activities took place.

A dare-devil clown at the Hemlock Grove carnival is walking the tight rope under the Maypole. (Alright, it's a plank, but it does the trick).

Cousin, Barbara (Harris) Friedman is standing next to some of Murray Louis's fantastic art work. This was the entrance to the carnival that year.

I'd have to say that the best attraction that was ever made for any carnival at Hemlock Grove was the children's roller coaster ride. Remember, this was way before you could hire a company to bring in carnival rides. Hand building an elevated track that the car could travel down was an extremely difficult undertaking. The track was about thirty feet long and about four feet high to accommodate a small car. It was constructed from a discarded baby carriage, scrap wood found around the colony, cardboard, and aluminum foil. A small child, as I was at the time, would climb into what looked like a "rocket ship" and with a small push would go traveling down the wooden trestle. It was the most amazing ride they ever made for any of the carnivals. How do I know? It had the longest line! I can vividly remember the excitement that was growing amongst all my cousins and friends in just hearing about this fantastic ride that they were going to construct for the carnival.

That year, my parents allowed me to sleep over the night before the great event with my cousin Ricky. His bedroom was on the second floor of the Main House and over looked the entire carnival grounds. We anxiously watched out the window as a few specially-chosen carpenters were busily constructing the track. As they hammered away, we couldn't stay up any longer, but the men worked all thru the night. At least, it seemed like they had, because the next morning when we awoke, there it was: the completed track with the rocket car sitting on top in position ready to go! Every small kid that attended the carnival had to ride it at least twice, or maybe it was three times!

Abie Wands Heat Um & Eat Um TV Dinners

Unfortunately, the Jewish Community Center in Monticello is no longer active because of a decline in membership. As the social meeting place for much of the Sullivan County Jewish population, it had been a place of constant activity for many of my friends. Some of my earliest interactions with girls took place there through dance classes. Our instructor, Charlie Gipps, was also the director of the Pied Piper summer day camp in Hurleyville. In addition to my coed experiences, many of my friend's bar-mitzvah receptions were held in the Center.

The Pinewood Derby, a Cub Scout activity that I really enjoyed, also took place in the JCC. It involved the construction of a small wooden racing car that sped down an elevated track. I never won a race but almost always received a trophy for best of show. As my Cub Scout career was ending, I made the jump to Boy Scouts, which played a big part in my life. This was where I met the two greatest troop leaders, Mr. "T" (Teddy), and Mr. "S" (Seymour), Feldberg, two brothers who loved the boys.

Being a Boy Scout involved mastering certain skills for which awards were then received. One skill, which was relatively easy for some of us, was preparing a full meal over a camp fire. (Coincidentally, while I'm writing this tale, I'm vacationing in a local campground in Woodridge with my niece, Jenna Blank, and my wife Lorrie. The fire is burning nicely, and I am getting ready to cook a fantastic dinner. Some things in life never change).

Getting back to my Scouting campfire, we actually cooked our meal behind the community center. At Tuesday nights' meeting, Mr. "T" asked my patrol, "Did you guys complete your assignment of making your campfire this past weekend?" We all pointed out the window into the woods. He could see the remains of our weekend project by the stones and ashes that were still intact. He couldn't believe that we did it behind the building but we answered rather quickly, "The three of us all live right around the corner, and how else would you know we had a cookout without seeing it?" Shaking his head he said, "You know boys, that actually makes sense."

We never let a little snow get in our way of any activities. In fact, one of the exciting winter activities was the Klondike Derby. This was a competition where different troops from the county had to complete various survival skills in the woods. My patrol had several months to construct a sled which was to be loaded with our equipment for the race. On the day of the event we were handed a map, and with our compasses we calculated the route to each checkpoint as we all took turns pulling the sled through the grueling course.

Our first test was making a fire for lunch in the snow- not an easy task as dry wood is hard to find in the winter. This meant searching for dead twigs that hadn't fallen off the trees yet and peeling birch bark that was dry enough to start the fire. We collected as much firewood as we could when one of my compadres, Barry Arfa, said, "Wait boys. I have something that will really help get things going!" After looking over his shoulder he pulled out a can of Sterno from his pocket. It was placed well under the not-so-dry firewood and in a flash we had a roaring fire! We all started *schlepping* whatever we could find to make sure the fire wouldn't burn out from the high heat and expose our magic-fire starter. We began cooking our hot dogs and beans right away, and while the other troops were still working on their fires we were enjoying our desert of Devil Dogs. One of the troop leaders came over to see how we were doing and congratulated us on being the first patrol to get a fire going. Good thing he didn't walk too close or he might have seen our little secret. We scored big on this challenge, and I couldn't believe that the Troop leaders never caught on.

One of the skills we were being taught prior to venturing into the woods was knot tying in order to lash logs together. This was in preparation for constructing a structure similar to a tee pee, suspending the sled underneath it, and pushing it over a stream. Sounds complicated doesn't it? Well it was, and my group had a problem. We were having too much fun at the meetings goofing off and didn't pay much attention to Mr. "T".

Inevitably, the moment of truth arrived for us to build our sled sling. The stream was narrow and the ice hard enough for us to walk back and forth getting everything ready. We tied the knots the best we could. The sling stood about fourteen feet tall when finished and it looked like we were going to do alright. With some of the other members in my patrol, like Barry Slyper, I felt that we might be able to pull this one off. The catching crew walked to the other side with stretched out arms in anticipation of grabbing the sled. Both teams were ready. "On three", someone shouted, and with one big swing, the sled started flying over the ice-covered stream. It was inches away from our hands when suddenly some of the knots started to unravel. What happened next seemed like a slow motion film. The logs begin to collapsed, and the sled went crashing through the ice into the water. Some of the receiving team also got quite wet from leaning forward too far in a last ditch attempt of grabbing our sled. Thank God the water was only about eight inches deep because it was cold, REALLY cold!

I think they call that payback for not paying more attention. Of course, after this monumental disaster, our chances of collecting more points at the remaining check points became rather slim because of our wet gear. Did it matter? Heck no! We just laughed our butts off and it was another great day being together with my friends.

The biggest gathering I attended was the Boy Scout Camporee held in Eldred, New York. My new patrol of six guys was getting prepared for this camping weekend. (Some of my friends had left Scouts at this point). We needed to take our sleeping bags, personal items, clothing, but most important, food for the entire time. Although it was a relatively simple list with items like eggs, bacon, orange juice, hamburgers, hot dogs, we wanted to make sure we had it all.

One of the members of our patrol was Abie Wand's son. Abie, owned a large kosher butcher market in the vicinity of where the Sullivan County Government Center is now located in Monticello. His son suggested that since his dad was in the food and meat business, we all give him our share of money, and he would take care of all the purchasing. Wow, we figured this was gonna be great! While everyone else would be eating Oscar Meyer franks, we'd be chowin down on delicious kosher steaks. Friday afternoon arrived and we all met in the parking lot of the J.C.C. except for his son who had all the food! It was starting to get late and we were worried that something had happened to him. Finally, he showed up with five large, heavy coolers that we threw in the pick-up truck, and off we went.

This was going to be a fantastic weekend, plus the weather was expected to be perfect. We were all good friends, and there was going to be great food! What more could we ask for? When we arrived in Eldred our first chore was to set up camp. We started with pitching our tent which could easily house eight adults. Someone's dad acquired several army surplus tents that were quite roomy, but with all that comfort, came the distinctive old, stinky canvas smell. Next we set up our campfire by gathering stones and finding dry wood. Sorry, no Sterno this time. It was time to prepare our first meal which was dinner. With great anticipation we went to the truck that contained the coolers and took out the first one to see what delicious morsels we had. As we opened it and slid the ice to the side, we exposed a layer of boxes that said Abie Wand's "Heat Um & Eat Um Kosher TV Dinners." We dug deeper into the cooler expecting to see some other items, but all that was there were the same colorful boxes containing Abie Wand's "Heat Um & Eat Um Kosher Dinners." "Okay okay, open the next cooler," someone shouted. We figured this one had the meat we were looking for. But it was the same deal; Abie Wand's "Heat Um and Eat Um Kosher dinners." The third and fourth coolers had the same contents! We were screwed!

Now, before going any further, I need to educate the reader about what is an Abie Wand "Heat Um & Eat Um Kosher TV Dinner". These were the first Kosher TV dinners of their kind and were designed for the airline industry. Each box contained half a chicken, a piece of *kishka* and some vegetables, all served in an aluminum pan with a cardboard cover that had a picture perfect photo of all the items mentioned above. I must say, it did look mouth-watering, and all you had to do was to remove the cover and place it in your oven. (Who knew from a microwave)? But here in camp, who the hell was going to cook a TV dinner? That wasn't what you did in Boy Scouts, and how many of those *fakocta* dinners could one person eat in one weekend?

We realized that Steve had gone into his father's freezer and just grabbed as many dinners as he could pack into the coolers. We felt we got ripped off. Abie's son waited a moment for us to cool down and then said, "Hold on guys, watch this." He grabbed a few dinners, walked over to the next campsite, and to our amazement returned with a dozen eggs, a pack of bacon, and orange juice! We looked at each other and realized we'd all have to use our entrepreneurial skills this weekend at the Camporee. This was not explained in the Boy Scout handbook. This was plain old street smarts!

As the weekend progressed, we were eating just as well as everyone else at the Camporee, since we were eating what the others all brought. As long as we kept trading further and further away from our campsite, we could *handl* the dinners for other food items. What everyone was doing was simply wrapping the dinners in aluminum foil and placing them on a hot bed of coals. It worked so well it actually became a Kosher Camporee; the first of its kind in Sullivan County. Funny thing was, the Scoutmasters were wondering where these TV dinner pans were coming from. They were all over the entire campground by weekend's end. I wish I could have saved one of the covers of these Catskill relics, the Abie Wand "Heat Um & Eat Um Kosher TV Dinners". Not only were they great, they also made history!

Let It Snow, Let It Snow, Let It Snow

All right, I've been going on and on about all these great stories that took place in the summer, but I would be remiss if I didn't talk about the other season, "the dead of winter." I was often asked the same questions by our visiting population: "How can you live up here in the winter? There's nothing to do!" Or, "Isn't there too much snow to get around?" And my all-time favorite, "How do you deal with the cold?" For all those questions I always answered, "That's what makes this place so cool!" (Pun intended). If you've never lived here all year round, those questions deserve some attention. So let's begin with the snow, the way it USED to snow in the Mountains.

It was 1957, and the Catskills were thriving. The Monticello Racetrack, which was under construction, became a life saver as you'll see later on. What a huge under-taking it was at the time. My parents just completed their own huge undertaking, which was the building of our new home on Lawrence Avenue in Monticello. My grandfather Irving kept saying, "How could you live so far out of town?" But, eventually the Rutherford School was built a block away and soon after that, the Monticello High School, so it all worked out quite well.

The view from our backyard allowed us to see the Monticello Court House dome. We had some elevation! Our neighbor, Lester Rosenberg, had nicknamed the top of our street, "The Hill of Wind". This was quite appropriate since there was always a nice gentle North wind blowing. What we didn't know was how strong a wind that could become.

Our first winter was coming to an end (or so we thought). But for several days in late March, the snow just kept coming and coming. It seemed like it was never going to stop, plus the wind was howling continuously under darkened skies. The snowdrifts grew as they accumulated around every object in their path. The highway crews hoped that they could start some initial plowing, but it was useless since the snow was coming down at an incredibly fast rate. It was decided that they would wait for it to let up before they made any attempt at the job.

Our home was located about 1200 feet from Route 42 as the crow flies, and because it was one of the few that had been recently built on the Hill of Wind, we still had a clear view of Route 42 from our large picture window. The storm was into its third day as the snow was finally slowing down, but the wind was now picking up. Through the white outs I could see the flashing lights of the snow plow on the big Oshkosh dump truck. The town couldn't wait any longer. Relief was finally on the way, but as the truck started coming up Wood Avenue something happened. Even from a distance, I could see that the truck stopped moving. It became stuck in the deep snow. I called my dad over to tell him. He looked down at me, and with apparent concern said, "Now that's a problem." The driver kept trying to "rock" the truck, but all we saw was the blackened smoke belching out of the exhaust stack. The driver must have radioed the highway department to bring their big grader to the scene to extricate the Oshkosh out of the snow drift. It was a struggle but they finally succeeded with lots of effort and heavy tugging. My dad figured they would use the grader to plow through the heavy drifts to come up our hill, but even with its massive strength, it also failed and had to turn around.

Now all this time my friends and I were happy as punch that we did not have to go to school, but we were snowed in like never before. We couldn't even go outside to play, so we just watched as it continued to get worse. I remember waking up the third morning after the wind had been truly howling all night long, looking out my bedroom window, and all I saw was snow up against the glass. Incredibly, it drifted to the top of the back of our house blocking all the rear windows completely. That's how bad it was.

Early, that same day, there was an emergency neighborhood expedition to get some badly needed supplies for each of our households. Items like milk, bread, and my dad's personal favorite in those years, Chesterfield cigarettes. I'm quite sure that toilet paper was also on the list, which was MY personal favorite, and actually still is! Our neighbors, Arty Kiss and Joe Selvin, showed up at our house and were dressed in the heaviest winter gear they owned. They were ready to embark on the journey to Route 42. There was a small grocery, Schoch's, located a short distance from our house which was their destination. With the wind still blowing about, there were occasional whiteouts making visibility extremely difficult. For some added protection, my dad grabbed a rope from the garage and tied it around everyone's waist to prevent these gallant adventurers from getting separated on the dangerous trek. Seeing all this at six years old I started crying and asked my mom, "Is Daddy going to come back?" She promised me that he would, and as they all walked out the door I glued myself to the front window. Finally, after what seemed like eternity, I could see several figures in the distance. I started yelling to my mom, "I see them, I see them coming up the hill!" They all made it home, thank God!

The sun eventually did come out to greet us on the fourth day as we all ventured outside to see the results of this blizzard. (By the way, this was before someone decided to call them Nor-Easters). My friends and I couldn't believe what we saw. My driveway had almost eight feet of snow on it, and the streets still had not been plowed making travel impossible. It was time for the Village to call in reinforcements. It turned to the biggest project that was being constructed in the area, the Monticello Racetrack. The horses weren't there yet, but the horse power was. There were several very large bulldozers working the site; these were the only machines that would be strong enough to push the snow off the roads. They were transported on huge trailers and unloaded at the bottom of the hill. They started clearing the snow away, but what resulted were enormously high piles of snow along the sides of the streets. Because they were so large and heavily packed from the dozers, some of them didn't melt until the end of May! So in the end, the track's purpose was more than just betting on horses.

This is the first day of sunshine after the blizzard of 1957. My dad is trying to shovel a path to the street through an eight foot high snow drift in our driveway.

If you ever visited Monticello in the winter back then, you probably remember how the snow was plowed into the middle of Broadway. This resulted in huge mounds that were much higher than any vehicle. As you drove down the street you weren't able to see the opposite lane. This became quite a challenge when you had to cross over into a side street like Landfield Avenue since you couldn't see any on-coming cars. It always took a few days till the State brought in their monstrous snow-blower to remove the snow mounds. Even after I got my driver's license in the late 60's, I distinctly remember my vision being blocked as I tried crossing the street.

As the larger hotels became all-year-round destinations, many of them developed their own small ski hills for their guests, like the ones at The Concord or The Pines. But for those who needed a lot more excitement, and let's not forget the locals, there was Holiday Mountain which is still in operation today. In its early years, my dad had the exclusive propane gas account, which meant the delivery of lots of single 100 pound cylinders. Some of them were used for the gas heaters inside the small chairlift operators shacks throughout the ski hill. Those guys had to be kept warm so they wouldn't freeze to death on a cold day, or especially on a frigid evening when there was night time skiing.

On one particularly cold night Holiday Mountain was closed, but my dad was called to fix a heater in one of the shacks at the top of the biggest hill. One of the workers brought him up in a snow cat (this was pre-snowmobile days). Just as they arrived at the *bootkey*, the driver was called back down on the radio. He told my dad he'd be back in a half hour to pick him up, which gave Hy more than enough time to repair the heater.

My dad got the heat back on, which only took about fifteen minutes. He walked outside and tried yelling and waving his arms hoping to grab someone's attention at the bottom of the hill that he was ready to go, but the large snow-making compressors by the chalet were making a loud screaming noise that completely drowned out his yelling. He was also at the top of the hill making it almost impossible to see him. He figured he'd wait a while, as agreed. Well, he waited, and he waited, and he waited, and after an hour and a half, he figured the guy just forgot about him. But how was he going to get down? There was no way he was going to walk it, because it was too steep and he didn't have any skis, not that he knew how to use them.

But there, up against the shack, was his ticket to being rescued: a shovel. He had seen how the guys would sit on them with their butts, hold onto the handle in front of them, and ride down on the shovel's metal cradle. He looked at it and thought to himself, "If I'm going home tonight, I better learn how to ride this thing right now." Since he didn't have a choice, he sat down, positioned himself carefully, hoped for the best, and off he went. At first things didn't seem so bad, but as he picked up speed, it started getting a little scary. With the handle of the shovel between his legs and flying down a steep hill, the last thing he needed was to fall to the side or hit a bump. With the grace of an experienced champion he slid right up to the main building.

"Where the hell did John go? I waited for almost two hours!" he said with disgust at the work crew. Someone told my dad that right after he came down, he had to rush home since his wife was having a baby. He was so excited, that he forgot to tell anybody that my dad was up there working on the hill. I guess it wasn't that bad, because that evening Hy was initiated into professional shovel racing. I don't think he ever did it again, but he did tell everyone what a hell of a ride it was!

Snow sledding is nothing special, even to a kid growing up in the city, but ice fishing is another story. My first experience of this outdoor sport took place while I was living at Hemlock Grove, which was conveniently located across the street from the Hey-Ru Trout Fishing Preserve. It was interesting that one of their trout ponds was constructed only inches away from our property marker, and during the summer season we would catch a trout or two, but we were on our property, I swear! My brother, Barry, had just moved in with me in the winter of 1977, as he was recuperating from a burst appendix mishap. We were low on food and he suggested we go ice fishing for some delicious fresh fish. We didn't have an ice auger, which is what you'd normally use for opening a hole in the ice, but after looking in pop's basement, I found the tool of mass destruction that I needed; a metal wheel axle that had a point ground off on its end. Maybe it was used by someone else for this same purpose at an earlier time. Who knows? It was heavy as hell, and I knew it would do the trick.

We also located some old fishing rods in the basement. (This was a basement that had anything you ever needed if you could just find it). I chopped two holes to start with, baited our hooks with some bread, and basked in the winter sun as we waited for the fish to bite on the big lake. A few minutes later, I looked over at my brother who was about twenty feet away from me. He was actually lying on the ice with his rod loosely held in one hand and snoring away, taking his daily afternoon nap. He had on so many layers of winter clothing that the cold was having no effect on his tired body. He was quite comfortable inside his nice cocoon and just lay there still as a mouse. The sudden movement of his rod awakened him enough to successfully pull out a nice size fish. That meant we had worked hard enough and it was time to head back to the cabin, for a delicious meal. (We still called it our bungalow but it was now winterized).

My ice fishing days weren't over yet. Later that winter, a group of my brother's friends and I decided to meet early one Sunday morning to go ice fishing on White Lake. The pivot man of this adventure was Billy Thalman, who was working as the main bartender at the Bend an Elbow, just down the road from the Ideal Bungalow Colony. You can recognize it today as Mr. Willy's. Billy told us we should meet him at the bar at about 4:30 AM after he closed down that night. Okay, actually it was Sunday morning. We were to follow him to his house to pick up all the ice fishing gear like tip ups and a gasoline operated auger, not the old steel axle! It was best that we didn't go to sleep that night, so we made the rounds at several other drinking establishments before meeting Billy at the bar. We all had one last beer as he was finishing the clean-up duties and off we went to his house.

There were eight of us going fishing that morning, so it was decided that we take my Chevy Blazer and Billy's custom van on this winter safari. As we opened the door to leave, a snow squall started to develop, but we all said, "No problem. It ill' blow over." We were going ice fishing, period! Hey, we're country boys! A little snow wasn't going to stop us. I followed Billy in the pitch black of morning to get the gear. We picked up everything we needed and we were now heading to White Lake where the real action was going to begin soon.

As we traveled down 17B the only thing I could see were the taillights on his van in front of me. The wind became stronger and the white outs became much more intense as we got closer to White Lake because of the openness of the lake. Thank God nobody else was on the road that night because we were all over the place. We hit one white out where even Billy's lights disappeared for a few seconds, but my brother and my other passenger, Dennis Deitrich, kept saying, "Yo Frish'. We're goin' fishing no matter what!" I remember Billy saying just before we got started, "You'd better stay close or you'll wind up in Narrowsburg!" A few moments later Billy stopped the van, jumped out, and said,

"Stay right behind me. This is where it gets tricky."

"Are you crazy? We're both gonna drive our trucks on the lake?"

"Of course, we do it all the time!"

"What about crashing through the ice?"

"Don't worry, Allen, it rarely happens."

And with a good buzz on I said, "What the hell." Billy must have had some sort of radar in his van since he knew exactly where the boat launch was for us to get on the lake. We drove a little further, and Billy stopped the van again. "This is it guys. It's a perfect spot!" Now, how he knew that was beyond me, since it was still pitch black at 5:30 in the morning. As the wind finally died down, we started drilling sixteen holes, two apiece, for everyone's tip ups.

We completed the last one as the sun was beginning to rise. It was now about 6:30 and there we were, parked in the middle of the lake. It was really beautiful but scary as hell at the same time. The ice was plenty thick, almost two feet, but every now and then you could hear a terrifying cracking sound which was the movement of the ice. I just kept thinking, "We're gonna fall in!"

It was pretty cold outside, but we were all warm as toast hanging in Billy's van, listening to great music. Someone looked out the window and yelled, "Frish, your tip up's movin! Get out there!" I opened both doors, jumped out of the van, ran to my hole, pulled the string on the tip up, and just as I got this fish out of the hole, it fell off the hook and flopped back into the cold water. I tried grabbing it with my hand, but all I got was a freezing cold bath for my arm. Not a smart move by any means. It turned out being the only bite we all had that morning. The day ended without any fish, but it was one great time that I will never forget. And it was then that I came to realize what was meant by, "A bad day of fishing is better than a good day at work!"

As I mentioned earlier, sleigh riding is nothing special, but in the country, because of the many back roads we have, we'd go "skiffing". This is sort of a take-off on sleigh riding except you don't need a hill. Oh, yeah, and you don't need a sleigh. You just need a good pair of winter boots before the roads were plowed and big *batesum*. Having the snow blow by your face as you picked up speed was unbelievably exciting. I almost forgot. I didn't explain how you skiff, right? Someone would become the designated driver and usually two or three of us would hold onto the driver's rear bumper as the heels of our boots slid on the snow. Now let me tell you. This was definitely the forerunner of "extreme sports" because it was super dangerous and we were nuts! Sometimes it felt like we were traveling twenty to thirty miles an hour holding on for dear life to the bumper, and praying that our feet wouldn't buckle on us. Yes, we were young and dumb, but if you had a great "skiff" it was really worth it.

Here's one more crazy winter adventure. A few friends stopped by one afternoon and asked if I wanted to check out the Glen Wild water falls. I figured we were going to tromp around in the snow and check out the falls from the edge, where we hung out in the warm weather. I readily agreed, of course. But to my surprise, one of the guys discovered a frozen pathway that lead behind the falls. This had occurred because of the super cold winter we were experiencing and the way some of the overhead rocks had shifted. We started walking down the edge of the gorge before we entered this amazing ice cave. This was scary enough, since we didn't have the proper spiked walking shoes! One slip and you'd go flying down the extreme drop to the bottom of the gorge. We all made it to the ice cave, but as we entered we saw there was nothing for us to hold on to or step into. There was only smooth, rounded ice everywhere! The roaring sound of the water was deafening so it blocked out our voices. The ice was beautiful with streaks of red and blue, resulting from minerals in the rocks bleeding out and becoming visible in this ice paradise. This was one of those times that I was so sorry I didn't have a camera. It was the most amazing winter hike I had ever taken. The sound, the colors, the encasement in ice, was a once in a lifetime experience.

When people asked me the age old question, "What do you do up here in the winter?" They had no idea how great it was being in this quiet, cold, and beautiful environment.

Food Glorious Food

Where's the Beef?

Even with all his *meshugas*, Louie Slamowitz, owner of the Ideal Bungalow Colony, made sure of one thing. He would always take care of his select group of tradesmen: his electricians, carpenters, and plumbers. These were the guys that he used every year for the construction of new bungalows or the general repair work that was needed on a constant basis. They were the same crew that built his casino, the largest one in the Mountains, which was referred to by the contractors as "Louie's Airport Hanger". It was that big. After working a long hard week, and once the roof was on, the crew would pack up at 4:00 on Friday's, break out the beer, and start playing dice. It bugged the hell out of Louie that they weren't working till 5:00 like the rest of the week, but there wasn't anything he could do about it. The men were exhausted and they felt they deserved it.

Above it all, Louie truly appreciated all the work that they did for him (or maybe it was because of all the grief he gave them). He came up every spring like clockwork, just before Passover, to distribute some special gifts to this group of hard-working men. For some unknown reason our house became Louie's distribution center. I think it was because we lived right off Route 42 in very close proximity to his bungalow colony or maybe it was because he knew my dad was responsible enough to be the drop off point.

My dad would get a call from Louie asking if he would be around to receive the packages that he was bringing up from the city. Upon his arrival, he'd pull into our driveway and announce his presence with the majestic sound of the horn blowing from his new Cadillac. But this was not an ordinary Cadillac. No, this particular model was a *schleper*. Typically, there on the roof, on top of some old blankets, would be a cast-iron bathtub that he needed for an up-coming job. It was always cheaper for him to purchase it in the city where he was already doing business, and could buy them wholesale. Or there might be two commercial washing machines carefully tied down with ropes run through the car doors. More on that subject later. When my dad once suggested that he buy a pick-up truck, Louie answered that he always wanted to drive in comfort and style. In addition he wouldn't have the notoriety he so desired; "A Jew in a Cadillac, *Hoo-Ha!*" So every trip made from the city served to deliver many important items that were needed in the colony. Now here comes the good part. Not only was the car loaded with all the supplies needed for the upcoming season, but he also had those gifts for his special contractors.

As Louie opened the trunk in our driveway, my dad went out to greet him. Louie would take out a rather large piece of fresh meat that was wrapped in brown butcher paper with the blood beginning to seep through. He'd place it on the hood of the car, go back to the trunk to pull out a large old butcher's knife, more butcher paper, and then would start cutting into the slab of meat. Typically he would bring beef liver. He'd wrap the first piece, and would instruct Hy as follows: "This one's for Murray (Graber)." He was Louie's carpenter for many years, and had a large family, so he was rewarded with the biggest piece of meat. Next was a piece for Joe (Wolfson), his garbage man. "And here's a piece for Ed (Motl)." Ed was the President of the bank. "You'll bring it to him, Hy." And every year my dad would answer by saying, "Are you crazy? I'm not bringing a package of meat into the bank. Forget it, Louie!"

After all the pieces were carefully wrapped, my dad would put them in his huge 10 foot long chest freezer in the basement, alongside the "cold cash" that was still in reserve from the summer's washer machine business. Louie worked as a prominent butcher in New York City which is where he had his meat connection. This is how he made his money so that he could dump, I mean "invest" it into the Catskills. In addition, he also provided everyone with bottles of what he considered to be great booze. He'd go back in the trunk for a case or two of Duggan's Dew Scotch and would further instruct my dad with, "Two bottles are for this guy, three bottles for that guy", and I'm sure you have the picture of what was going on at our house.

Right after Louie drove away, my dad would call all of the tradesmen on the phone, inform them that Louie had left them their "booty," and that they could come by and pick it up.

One of Louie's earlier tradesmen was Maxie Feldman. He was his first plumber when he opened the colony. Maxie was getting on in age and the work was becoming more difficult for him, especially as the colony was growing in size. So after a few more years of working for Louie, he referred my dad and my grandfather Irving to take over the job that he was relinquishing. Louie still had an appreciation for Max, and that's why he remained on his "special" list.

Now one year, for reasons that are still unknown, Louie broke the tradition and didn't show up with his thank-you gifts. Actually, nobody really cared about getting the meat anymore, and the Duggan's Dew was not top shelf. Nobody cared, that is, except for good old Maxie. He kept calling my dad asking if Louie had been there yet. I'm not talking once a week, but this became a nightly ritual with Max inquiring about his meat and booze. I believe he thought Hy was keeping it for himself. So after three weeks of constant phone calls, my dad figured the only way to satisfy Maxie was to buy him some Passover wine. He called him the next evening and told him to come to the house because Louie had finally brought up some wine.

When he showed up at the door Hy handed him two large bottles and said, "This is what Louie was giving out this year and apologized for getting up here so late." Maxie didn't seem to care that he didn't get any liver as long as he got his booze. He was finally happy, the evening phone calls stopped, and my dad had another satisfied customer.

When Louie made his pilgrimage back to the mountains it meant the coming of a new season. It also indicated that he was going to start bringing up some help to work at the colony. Owning the biggest in Sullivan County translated into having the biggest work force to do the painting, lawn cutting, raking, cleaning, etc. There were several employment agencies in Monticello, but Louie was always trying to save a buck by not having to pay for their services. Because he had to continuously go to New York City to check up on his many apartment rentals, it made great sense for him to recruit the men we referred to as his "soldiers" while he was down there. His methods were unusual, to say the least. He'd drive to the Bowery in his Cadillac, literally pull guys right off the streets and load them in his car. They were stone drunk and had no idea what was happening, but as soon as he had three or four *schlepers* for his "army", off he went. Most of them recognized Louie from all the past years that they had worked for him, and I think they knew they were actually in good hands. He gave them a place to sleep, not that the rooms compared to the Holiday Inn. They were more like the Holiday Out. Shirley, Louie's wife, would cook them a meal or two a day, plus they would eventually make a few dollars. Unfortunately for some, after a short time of being sober they would blow the money by going into Monticello to get drunk again.

The following morning when he was giving out job assignments he'd ask the guys, "Where's Joe?" "He stayed in town," another laborer would comment. That meant that Louie had to go to the jail and bail out Joe or some other soldier who got drunk the night before. For some of these guys, the cycle would continue throughout the season until they got fed up with Louie's *shtick*, and would take the bus back to the city. In some ways, Louie's place was sort of an unofficial rehab center for Bowery bums, but with a poor success rate.

One afternoon, after Louie had finished with his city business, he loaded up the car with some fresh recruit's, a bathtub strapped to the top of the Cadillac, a full bag of cash with about $3000.00 under his seat in just collected rent money, and headed back to the Catskills. It must have been one hell of a ride with the car stinking of alcohol and God knows what else. It was mid-April and the weather in the city was really nasty, with a steady rainfall all day long. As soon as they crossed the Wurtsboro Mountain, the change in temperature created a wet and heavy snow which is so typical. Maybe it was because of all the guys inside, the extra top heavy load of the bathtub on the roof, and the slippery snow, that the Cadillac started sliding off the road. Even with all of Louie's efforts the resulting accident was inevitable. He landed in the median of Route 17, and couldn't get out of his car. His "soldier's" didn't even know what had happened since they were still flying high! The State Troopers arrived at the scene almost immediately as some of the guys were beginning to crawl out of the car. They were all, well almost all, stinking of alcohol, and for sure weren't the best dressed crew of men. Actually, Louie's attire was quite similar to theirs, since he had just collected rent and this was his way of not standing out in the city. When they assessed the situation their immediate reaction was that the car was stolen. When a trooper crawled in to get to the driver, Louie grabbed him by the arm, and demanded, "There's a bag of cash under the seat and I'm holding you responsible!" Seconds later he passed out right in the car.

They were all brought to the Monticello Hospital for evaluation and identification. Louie, looking just like his workers, was put in the same ward until Bob Selps, the Hospital Administrator, just happened to walk by and saw Louie lying there. He grabbed the head nurse by the arm and sternly said, "Do you know who that is? It's Louie Slamowitz. He donates a large amount of money to the hospital every year! Call his wife Shirley, and get him in his own room, now!" She knew that Louie had lots of cash with him from the rent and asked my grandfather Irving to accompany her to the Trooper barracks to get back her *gelt*. It took some time to straighten things out with the authorities, but when all was said and done, the first words that Louie spoke when he opened his eyes and saw Shirley were," Did you get the money?" "Yes, yes it's all been taken care of," she assured him. And it wasn't a day later that you could hear him on the loud speaker saying, "Hy, come to the office, I have the list for you, Hy, come to the office," which translated to Louie was ready to go again.

The Green Thumb and Magic Tomatoes

Beautiful and elaborate landscaping always surrounded the hotel entrances in the Catskill Mountains. Likewise, many of the bungalow colony owners took pride in their properties by using native shrubs and flowering bushes to create beautiful walkways to the swimming pools or to show off their casino entrances. One of the most common shrubs used were the Forsythia. The delicate bright yellow flowers that bloomed in early May were a definite sign that spring finally arrived after a long hard winter. Next to bloom was the Lilac, which grew in perfuse lavender clusters. Occasionally, while driving through the countryside, the rarer variety of White Lilac would be seen. Their familiar aromatic scent could be detected in many homes around Mother's Day.

Most of the summer visitors didn't witness this beautiful time of year because of their late arrival to the Mountains, unless they were searching for a bungalow to rent. However, they were able to see the blooming of the Rhododendrons. I vividly remember walking along the trail next to the creek at Hemlock Grove during an early summer day, and passing shrub after shrub of large pink clusters of this natural beauty. It truly added to the sometimes surreal feeling when I was in the woods. To this day many of the decorative plants, shrubs, and trees still survive, lining a partially grass covered sidewalk to nowhere, or along the edge of the road, planted there by an earlier resort owner in the 40's or 50's.

My grandparents Sam and Celia, and many other "old world" bungalow owners often planted vegetable gardens. Not only did this give my grandfather an excuse to get away from all the *tummel* of the bungalow colony, it also afforded the family fresh vegetables that were immensely enjoyed. Meantime, on the other side of town, Grandma Shirley could be seen every morning watering her several tomato plants, which she grew in five gallon plastic buckets on the porch of her apartment.

Grandpa Frishman's garden was started from seeds rather than purchasing starter plants from the local nurseries which of course saved money. Every spring there were rows and rows of small paper cups all filled with tiny newly sprouted seedlings on their porch. These were later transplanted into the garden. Several perennial herbs also had a place on the farm. The cluster of chives was the first to rise from the warm ground in early spring. No one ever could seem to remember how they got there, and were probably planted by the Andrews family, the prior owners. It was great to be able to run outside and pick the chives to enjoy with a baked potato and sour cream. There was also the culinary treat, well, for some people, of the wild grass that grew on the main lawn known as *Schav*. It was sometimes referred to as sour grass. Many a late afternoon, just before dinner, my grandmother and her sister, Tonta, could be seen picking the leaves and filling their apron pockets. After they were cooked in water with a little salt, the pot cooled, and some sour cream was added making what they thought was a delicious cold soup similar to borscht. I would try anything, but the bitterness of the *Schav* never made it to my top ten or even my top thirty, Yuck!

When the property belonged to the Andrews family there was one outbuilding used exclusively for their chicken coop. After my grandparents bought the farm they continued using the building for raising chickens. Next to the coop was the outdoor pen, which contained valuable composted chicken manure-a commodity that gardener's still purchase to this day. When the farm was converting to a resort, having the minimum requirements of four walls and a roof, the chicken coop was soon transformed into a casino (which is where my parents eventually held their engagement party). Several years later, after a larger casino was built, the building then became a bungalow. It was common to continually reinvent structures for new purposes at the colonies. After its renovation, it was rented to my cousin's Benny and Rosie Bailin.

The soil around this particular bungalow was super fertilized because of its "past tenants". That's where pop planted horseradish and it grew like crazy. However, there was one problem. Rosie hated the huge leaves that grew past the bottom of her kitchen window. I don't know if she could smell the horseradish or if she just hated looking at the leaves, but she always *hochted* my grandfather to cut them back. He generally ignored her requests knowing that it could affect the growth of his prized horseradish. Since I lived in the adjoining bungalow she would come over and say, "Darling, would you please cut those leaves down, they're driving me crazy!" I wouldn't dream of such a thing, but every once in a while someone gave those leaves a "haircut". Thank God there was no way of killing the "White Lightning". It just wouldn't die. The plants always came back year after year, and we continued to enjoy the horseradish that my grandpa made for Passover even with Rosie's continuous *kvetching*.

Before Hemlock Grove was sold, my parents made sure to dig up some of the horseradish root, and they transplanted it in the back of their Monticello home. It grew surprisingly well there even without the heavily composted soil. Occasionally, we would dig up a piece, grind it on my mom's *ribeisen*, and enjoy our very own homemade killer horseradish. To continue the cycle, just days before my parents sold their Monticello home, I made sure to transplant some of the root back in Mountaindale at my current home. It's doing nicely and still makes great *hain* for Passover Seder every year.

Getting back to Pop's garden at Hemlock Grove, he would always throw out his food scraps in the garden during the fall months to create compost as was done in Europe. This was long before composting became popular and people became "environmentally conscious". He was also a recycler of materials like old iron bed springs which served as fencing to keep out the deer from eating his vegetables. Attractive it wasn't, but it was functional and free! He then tied eight foot saplings to the fence posts, ran string at two different levels and hung various objects like tin pans, strips of shinny material, and colorful items which discouraged the deer from jumping the fence.

I often wondered how grandpa kept some of the critters from sneaking under the fence. Years later, while I was living at the "farm," my cousin Stevie and I wanted to expand the garden. As we were dismantling part of the fence, we discovered his secret. There were lots of pieces of broken glass buried beneath the soil. My grandmother explained Grandpa's theory that the sharp edges dissuaded the woodchucks and rabbits from burrowing under the fence. This was his environmentally friendly method of protecting his garden: no electric fence, no chemicals, just good old recycled glass. On occasion though, when a critter did sneak in I would ask Pop if he was upset by them eating some veggies. His answer was, "You know, they have to eat too and we have plenty." That was his good natured attitude towards life.

The garden flourished for a few more years with the newly expanded growing area. After pop passed away and it became harder for my grandmother to maintain the garden by herself, I stepped in and became the new "Head Gardener". It made sense since I was living permanently in my newly renovated bungalow at Hemlock Grove. This was also about the same time that I was occasionally using recreational drugs like Marijuana. There, I said it. But because of the resourcefulness instilled in me through my grandfather, I figured why buy the stuff when I could grow it.

It was becoming hard for my grandma to do any work in the garden, but watering the plants was easy for her since the hose was right there. This gave her some satisfaction that she was still a part of the "Good Earth". But mixed-in with some of the regular vegetables, in the lower corner of the garden, were some strange looking plants which I told her were "hybridized" tomatoes. They were so unique that they didn't yield fruit until September! This was actually my pot plot. As the summer season was coming to an end, she kept asking me, "Allen, vat's mit these crazy tomato plants? Vil the tomatoes have time to ripen? They're not even showing yet."

What was I going to say to my sweet grandmother? "Don't worry. You're helping your grandson grow pot." Not that she even knew what it was. Luckily for me, she would leave for Florida right after Labor Day, a few weeks before the hard frost, and never saw any of the "ripened tomatoes". Something else of interest about the marijuana was that one of my aunts had developed glaucoma and was experimenting with making tea for relief. I would always make sure to have some put aside for her use upon request. So you see I was really growing it for medicinal use. Oh, and I never inhaled! Really, and I never had sex with that girl.

One from Column A, Two from Column B, and the Third Sedar

Some people in this world eat to live and others live to eat, I am of the latter, just like everyone else in my family. To this day, my parents still remind me that as a small child, if I started crying or I became irritable, they just had to put some food in my mouth and I would immediately quiet down. That's probably why one of my favorite treats as a kid was going to Hemlock Grove at dinner time. Almost everybody there was related to me in some way: aunts and uncles, cousins, or my grandparents, and I would visit them all, going down the line from bungalow to bungalow. I'd start with my Aunt Ceil. After I knocked on her door and said hello she'd welcome me in. The first thing she'd say was, "Did you eat dinner yet, Allen?" And with a quick reply, "No, I just got here!" "Good, then sit down and have something to eat with us," and I would have a little *nosh*. Maybe it was a piece of stuffed cabbage or if it was my Aunt Mary it was usually a Velveeta grilled cheese sandwich that she made in her special small aluminum frying-pan with a little margarine.

After finishing the delicious morsels, I'd thank them very much and tell them that I had to say hello to the rest of the family. They totally understood since I had just come from Monticello and wanted to see everyone. I'd literally eat and run to get to the next bungalow, knock on the door, and waited to hear, "Allen, come on in. Sit down with us, we just started dinner. Did you eat yet?" "No, I didn't have a thing." And as I said that, a plate of delicious egg noodles and cottage cheese would be placed before me. I'd finish up and politely say, "Thanks, I got to go see Aunt Helen." I would go to her bungalow, knock on the door, and with a big smile she'd say, "Allen, it's so good to see you. We're having dinner. Please come in and join us!" I would sit down and she would feed me like I was her own son. You know, nobody caught on to this routine for several years. But, when they finally did, they weren't mad at all. All right, maybe my mother was embarrassed since it looked like she never fed me, although she always gave me something to eat before I left the house. The real question was why wasn't I fat because of all the food that I had consumed?

Neither rain, nor snow, nor sleet could stop my family when it's time to eat. L to R: Melvin Bailin, Mary Fox, Ceil Bailin, George Bailin, Rose Bailin, Dave Bailin, Rosie Bailin, Grandma Frishman, Stanley Bailin, Susan Bailin, and Meredith Bailin-Hull enjoying lunch in front of my bungalow at Hemlock Grove while it rained.

It was my early upbringing of always having great food that nurtured my appreciation of it today. Even my mother-in-law Gloria, after serving me dinner, will quite often comment, "I love watching you eat Allen." (Although according to my wife, Gloria tells her, "You should feed him before he gets here." Now isn't that what a nice Jewish boy is supposed to do)?

While working with my Dad on a nasty sewer job, lunch time would inevitably arrive, and some of our customers would ask, "How can you guys eat now?" We'd tell them, "Its mind over matter and right now what matters is we gotta eat!" Lunch was not only for nourishment, but sometimes it felt like the most rewarding part of the day.

My earliest recollection of eating out with the crew was going to the West End Diner which was on upper Broadway in Monticello, almost in the same spot as the present-day Sullivan Internal Medicine Office. Coincidently this is the location of my doctor's office. Maybe there's some kind of karmic connection here since it's the same spot where I go now and used to go back then to make me feel better.

Eating at the West End Diner was like eating in someone's house. Herman and Sadie Luster were the proprietors, and never talked to each other much when they were busy. When the restaurant was slower, however, they continually yelled back and forth at each other except when I walked in with my dad. Sadie always made sure that I had enough to eat and seemed to cater to my every need. "Allen, *boychick*, what do you want to eat?" Sadie would ask in a loving voice. "A nice lamb chop, some soup, what'll it be?" She was wonderful. Their son, Jack, just told me how his dad often joked, referring to the diner as "The Gold Mine." Yeah right! They both worked from 6:30 am to 8:30 pm, six days a week and seven in the summer. They made so much money that they had to close from January thru March because they couldn't afford to stay open. Yeah, what a gold mine.

The diner and other businesses like Rosenberg's Furniture (our Hill of Wind neighbors), were razed to make way for Urban Renewal. That whole area of Monticello is entirely changed from the way it looked back in the fifties.

Often, we were working a distance from any eating establishment. It would take too much travel time to go to one of the places that we usually patronized, like Lefty's for a steak sandwich or Kaplan's for a corned beef sandwich. What this meant was that we would have an "Irene lunch," which never consisted of just a sandwich with a drink. No, her lunches included dinner leftovers with sides of salads, sour pickles, knishes, chips, dips, puddings, pie and fruits: a real Jewish mother's lunch. She always made sure that her boys wouldn't go hungry. When we could, we'd choose the nicest locations to eat, whether it was by a lake, a beautiful waterfall, or in the shade under a large tree. The problem was that lunch went by so fast and the rest of the afternoon dragged on forever.

During the season, while working in the sleep-away camps, we were usually offered food to eat from the kitchens. Not a bad deal at all! I remember being sent on a service call with Larry Cardini, one of my dad's helpers, to a camp because the main triple bay sink was plugged up. We arrived shortly before lunch as the cooks were yelling, the waiters were running around, and someone was trying to wash things in buckets to keep the food flow going. It was a zoo in there! Now just because there was a technical problem in the kitchen didn't mean that lunch was going to be cancelled for the entire camp! The sink had been out of commission since dinner time the night before and it took about twenty minutes for us to get things moving again. The head chef was ecstatic that he could finally work in a fully operating kitchen.

We hadn't eaten lunch yet and our stomachs were beginning to growl as the smell of fresh-baked donuts wafted through the kitchen, and it was killing us. Tray upon tray of hot jelly-filled delicacies that had just come out of the oven were being stacked in cooling racks for the campers' dessert for that evening. Without any hesitation, when we were offered a donut, we graciously accepted. The baker just kept saying, "Take, take." So of course, we took and took and took. There's just something about a freshly baked donut that can't be beat. After eating, I mean gulping down about three or four of them, our stomachs starting saying, "Hold on, what the hell is going on up there? Are you crazy?" You're really supposed to let fresh baked goods cool first before you eat them so they don't expand in your stomach. Forget about waiting. The smell was wonderfully delicious and we were starved. You know how they say, "Don't go grocery shopping when you're hungry?" The same thing holds true when you are doing a plumbing job in a kitchen and they're baking. The two of us finished the job, and a little while later the donuts finished US for the rest of the day. Boy, were we hurting, and it took me a while before I wanted to eat a donut again hot or cold!

As the bungalow colonies and hotels starting dwindling in Sullivan County, our work shifted towards Quickway Metals, Marc Lerner and Hank Pavlick's company, located in Monticello. An earlier division of that company known as Fountain Pools was responsible for the construction of many steel swimming pools in the local summer lodgings'. They were the fabricators of the famous swimming pool at the Concord Hotel that incorporated a waterfall, and was later copied by Louie Slamowitz, at the Ideal Bungalow Colony. Upon a visit to the Concord he saw their pool and immediately said, "I have to have that for my place." It's a smaller version, but the identical design.

This brings me to a particularly funny story that happened while on a job at the Newburgh plant. We had to work after the daytime crew left so that we wouldn't get in their way. My mom knew that I didn't drink coffee like the rest of the crew which at that time consisted of my brother Barry, Larry Cardini, Joe Lorino, and my dad. She'd make me a thermos of hot chocolate instead. It was about 7:00 pm. and we were taking our first coffee break. Knowing that I had hot chocolate to drink, I eagerly grabbed my thermos and poured some into my cup. But it looked a little strange. It was unusually thick and there was something odd about its consistency. After taking a sip I said, "Dad, there's definitely something wrong with this." He looked in the cup, rolled it around swirling its contents slightly, and remarked, "She must have used bad milk. Maybe it turned sour. Don't take a chance of getting sick." Because I couldn't drink it I had water with my piece of cake. Yuck. The following afternoon, while she was preparing our food, my dad told her about the hot chocolate. This time she made sure to use fresh milk. That night, when we took our break, I opened up my thermos, poured some into my cup, and it came out in that same lumpy and gooey consistency. I said, "What the hell is going on? It happened again!" Hy said, "I know she changed the milk. So I am not sure what could be wrong." That night I was forced to drink coffee. Ick. My dad told her that the hot chocolate was bad once again, and she felt awful. What could be the problem? She thought that maybe the hot chocolate was cooling off too fast so on the third night she made sure it was going to remain extremely hot. She wrapped the thermos in aluminum foil, but again, the thick, gooey chocolate glob came oozing out of the mouth of the thermos. What a bummer. Could this really be happening? The following day when I saw my mother I asked her, "What are you making me Mom, because it's definitely not hot chocolate?" Very apologetically she said, "I went to Lloyd's Shopping Center in Middletown and I bought hot chocolate mix in the bulk section." I suggested to her that we check the bag. When she saw the label which read brownie mix, the mystery was solved. Not surprisingly, as a result of the experience I became a tea drinker.

During this time in my life my brother and I were both living in downtown Mountaindale. We would frequently patronize one of the town's last remaining businesses, Fried's Bakery. By that time, it was only opened during the summer season, and was conveniently located just a few doors down from our newly acquired property. For me, this was one of the greatest pleasures about living on Main Street. After working on our building, I always made it my business to visit the bakery.

On afternoon Barry and I went for some treats. The owner's daughter, Rita, was working the counter when I asked for my daily ration of sprinkle cookies. Barry was looking through the glass cabinet in search of his own sweet satisfaction. His eye caught a tray full of round dough balls, about the size of Dunkin Donut Munchkins on top of the cabinet. He inquisitively asked, "What are those?" to which Rita curtly replied "Barry, you wouldn't like them." Barry pressed her, "Why not?" Rita, shaking her head said, "They're dietetic *kichel* and taste awful. I know you wouldn't like them." "Okay, then I'll have a half a pound please," he said defiantly. "Are you sure," she asked? "Absolutely," he affirmed.

Rita looked at him with a puzzled look but realized he wasn't going to change his mind. She weighed out a half pound of those dough balls on the old porcelain scale, placed them in a brown paper bag, handed them to Barry and kindly said, "Enjoy!" While all this was going on, I had already eaten about five sprinkle cookies one after another. It was time to pay up, so I pulled out some money from my pocket, paid for our afternoon treats while Barry took a *kichel* from his bag, and proceeded to delicately place it in his mouth as if it was a gourmet treat. He raised his lips in a wide smile, looked at Rita as he was leaving the store and murmured, "Um um." We stepped out of the bakery, walked past the first alleyway and I heard this huge spit as the entire glob of *kichel* dough went flying out of his mouth. "Holy sh-t, these things taste like crap," he said empathically. I looked at him in shock and said, "Then why the hell did you buy them? She told you in the store you wouldn't like them!" Barry looked me in the eye and said, "Nobody tells me what I like or dislike," an edict that he still lives by today.

I bet your getting hungry by now and that's what happened to my cousin Robby at the White Rock Bungalow Colony one early spring day. He'd gone there with my dad to begin the first stage of opening the water. It was almost lunch time and he was getting real hungry, and having not brought an "Irene lunch", he figured they were going to leave to eat. Somehow my dad convinced him to work another hour before leaving so they could complete the job without having to return.

They split up and as Robby entered the next bungalow he heard the familiar humming of the refrigerator. He wondered what it was doing on, but figured that someone must have forgotten to unplug it last summer when they closed down the place. When the electric was turned back on it started right up again. Because he was starving he hoped there might be something edible, a sandwich or maybe an apple to tie him over. Well, there on a plate, was a single piece of matzah and two pats of butter. "Could this be a mirage, did I really find something with nourishment in this forsaken plumber's battleground?" What he didn't know was that the owner's had been up a few days earlier to check on the place during Passover and this is what was left of the lunch they brought with them. His next step was to find a utensil to spread the butter. Jackpot! There in the kitchen drawer was a plastic knife. Things couldn't be better as he carefully spread the butter as to not break the matzah. His anticipation was overwhelming as he brought the piece of matzah to his mouth. At that exact moment my dad walked in and saw the matzah that was about to go in Robby's mouth and shouted out, "Wait a minute that stuff could be rancid!" He was looking out for his nephew as he took the matzah out of Robby's hand, gave it whiff, and then said, "You know, this doesn't smell right." He then took a big bite and said with concern, "The butter tastes funky. It might be bad. This could be from last summer, you don't know," and with that proceeded to gulp down another big bite. Before long there was no more matzah and Robby realized he'd been scammed. He chased my dad around the colony for almost a half hour before they both collapsed on the ground. "Come on. Let's get some food," Hy said, and from that day on, it became known in my family that if the food was good it was rancid. We'd all be in a restaurant complaining that the food we were eating was rancid, but we couldn't put our forks down. Talk about confusing the waiter and the customers around us.

So now it's time to take a ride to Brooklyn to be with the family for the tradition of celebrating the Seder of the Third Night of Passover. "What are you talking about, Allen?" the reader may ask. Well, let me explain. If my parents decided to stay in Brooklyn for several nights during the Passover holiday, it meant a third night of getting together with the whole family for another food fest. By now, several family members were craving something a bit different from the traditional holiday dishes and the matzah that we had been eating. It was time for the "other" Jewish food group that our culture loves, Chinese food. Typically, when there was a large group of people ordering, it could become a nightmare because you had the option of ordering, one from column A and two from column B. That was a way to save a few dollars and get a bigger variety. But on the Third Sedar in New York City no one was better able to direct us to the best Chinese restaurants and deals in Manhattan than my cousin, Dave Bailin. He was the connoisseur of Chinese food in our family. After lengthy reconnaissance he became acquainted with the not-so-popular restaurants by visiting some of them on the lower levels along Mott Street, or down alley ways where the general public wouldn't venture. This is where the tastiest Chinese fare was being prepared by the best chefs in the city. So off the family went on a jaunt to Chinatown. When we got to our restaurant of choice, all my younger cousins and I were given our own table where we were free to make fun of the Chinese waiters until being caught by our parents, at which time a good slap was in order. Come on, you never did that as a kid? We would then revert to playing with the chop sticks until our food was served. As the adults discussed world news, baseball, or the Mountains, we giggled and poked at one another, celebrating our last night together before returning to our respective homes. We knew it would only be about two months until our joyful reunion back in the country. I used to love the Third Sedar. Did your family have one?

Now That's Entertainment

Thank God for the American Flag

Because the crowd was, shall we say, "hipper" at Sadownick's, they needed to have professional entertainment booked on Saturday nights. In those days anyone who was anyone tried to get work with the Charlie Rapp Talent Agency, the agency that my grandparents used until the year they sold the colony. It was routine that many smaller acts were booked to play an early show on a Saturday night at a bungalow colony, before performing in a hotel at prime time, so they could make a few extra bucks that evening.

This was one of those Saturday nights, when my grandmother was able to acquire a rather well-known show band for her very anxious crowd. When the band arrived they were accompanied by a woman who was probably in her early 30's. She was very pretty, provocatively dressed, rather *zoftig*, and you could tell that she already had a few drinks before she got to Sadownick's. My grandmother said to the band leader, "So, who is this lady, your wife?" "No, she's a friend of mine who sometimes performs with us as a percussionist and also does some singing," he answered very convincingly. This impressed my grandmother, but her woman's intuition told her something was amiss. The band set up quickly and began playing. They were starting to get good and hot and the crowd was getting into it. The drunken lady friend was just standing, well more like leaning, next to the upright piano which was on stage. She was neither singing nor playing any instruments. Nobody was paying any attention to her until about half way through the first set, when she started playing the tambourine sort of off-beat. After a few minutes, however, her musical abilities were no longer an issue, as she began dancing very provocatively. Soon, this evolved into a strip tease which was a total surprise to everyone.

My grandmother had left the room a few minutes earlier to prepare the grocery for the first break. She had absolutely no idea what was going on. The lady, who was now in just her under garments, proceeded to walk... actually it was more like a stagger... off the stage, and asked one of the gentlemen in the audience to help her remove her stockings from her garter belt. She grabbed hold of the arms of my cousin Sam Cohen, who was probably one of the shyest guys in the casino that night, to help her out. She had already gotten one of her stockings most of the way down, but wanted Sammy to take them off completely. As he bent down to assist her, she leaned over him in an effort to keep her balance. Her large boobs practically engulfed his head. He got so nervous that he forgot to take off her high heels first, and started pulling the stockings right over them. The audience was hysterical with laughter as they watched Sammy, who at this point had turned a vivid shade of red. He was becoming more and more tangled in the lady's stockings and her high heels. By this time she was partially lying on top of him because she was so drunk and could hardly stand up anymore.

My grandmother, hearing all the howling and craziness of the crowd, had to see what was so funny. Actually, a few of the tenants tried to block her path knowing what was going to happen next. As she finally ventured into the main room, the dancer had her bra off and was in the process of trying to take off her skimpy panties. Shirley started screaming out,"Vhat the hell are you doing! You can't do that stuff here, this is ah clean place!" And with that my grandmother grabbed the closest piece of material available to cover the strippers exposed body. That was the American flag that was neatly folded on a table right next to the stage. She ran over, wrapped the singer, I mean stripper, the best she could, and proceeded to throw her out of the casino yelling in Yiddish and in English, "This is ah clean place! How could you do dat here? How could you do such a ting? Get dalot a here!" (That was her way of saying get the hell out of here). My grandmother kept ranting on and on. Meanwhile the crowd was still rolling with laughter between my cousin's performance and my grandmother's reaction. Someone immediately scooted her off to the next show, and she was never seen again. Neither was that flag.

That Monday morning, when camp began, the ritual of raising the American flag had to be canceled due to the fact that there was no flag. The rumor amongst the kids at the colony was that there was a stripper in the casino Saturday night and somehow she stole the flag. Now, she might not have stolen the flag, but she sure as hell stole the show!

Helpful Tip #2- This one's really important. When you are going to hire someone who says they are a professional dancer, always, and I mean always ask what type of dancing!

Here's my grandma Shirley resting after the summer's *tummel* at her home in North Miami Beach Florida. This area of Florida became a popular winter retreat for many of the Catskill Bungalow Colony owners.

Games People Play

The front lawn, or main lawn as it was sometimes called, was a gathering place for all sorts of activities. This is where the children often congregated to play running games such as Ring-A-Leveo or Stick-Ball. Typically, on Saturday afternoon, the men held their "beer party" there with plenty of cans of Reingold beer and lots of herring. During the week the women would sit under a tree or at a table with an umbrella, playing Mah Jong for hours, and you'd hear them say," Crack, dot, bam", along with the distinctive sound of the tiles knocking against each other.

Shirley Boker, one of the tenants at Sadownicks' told me a great story about a game that was very similar to the current version of Truth or Dare. The women would gather around in a circle, and the leader would ask each lady a question one at a time. Now, it was not uncommon for a married woman to have a flirtatious affair during the summer season. During this game, after the easy questions were asked they became more daring. "Did you suck, did you suck?" And one by one, they'd answer, "no." But one day, before she knew what she was saying, one lady answered, "Yes!" Realizing what she had just blurted out, she immediately followed with, "But only on the tip." This brought the ladies to tears as they literally fell off their chairs, thinking how she had just let the cat out of the bag.

Another popular game played on a Saturday night in the casino was "Pick Out Your Husband". Five women would be blindfolded and five corresponding husbands would take off their shirts. The women, by feeling the men's chests and backs had to choose which partially naked guy was their own husband. There was one gentleman who resided at Sadownick's who was extremely hairy. They would use him as a ringer, even when his own wife was not in the contest. As the ladies were guided towards him and their hands touched his hairy back their reactions were always a shock as they pulled back and screamed in disbelief. It made for great laughter and great fun that all the tenants enjoyed.

In making their own form of entertainment, someone would initiate a "Come As You Are Party". A chosen group of judges would arrive at your bungalow at an unspecified and often inconvenient time of day or night, and whatever you were wearing or however you looked at that moment, curlers in the hair, no make-up, wearing only your boxer shorts, was the way you had to come to the casino for the party. The judges knocked on one of the tenants' door, and his wife said, "*Oy vey*," which usually means oh no, but in this case it meant something like oh sh-t! Her husband was on the toilet. That became his moment of fame, and he showed up at the party in a diaper.

I had one cousin Sheila Needelman, who never left her unit, and I mean not ever without her make up on! In fact everyone thought she slept with it on. Her husband, Herman, had worked out a signal with the judges and just at the right moment which was something like 1 o'clock in the morning, came knocking on the door. She was caught like a "deer in headlights". He never heard the end of it, but she did arrive at the party without her makeup. She couldn't stand it, and after a few minutes of embarrassment, she ran back to her bungalow to get her face on.

Prevalent throughout many of the smaller colonies was the performance of a mock marriage which was a spoof on a hillbilly shot gun wedding. What made it particularly funny were the reverse roles that the men and women played. Dolled up in their wife's dresses, the men, oops, the brides were always buxom and were *schlepping* several babies out of wed-lock. The bridesmaids may not have had matching dresses, but they looked funny as could be in their wigs and make-up. The ladies, the groom and best man, were wearing their husband's pants, shirts, ties, jackets, and of course an added mustache for realism. Sometimes one side of their mustache would begin to fall off during the performance which brought on more laughs. Also included in this crazy cast of characters was an officiating Rabbi, who also worked as a *moel* with a name like Rabbi "Kutapeckeroff". The anticipation of seeing all the dressed up spouses made for a great nights entertainment. The skits were typically cast as the groom trying to run away from his future bride with a gun toting Sargent of Arms standing guard. With lots of improvised jokes, funny names, and a great deal of laughter, Saturday night was a time to let go of all the stress from the past week after working in the city. The humor was never offensive, and everyone enjoyed each-others company in post war celebration and the coming of the baby boomer generation.

Preforming a Mock Marriage Wedding at Hemlock Grove. L to R: Bessie Krupp, Harry Balch, Aron Harris (the bride's mother), Rose Bailin (Sargent at Arms), Lou Abrams (brides maid smoking a cigar), behind him unknown, Ceil Bailin (the Groom), Bill Supree (the lovely Bride), Sam Anger (the Maid of Honor), and Manny Krupp (the big baby).

Men at the bungalow colonies, the weekend warriors, enjoyed the team spirit of baseball and competition with other colonies. Games were always played on Saturday mornings against opposing teams, typically before going into the pool. On one occasion, however a game had to be played on a Sunday, not because of a conflicting pool activity or inclement weather, but because the opposing team was a group of young Hasidic men. This was very unusual for that time since there weren't many religious colonies, especially one that had an organized baseball team. Someone at the colony heard about these guys and set up a special game, and because Sadownick's team was a well-oiled fighting machine they figured they'd give these guys a run for their money. When the team arrived at the Hasidic colony, they were surprised to see the home team rigorously practicing for the showdown. "You know, they look pretty damn good," someone remarked. "Yeah, but we got the power to kill um!"

It was now the last inning and Sadownick's was losing by 1 run. The captain gathered his team for some encouragement. They formed a huddle, and he began. "This is it guys. We've got the top of our batting order. We gotta give um hell. If we lose what are we gonna tell our wives?" The game resumed and one of the guys hit a nice double. It seemed like Sadownick's was going to pull this one off after all, but when that last shot was hit into the outfield, their little center fielder, Yossi, went chasing the ball. His *yalmuka* went flying off his head, he made a flying leap, and by some miracle of God, his glove magically grabbed the ball. The field turned into mayhem for the Hasidic guys, because they knew the reputation of the Sadownick's team before they started. It was a tough and surprising loss for the men from Sadownick's, and a rematch was immediately scheduled for the following Sunday. How could they live with that humiliation that they lost a baseball game to a group of Hasidic men?

Well, the week went by and a rugged practice was held Saturday for Sunday's big game. There was absolutely no way that they were going to lose again. This time they were playing at Sadownicks. When the visitors arrived the men didn't take anything for granted and were well into their practice. They knew if they were to win, they'd have to pull out all the stops and play like this was their very last game. This time they would use a very complicated psychological strategy and would bring out their secret weapon: the Ladies of Sadownicks! They were going to become a part of the team. Wait a minute. You didn't think they were going to play on the field did you? No. They had specific instructions from their husbands: "Wear the skimpiest clothing… short skirts, midriff tops and bikinis if you want. You are now our official cheer leaders." All that week the ladies practiced making up great cheers for each of their husbands.

It all seemed to pay off since the Hasidic team played with so many inconsistencies, that they didn't seem like the same men from the week before. The Sadownick's cheerleaders were such a distraction that it became too much for the opposing team to concentrate and they lost the game. Several weeks later the Sadownick guy's went back to the Hasidic colony with members of their "special team". When they got out of their cars and approached the playing field, the main Rabbi saw the women dressed in their provocative outfits, and started yelling, " Vat is this? You can't have dis here! Dats it, you gotta go now!" It was all over, and they never played against each other again.

One of the most historic, I think we'll change that to outlandish baseball games ever played in the mountains was held up the road from Sadownick's at the Delano Hotel. Because the Delano was in walking distance from Sadownick's, the day camps as well as the Weekend Warriors quite often played each other in a competitive baseball game. But unlike Irving's field, which was located behind the colony, the Delano's was right next to the Old Liberty Road for all to see. As a matter of fact I was always distracted by a passing truck or car coming down the road while I was stuck playing right field; the official position of a lousy baseball player on a kids team. Today was different. It was a women's team playing against the men. Jeffery Newman from Sadownick's organized the game to help a group of women from a local bar that needed to raise some emergency money for one of the ladies. It was a bunch of lucky guys, playing baseball against a women's team. And why were they so lucky, they were topless: not the guys the LADIES! They were bouncing all over the field as they tried catching the baseball or running the bases. It wasn't like the men were really playing hard, more like hardly playing. The sight of these beautiful semi-nude women being so close to the road nearly caused several car accidents as drivers suddenly hit their brakes. You have to be wondering why this game was taking place topless. It was a time when topless dancing was fighting for its existence in the Catskills, and this was a way that the ladies were making a stand that it should be allowed in the local nightclubs. And what a point it was! The game didn't last that long because the local cops and State Police were called and "busted" up, (all right, pun intended) this classic game. The details of this event were explained to me in explicit graphic detail by my young day camp friend, Eugene Gorelick. As soon as he heard about the game, he, along with some of my other young friends, hid in the bushes next to the edge of the baseball field to enjoy what lied ahead. Boy, I wish I could have attended THAT baseball game!

The 1968 Tomato War

What's nicer than picking fresh vegetables from a garden on a beautiful fall day? The sun was shining, there was a slight cool breeze, and we were at Reinshagen's Farm in Bethel. It was 1968, the early part of September, and Labor Day had just passed, which meant that there was time to breathe again. (Who could have imagined that in one year, the biggest rock concert was going to be held just down the road).

My family was gathered to celebrate my brother's Bar-Mitzvah at my parents' house, and we were all having a great time. After a few hours some of my cousins were getting a little restless, when our parents suggested we all take a ride to Reinshagen's to pick fresh tomatoes to bring back to the city. This was one of those special things we did after all the summer residents had gone home. "What a great idea!" someone remarked. We'd get out of our parents' hair for a little while and have a great time being with all the cousins in the country.

Because there were so many of us, we piled into two cars and headed out for our adventure. My cousin, Robby, and his girlfriend had come up to the Mountains on his motorcycle, so they rode to Reinshagen's by themselves.

When we arrived at the farm we were directed to a specified field where we could pick. The farm hands had already made their final harvest of the season, but there were still plenty of tomatoes that would further ripen even if they were green. You just had to be careful not to pick the overly ripened ones that were beginning to rot by this time.

We were all given small wooden baskets as we headed out to get to work. Along the way we were goofing with one another, but when we got there, the picking fest began. Everything was going fine until the first rotten tomato was thrown at someone's shoe. We were never quite sure who the instigator was, but all fingers pointed to Robby since he was wearing his motorcycling leathers. The problem was whoever received the first splat wasn't going to let it go, so they picked up a rotten tomato (of which there were plenty), and tossed it back at Robby. And so it began that in a matter of seconds the field became a free-for-all of flying rotten tomatoes. Robby's black leather outfit resisted the tomato splats easily. Most of us changed into play clothes except for my cousin Marty Fox. For some unknown reason he was unable to change, and was still in his brand new gray suit. His attire was now customized with shades of red after the tomato war!

We never got the fresh ripened tomatoes, because the owners came running out to the field when they saw the tomatoes flying, and threw us off the property. It wasn't because of any damage done to the field, but during the war we were occasionally grabbing good tomatoes as well as rotten ones. Hey, that's what you do when you're in the thick of it.

Our tomato incident didn't sit well with the Reinshagen's, and looking back, who could blame them? We were permanently banned from the farm. After cleaning ourselves off the best we could, we headed back to Monticello without the requested tomatoes. As we started piling out of the cars, the family quickly realized what had happened. Marty got the worst end of the stick. When Robby finally arrived on his motorcycle he got an earful from some of the parents for starting the ruckus, although he never admitted to the deed. It didn't take too long before all was forgotten, as we continued to eat and to celebrate my brother's Bar Mitzvah. One thing that did impact the mountains that day was the end of "Pick your own tomatoes" at Reinshagen's farm. For the rest of you, we're sorry about that.

Helpful Tip #3- If your ever invited to pick fresh vegetables, never feel that it's a formal occasion where you would need to wear a new suit.

Groupies, Bimmies, and Chopped Liver

Music was a very big part of my life while growing up in the Mountains and it still is to this day. On special occasions, I perform with my comedy jug band, "Chicken Lips." That's right, "Chicken Lips." Let me tell you how it all began.

I come from a family of musicians and artists on my father's side. When my grandfather Sam was a young man, he had a small band in which he played the drums, and was accompanied by a violinist and a guitarist. On this one particular job his band performed for a fancy affair in a hall in Brooklyn, and at its conclusion, when it was time to get paid, the owner handed one of the band members a case of raw chicken. He looked at the owner and remarked, "We never got chicken as a tip before!" The owner quickly replied, "No, this is how I'm paying you tonight. I didn't do too well, so this...," and before he had a chance to explain himself, one of the band members threw the case right back at him and shouted, "We don't need your lousy chickens! And you know, the food you cook is lousy, too! That's probably why you don't do so well!"

As the years went by, Sam got a steady gig on Saturday nights performing at Hemlock Grove in the casino, and was now playing the mandolin. Morris Slutsky was his accompanying violinist, and of course, there was always cousin Dave Bailin on the upright piano. Occasionally, my dad would accompany the band with some trumpet playing.

It's the original Saturday Night Live at Hemlock Grove. L to R: Shelia Brenner, unknown, cousin Mary Fox, her daughter Arlene, Grandma Frishman, Mildred Slutsky, Morris Slutsky on violin, cousin Sadie Bailin, her son Gary, cousin Dave Bailin on the upright piano, and Grandpa Frishman playing one of his hand-made mandolins'.

My Aunt, Helen Harris, was also a wonderful artistic influence at Hemlock Grove. She directed musicals plays in which the children sang and performed, and would accompany them on the upright piano. On Saturday nights she taught everyone folk dancing in the casino. There was also Helen's husband Aron who was the colonies natural born comedian. I think being around so much creativity, brought out my own natural talents.

My first consistent gig was in Sadownick's after day camp ended on Friday afternoons. My grandmother Shirley would have me sing "*Adonalum*". At age seven, I was already a star in my grandmother's eyes. This tradition of singing *Adonalum* continued for several summers. Even my grandfather Irving, who was Vice President of the Liberty Street Synagogue (it's now a church), took me to a small synagogue on the Cold Spring Road, and at the conclusion of the morning service had me lead everyone in the song. But this guest appearance wasn't enough for my budding talent. The taste of wanting to be on stage was increasing, and I needed more.

I'm about 7 years old when this photo was taken of me singing *Adonalum* in Grandma Shirley's Casino. Eventually I would become a rock and roll star on that same stage. It's like they say, "It's who you know, not what you know." Note the standard bungalow colony upright piano on stage behind the lamp. Every kid in the Mountains' *clopped* on one of these to play chopsticks or Heart and Soul in a round with a friend.

I developed the desire to learn to play a musical instrument, and my dad suggested that I try the trumpet, just like him. After a short stint in the school's band, it just wasn't working out. It didn't feel comfortable. I searched for another instrument for me to learn, Accordion, that's the ticket! Yes, I was going to become an accordionist. (Believe it or not, my parents recently informed me that I was the one who chose the accordion).

The decision was made. Now, where does one purchase an accordion? At Blimpy Blank's shop, of course, and incidentally he was no relationship to my wife's family. He was a good friend of grandpa Frishman. Yes, Blimpy Blank was his name. Can you guess why they called him Blimpy? You're right; he weighed around 380 pounds without any exaggeration. Blimpy's store was located in downtown Manhattan where he sold a variety of used instruments. I went on a road trip with my dad and my grandfather to visit his music shop. I was young at the time, which also meant I was short, and as we entered his store I was mesmerized by the hundreds of string instruments loosely stacked on both sides of his narrow shop. I'm quite sure there were antique Stradivariuses mixed in those piles, but who could tell? There were so many of them! It was incredible. There was just enough room for Blimpy to waddle through the maze of instruments to get to the back of the shop. Finally, after following him through this mass of wood and strings, there in the corner of the rear of the store was a beautiful small red accordion which seemed to call to me. "Allen, take me home!" And that's what we did.

The problem I had in learning to play the accordion was that I developed the uncanny ability to easily learn music by ear. The chord buttons, which are usually the most difficult for people to master, became very easy for me. But I always fought with my teacher, Mr. Selig, about learning how to play the keyboard by reading music. It's interesting that in later years he became a big donor of money to the local hospital where his face is prominently displayed in the entrance hall. I get chills every time I go in, see his picture, and still hear him say, "Did you practice this week, Allen?"

When the mid 60's arrived music was really changing, and it had become an exciting time for me. Rock was making a huge transition with groups like the Beatles, the Stones, and of course, Jimi Hendrix. They were a huge influence on my desire to create a rock and roll band and give up the accordion. Let's face it. It's not a hip instrument unless you're Weird Al Yankovich! I finally convinced the 'authorities', my parents, with a lot of *kvetching*, that I wanted to learn the guitar. This change of instruments made a permanent impact on my life. My career in the entertainment business was about to unfold.

I was starting to master the acoustic guitar, but an electric guitar is what I needed to become a rocker. This was not going to be a freebee like the prior instruments that I dabbled with. No, this time I had to work for my dad; running back and forth to the truck countless times to get a tool or a part, crawling through the muddied water under the bungalows, and of course my 'favorite', pumping out toilets! This earned me the quota that I could now purchase my first electric guitar from a mail order catalog.

A week later, I walked into the house after school, and my mother said with a big smile, "Your new guitar is in your room!" I ran in, ripped opened the cardboard box, tuned the strings, and tried to play it. I was in shock as I tried pressing down on those heavy steel strings compared to the nylon strings that were on my acoustic guitar. This baby was a beast! It had terrible "action" since it wasn't well made (hey, it was a "cheapy"), but I was determined to master this instrument, and eventually it started to pay off.

My first rock and roll band consisted of several school mates. One of my buddies with whom I formed the band was Mark Streifer, whose dad owned the Dependable Employment Agency on Broadway in Monticello. He became the drummer. Glenn Vandervoort was next in line to become famous (okay, just in Monticello), and was our rhythm guitarist. Gary Sommers, who in recent years became the Mayor of Monticello, played bass guitar. It was Mark, Gary, Glenn, and me. Someone came up with the name "The Predominant Four", which was short-lived.

We soon changed it to "The New Generation," and it shall be. After a few months of rehearsing, our first gig was... where else?... In Sadownick's casino. See how convenient it was to have my grandmother own a stage? Well, we stunk with a capital S, but my grandmother was beaming, knowing her grandson was performing on her stage. This is where my rock and roll career all started.

Because Sadownick's was a large colony this required my grandmother to supply some entertainment for the teenagers. During that same summer that we played, she booked a really good rock and roll band with a young man named Wayne who changed my life. (Believe it or not, even to this day he doesn't let me forget it). His fantastic guitar playing ability convinced me to ask him for some guitar lessons, which really paid off. Coincidentally, his son, Gavin DeGraw was also nurtured by Wayne, and today Gavin has become a famous rock performer. Wayne showed me the path by teaching me bar chords, and with his instruction, and the other members of my band practicing a lot, we were starting to sound like a cohesive group of musicians.

The following summer, when we made our return engagement to Sadownick's, all the kids were shocked that we actually sounded good. What a difference a year makes! Guy Lagerway had become our new bass player, and we kept sounding better and better. Plus we had our own trumpet player, Ricky Hughs. Songs from the group Blood Sweat and Tears songs became one of our specialties. We had become one of the best bands in Monticello, and started to get a following or "groupies" as they're called in the business.

Thankfully, this area had hundreds of bungalow colonies and hotels that all needed some form of entertainment. This was evident by the simple fact that no matter how small the casino, a stage was always present. And that's just where I wanted to be. The first bungalow colony where we performed other than Sadownick's was the Capital Inn located in Monticello, just before Downs Road. Mark's dad, Harold, had a connection with the owner through the employment agency. Harold asked the owner if he wanted some entertainment for the teenagers. He agreed to have the band perform, and for twenty bucks, how could we say NO? The Capital Inn became our first paying gig.

We were starting to perform at different colonies around the area, and one that stands out was Slaters, on the Cold Spring Road in Monticello. We were playing there on a Friday night and the crowd fell in love with us! The hit single that summer was "Good Lovin" by the Rascals, and when we performed it for them, they went through the roof! We had to play it over and over again for that crowd. They couldn't get enough of us, and the song. When we told them the show was over, the young audience collected money so we could entertain them for an additional half hour. Not bad!

The night went great except for one small problem that we encountered with the owner, Mr. Slater. Someone told him about the additional money his tenants gave us, so he felt he didn't have to pay us what we had originally agreed upon. In his eyes, we were just a bunch of kids and it didn't matter. We left quite disappointed, but when my grandmother Shirley, our biggest fan, found out what had happened she said waving her finger, "I'll take care of that *gonif*. He operated a fruit and vegetable truck that he drove all around the area. Wait till the next time he shows up here to sell his *fakockta* fruit." (I think Slater took lessons from Mr. Kesten).

The following week, when he arrived in his vegetable truck (there were peddlers for everything, since most of the Bungalow Bunnies didn't have cars), my grandmother came running out of the office, gave him hell, made him pay the remaining amount of money that he owed us, threw him off the premises, and yelled at him, "*Zolsta voxum vee a zibala mit in cup in drear un feese a roof, a*nd don't you ever come back here!"

The band was gaining popularity, and it was decided that we needed a manager. "Hey, Mom, are you busy?" Irene agreed, but now it was time to get serious, and the first thing she did was to buy us new outfits. They were matching Nehru shirts and bell bottom jeans. What an impact we made in the Monticello High School when we were the first ones to come to school wearing bell bottoms. I'll never forget how we were ostracized for a few days until it became a really big fad; we were ahead of our time!

The New Generation, bottom row, Guy Lagerway, and Glenn Vandervoort,
top row, Mark Streifer, Ricky Hughs, and myself. My mom, as manager
of the band, always made sure we looked professional
in our outfits whenever we performed.

We were playing lots of Sweet 16's, high school dances, and for the Monticello High School student presidential candidate's parties. I remember playing for Marty Miller's party when he was running for student office, and he has since become a successful attorney in Monticello. (In fact, he's MY successful attorney.) Funny how some connections are made in life.

Do you remember "Sha lala lala la la la Happy Birthday Sweet Sixteen"? Okay. Do you remember who made that song famous? It was Neil Sedaka. Michelle Mason, a good friend and big supporter of our band, requested that we learn to play that song for her sweet sixteen. And what a great idea that turned out to be since we were being asked to play it at every sweet sixteen we were hired for, which turned out to be quite a few. All the young ladies in the

60's wanted a live band for their parties. You couldn't hire a D.J. because they didn't exist yet!

Another mutual friend and classmate of mine was Phyllis Asman. Her mother Irene and her aunt Esther were the owners of the Esther Manor Hotel that was located on 17B just past the Race Track. A bunch of my friends were getting together with her to go bowling one afternoon. We went to her house to pick her up, and her mom answered the door graciously welcoming us in. Phyllis appeared a few moments later and the first thing she said was, "Allen, you'll never guess who's here!" "The President?" I answered with absolutely no idea. She smiled back at me and said, "I'd like you to meet my cousin." Hoping it was a young lady she might be trying to fix me up with, I was quite shocked to see who was sitting on an easy chair as we entered the living room; Neil Sedaka! We were all introduced to Neil, but for me it was especially significant. What came next floored me. Knowing that I was coming by, she had a conversation with him earlier about my band performing his song and how I sang it so well. She turned towards me and said, "Allen, why don't you sing 'Happy Birthday Sweet Sixteen' to Neil?" I was absolutely stunned by her request. "You want ME, to sing HIS song to HIM, the song HE made famous? Are you crazy?" I blurted out without any hesitation! But all my friends wouldn't stop. "Come on, Allen, we want to hear you sing it. And that's when Neil said, "Come on, Allen, we'll do it together." Like I was going to say no to singing WITH him! We both walked over to the piano that was in the living room, Neil started playing, and we both sang the song together. I could not believe that I was singing this song with Neil Sedaka, instead of singing along with the record. Now that's something I'll never forget!

One of our biggest moments during the summer of 1967 was a big battle of the bands contest that was held in Monticello on Broadway. We knew we were going to blow the crowd away, not only with our music, but with the light show which had become our signature and set us apart from the other area bands. It was a psychedelic time in history, and we weren't going to miss out on that opportunity. We had day-glow posters with black-lights, a hand built mechanical strobe light, 16mm movies that were projected behind us as a backdrop, and all sorts of props to help enhance the show. Some of our fans would tell us that they came to see our light show more than listening to our music! We didn't care. What mattered was that they showed up to support us. For our finale, when the last note was hit, we always ended with a huge flash that was constructed with electrical wiring and magnesium flash powder. It was an exciting effect that always took everyone by surprise! But this time we had a problem.

A four-foot fence separated the crowd from the bands with a string of construction lights strapped to its top edge. This was used to light up the general area that evening. I remember talking to my mom just before we went on stage and asking her what we were going to do about the lighting up front, and how it was going to interfere with our light show. She replied confidently, "Don't worry about that, it's been taken care of. You just play the best you can!" And just like she said, the moment we hit our first note, every bulb mysteriously went dark. She had gotten the kids at Sadownick's to stand by all the lights, and that was their cue to unscrew them all along the line. We did great that night not just because of our musical talent, but also because of the help we got from our fans and my mom's resourcefulness.

As winners of the contest, we were hired to play at Clearwater Bungalows on the Old Liberty Road for the following weekend. One of the owners, Irving Baval, arranged to have the band's photo taken for the Panorama Magazine, which was the local entertainment guide. It featured photos of people while they were in restaurants, shopping in local stores on Broadway, or maybe lounging by a hotel swimming pool. It was a combination of advertisements and "candid shots" taken at various businesses throughout the Mountains.

The band was developing a problem with the amount of heavy equipment we now had, like amplifiers, large speakers, and in particular Glenn's Hammond B-3 organ, which weighed a ton. There were also lots of smaller items that had to be loaded and unloaded at each gig. The answer was to hire two *schlepers*, or as we affectionately called them, are *bimmies*, Jeffery Karasik and Steve Moss. (Wait a minute, that's not Yiddish, but it was a local hotel term). What a relief is was to have their additional help to move all the stuff, and help set it up. We were the real deal now with two "roadies".

With all the great places and some not so great places we played, the band finally made it to the crème de la crème when we were hired as the steady rock band for Kutcher's Country Club. This was a true milestone. We took over for the band "The Sting Rays" (of Newburgh), whom we idolized. During our stint in Kutcher's, the song "Hey Jude," by the Beatles, had just been released and was extremely popular. We found out that one of Mrs. Kutcher's daughters, Mattie, loved the song. So anytime she entered the "teen room" (this was the official room that was dedicated to the vacationing teenagers), it was mandatory that we play the song, even if we had just played it five minutes earlier. It was all part of pleasing the owner, or the owner's daughter in this case, in order to score some brownie points. You did what you had to do!

But the best part of being in the hotel rock band was the requirement of socializing with the young ladies. Yes, it was a tough job, but somebody had to do it! A teenager's experience could make or break a family's return to a hotel. It became difficult at times, since we never resided at the hotel like most of the staff members did. Remember, we all lived locally. Plus, some of us had steady girlfriends, but a job's a job, and we gave it our best shot.

On many occasions, after we performed, we would meet a few young ladies and somebody would suggest that we all go to the coffee shop for burgers and fries. We were the big *schtockers* now! One night, we were all sitting around a table with some female admirers we had met earlier. Mark and I were checking out one of the girls in particular, especially since she was wearing a very low cut blouse and man were we hormonal at the time. Who wouldn't be at seventeen, right? Glenn, who was the most reserved of all of us, began playing with a small ketchup packet. To this day, I still don't know how he did it, but the packet blew wide open and a blob of ketchup flew across the table and landed right in the middle of this young lady's cleavage. Talk about embarrassment! I don't know whose was worse, Glenn's or the young lady. We never laughed so hard in our lives. He got redder than the ketchup, and the young lady was never to be seen in the coffee shop again. I'm sure she's a mother now somewhere on Long Island, and has taught her children a valuable lesson to never, ever fool around with ketchup packets, since they have the ability of becoming dangerous instruments of destruction.

While working at Kutcher's, as we were *schlepping* in our equipment one evening, an older gentleman with bright red hair walked into the hotel through the side entrance that we were using. I politely asked if he wouldn't mind holding the door open for us for a minute or so. "No problem," he said with a smile on his face. My mom, who was still managing the band, came over to see how we were doing, and saw the man holding the door for us. We finished moving all the equipment, and thanked him for his help. As soon as he left, my mom couldn't wait any longer and said to us, "Do you know who that guy was?" No one had a clue. We assumed he was just a nice guest staying at the hotel. Surprisingly she remarked, "Are you kidding? That was Red Buttons!" She recognized him immediately. He was performing in the hotel that evening but we had no idea who he was. So, I guess you could say that Red Buttons inadvertently worked as a bimmie for the band.

It was time to leave Kutcher's for our next steady gig which was the Pines Hotel in South Fallsburg. The convention hall or teen room, depending on what activities were taking place, became our new home for the next season. Because it was relatively easy to sneak into the hotel, locals and bungalow colony tenants loved enjoying the hotel's activities. That's how we meet Ivy, her twin sister Ellen, and the girls from Skopps Bungalow Colony who came to see us preform almost every night we were there. There was so much hotel life shared by people that necessarily didn't stay in any of the hotels.

The Pines, one of the last big hotels to close, has been abandoned for almost 14 years. Several years ago, through the course of my job, I had to do a walkthrough of some of the vacant buildings. Even with the ceilings collapsing and graffiti sprayed all over the walls, I could see the band performing on that small stage for the weekend guests. It was definitely a déjà vu.

Our last steady weekend gig was working in the Homowack Hotel in Spring Glen. When I started writing this book the hotel was still operating, but a few years ago it had to be closed because of so many serious violations that were not corrected by the new owners. But let's get back to the good times.

Mark left for college, and was now replaced by Sammy Gold whose family owned Gold & Rados Bungalows in South Fallsburg. When we first arrived at the hotel, my mom was talking to the hotel manager, Mr. Herringer. His conversation with my mom focused around the prior teen band playing too loud, and how it became a problem. Her remark was simply, "My boys don't have to be loud to be good." And with that she told us of the conversation, and that it would be a good idea to repeat that statement to the audience. Hey, we had to listen, she was still our manager. This was our first night there and it was going to be our introduction to the hotel staff and guests. All right, we're ready to go on and here's what I said to the crowd, "We just want you to know that we are The New Generation and that we don't have to be GOOD to be LOUD." Boy did I blow it. All the guys in the band looked at me with that, 'what the hell did you just say' look, especially my mom. Thank God we performed well without making everyone deaf. The hotel was happy and we became the rock band for the next year. Unfortunately our secondary responsibility, being part of the social staff, was becoming more and more difficult. We all had to make extra money during the summer and the hotel gigs were never enough. Plus, we wouldn't even consider staying in those nasty staff rooms, and if we did, we would have had to give up some of our pay for the stay. No way! We didn't make tips like everyone else so we would have gone home with hardly any money. We killed that idea really fast! Playing was fun, but not for free.

It was 1970, Friday night, Christmas vacation, and we had just finished performing our evening gig at the Homowack. After storing our equipment for the next night's show, we went outside, and saw that there was no way that we were driving back to Monticello. It was snowing like crazy! We weren't going any place, but hey, that's no problem. It was a hotel, right? There must be a room somewhere that we could all share. NOT! The hotel was so busy this weekend that they overbooked. They didn't even have a closet for us to sleep in! We said, "Wait a minute, it's not private, but we can sleep in the lobby!" There were plenty of large couches we can sleep on." So each one of us settled into a nice couch or a big cushion seat in which we could grab a few hours of sleep, but as soon as we got comfortable, we were told by head of security, a lady named Marie, that we had to remove ourselves from the lobby. "There's no way we could make it home. You see what's doing outside," someone explained. She just replied, "It wouldn't look good if the guests came down in the morning and saw you sleeping all over the place."

But we had to find someplace to catch some zzz's. After walking around the hotel for a while our search finally ended. We found some solace in the locker rooms. Besides only having the narrow wooden changing benches to sleep on, just the smell of the room could kill you over time! Talk about a lousy night's rest! When we woke up in the morning, not that we got much sleep, we looked great for the female guests. Incidentally, that was the only time the entire band with our bimmies' stayed overnight in any of the Catskill hotels.

We tried working every weekend since that was how we made extra money. On the "off" weekends from playing the hotel jobs, we would get gigs to perform at special events. For example the Livingston Manor Senior Prom which is about 40 minutes from Monticello. We arrived at the high school and started setting up our equipment when I realized that we had forgotten almost all the microphones in my basement. Luckily, we found one extra microphone that Glenn and I had to share. We knew it was going to be difficult because he was playing the organ and couldn't stand up next to me to share a mic stand. Norby Raush, who replaced Jeff and Steve, was working for the band as our new bimmie, not as our future bass player yet. He quickly replied, "Let me borrow your car Allen. I'll run home, get the mics, and bring um back." I said, "Sure, Norb, but just take it easy." I owned a 396 Chevelle Super Sport, and even by today's standards, that was considered a fast car. (I hope my son isn't reading this Chapter).

It was time to start playing using the one microphone, but what a challenge! Miraculously, in what seemed like fifteen to twenty minutes, Norby reappeared with the rest of the microphones. We announced that we would take a very short break as we quickly set up the missing equipment, and continued with the show. Of course, we saved all of our good songs that had multiple harmonies making the rest of the evening a great show. During our first regular break I asked Norby, "How the hell did you get back and forth so fast? That ride normally takes forty minutes each way!" He looked at me and said, "Did you ever drive your car at 100 miles per hour?" "Are you kidding me?" I blurted out. "Well, I did it tonight," was his answer. Fortunately, he saved the show, but unfortunately, the car was doomed since riding it at that continuous high speed did something to the engine, and it never rode the same again.

There was something additionally noteworthy at that job, which was the strange effect our equipment was having on the male attendees' attire. This was a very fancy affair and many of them wore black tuxedos along with black shoes and white socks. Yes, white socks. There was just something about those white socks, but what really made them stand-out even further, was our use of the black lights, a major part of our psychedelic light show. Fact: black lights make white clothing really jump-out because of the phosphorus in the detergent. Some of the guys on the dance floor were wearing "high-waters". You know; pants whose cuffs are much higher than normal because of the expected flood waters. There they were with those blinding white socks in the darkened room. It was a night, and a sight to remember.

On a rare occasion, we were hired to play at a sweet sixteen party at the Concord Hotel. Not that playing a sweet sixteen was unusual for us, but the Concord Hotel's teen band was the Ebb Tides, and we were playing in their turf. The young lady insisted that she only wanted us to perform for her party, and that was final. During one of our breaks, as we explored the unfamiliar hotel, we discovered a room where a party was in progress and there was a typical smorgasbord table set up for the guests. One of the items on that table was very foreign to Glenn's palate: chopped liver. Glenn, our resident *goyim* of the band, had never eaten Jewish soul food before, and he immediately became a chopped liver junkie. We couldn't pull him away from the table. At each break, he ran back to that room to fill his face with more and more. It was Ritz crackers and chopped liver for the rest of the evening. He had a funny habit when he found something new to eat that he liked, and I remember this happening with Goobers Peanut Butter and Jelly in college. One night, after class, I brought home an unopened jar with a loaf of bread. The following morning when I saw the empty jar, he looked at me and said," Allen, I couldn't stop eating this stuff, it's great!"

It was time to get some good publicity shots for my latest band, Xanadu. Jeffrey Karasik, who was occasionally still *schlepping* for us, became our official photographer. This was becoming his expertise so why not? We drove around the area taking pictures at a bunch of good spots. One of them was Cimarron City, which in its heyday was a great "western town" attraction constructed in the late 50's. One of the partners of that venture was Alvin Adler, a good friend and local professional engineer. One of the signs from Cimarron City is still hanging in his garage as a reminder of his efforts. By the late 60's, because of a lack of attendance, it had been abandoned, but made for some interesting backgrounds for our photo shoot. One shot that Jeff took was all of us in front of an old store front where the windows were missing. Some of the guys stood outside on the porch while Norby Rausch, who had become our new bass player, and I stood inside the building right behind them. He graduated from a bimmie to playing bass guitar. There was an old mattress in the building that we dragged over to the window and stood on it to gain some more height so that we could be seen above the other band members. The shot came out pretty good, except for a minor technical problem. The next day I developed a tremendous number of bug bites on both my legs that were unbelievable. It didn't take my doctor, Seymour Cohen, too long to figure out that there was something living in the mattress that we had used the day before, like fleas or some other critters that took up residence on my legs. He gave me some heavy duty itch cream, but boy it drove me nuts for several more days.

The members of my last rock and roll band Xanadu. L to R: Me, Norby Rausch, seated, Glenn Vandervoort, Bruce Bleach, and Steve Fornell posing at Cimarron City. Long hair was in, could you tell?

We were having a rehearsal when I noticed Norby was scratching the hell out of his legs. I said, "Norby, lift your pant leg." I walked over and lifted mine. "Looks like a match to me!" He said, "How'd ya know?" "Remember that mattress we stood on in Cimarron City?" I quickly answered. "I couldn't figure out where I got um, but it's all coming back to me now!" he said sort of relieved as I handed him my tube of itch cream.

During the late sixties, because of the rock music explosion, there were several promoters who held concerts of some very popular and soon to be popular rock groups at different venues (hotels and even bungalow colonies), throughout the Catskills. The Gibber Hotel in Kiamesha, which has become a yeshiva, had a summer series of concerts. There were some hot groups like the Chambers Brothers. Another fantastic concert held there starred the Blues Project with an up and coming group known as the Vanilla Fudge. The Fudge soon became a huge success right after their Catskill performance. The room has been converted to a Shul and it's rather strange going in there seeing only students, and wondering where the Hippies went. Here's one for you: Led Zeppelin played the Delano hotel, and there, directly in front of one of the speakers, I mean no more than two feet away, was a guy lying on the floor passed out the whole time. And when I say this concert was loud, I was playing rock and roll myself and for ME this baby was LOUD!

Even the bungalow colonies wanted a piece of the action, like Breezy Corners in Monticello, with groups like Mountain (not to be confused with the "Mountains"). Also performing in their casino was Jethro Tull. Yes, Jethro Tull before they became very popular. What was so amazing about this concert was that there was just a handful of people who came out for the early show, and before the late show started, those of us who wanted to were asked if we would like to stay for the late show at no extra charge, because they wanted to try and fill the room up for the band. Yeah, like we were gonna say no! Could you imagine doing that for a Tull concert today?

Look at the performers that played at the Breezy Corners Bungalow Colony. Not many people were familiar with Jethro Tull yet since the group was just starting out. Check out the cheap ticket prices! And you thought I was kidding. Didn't you?

Another hotel that ran a very successful concert series was The Tamarack in Greenfield Park. Some of the band members and our good friends Sandy Speigelman and Arlene Kaminsky went to see the Who there. What? Never mind. But the one unforgettable concert that we all attended at that hotel featured Jeff Beck, Rod Stewart, and Ron Wood all playing together.

The evening started with hanging outside the building, and getting to know all the other people around you since we were waiting, and waiting, and waiting, because No concert ever started on time. When the doors were finally opened, it was a mad rush getting inside as everyone tried to get up front. There was no reserve seating, just pack um in! The warm-up band had a new drummer, Sammy Gold who just left our band. So we were there to see both acts.

The concert was way behind schedule, but just before Sammy's band was about to begin, Jeff Beck and the other members wanted to perform first, simply because they could. The MC made the announcement that there was going to be another delay since Beck wanted to open the show. Of course, that meant "breaking down" all of Sammy's group's equipment, setting up Beck's group's equipment, and waiting even longer till any live music was happening. The result was a really pissed-off crowd with lots of booing, but we didn't have a choice. The crowd waited an additional half hour or so as all the roadies took down the equipment and finally finished setting up for Jeff Beck. They took the stage, and I wouldn't swear by it, but Stewart and Beck seemed drunk as hell, as they received a not so warm welcome, which was to be expected. They played about three songs when Rod Stewart was trying to get the audience to clap along to one of Beck's popular song, "I Ain't Superstitious". The problem was, the audience was still upset with their delaying the concert, and a lot of people weren't ready to join in. After some further attempts by Rod Stewart to get some clapping going, he stopped singing, walked off stage, and moments later returned with a fire extinguisher which he promptly set off over the crowd. The people up front were taken by surprise as he expelled the white powder in an instant, and just as quickly the entire band took off in their limo. At that point, we were all glad that we weren't so close to the stage after all.

"Holy smokes, what the hell just happened?" everyone was saying. I immediately grabbed the girls and tried to get to an outside wall of the room, anticipating there was going to be a nasty riot, but through some miracle the MC was able to calm the audience, and get the room under control. Sammy's band ended the evening as a very sympathetic crowd cheered them on.

About 2 weeks later I got a call from Sammy inquiring if I was still interesting in getting a new guitar. I said to him," Yeah, I am, but it's got to be a Les Paul." He answered, "I thought so. My friend has a used one that he wants to sell and it's really sweet. You should really check it out Allen. Why don't you pick me up at my house and we'll go over there." When we arrived, I was introduced to his friends and followed them into the basement. They looked around the room like someone was watching, which I thought was rather strange, but when he opened the guitar case, I could see why. My eyes almost fell out of their sockets. There, right in front of me, was Jeff Beck's guitar. I'm sure you're asking yourself, how I could tell it was his? It wasn't like I was up close at the concert to see any specific details on his guitar. Well, there on the neck, in inlaid white pearl, was Jeff Beck's name. My reaction was," HOLY SH-T! There's no way I can buy that! Are you crazy? That guitar is so hot and so well marked! But how the hell did you get it?" Sammy's friend told me that right after Rod Stewart blew off the fire extinguisher, Jeff Beck immediately put his guitar in his guitar case and figured one of his roadies would grab it, but instead, we were working on stage for Sammy that night and were so pissed off like everyone else, we just grabbed it and ran. I couldn't believe they had the *chutzpa* to do that, but there it was, right in front of me.

"Can I play it?'" I asked with great anticipation. "Sure, you're the first person we showed it too. We don't know how to play. Hell, maybe you'll decide to buy it, after all!" Sammy's friend said with great hope.

Let me tell you, it was one of the sweetest guitars my fingers ever touched. The action was incredibly smooth. I was so tempted to buy it because of the way it played, but what was I going to do, tape over the name? I don't think so. I was sworn to secrecy that day, but by now, I figured the statute of limitations is over. It's been over forty-four years and I couldn't even tell you the guy's name that had it, really! What a thrill it was to play that guitar. And you know, ironically, I played it longer than Beck did the night of the concert.

Leaky Faucets or Someones Gotta Make this Place Run

That's One Strange Collection Guys

Being in the plumbing, bottled gas, and the washing machine business meant one thing: saving, saving, and even more saving of an enormous amount of different items. As the sixteen foot garage door opened in our house it exposed what looked like the aisles of an old hardware store. On one complete wall were a huge number of various sized bins that contained new and used pipe fittings, washer machine parts, gas valves, specialty tools, pipe dope, (funny name isn't it?), rolls of Teflon tape, and on and on. The other side of the garage had a rack that held long lengths of pipe of various diameters, and all this was just what was in the garage!

In the summer, as you walked downstairs into the basement, you'd feel the temperature change as the cool air touched your skin. What a relief that was on a really hot day, but you had to be careful since there were items on the sides of every step like an old can of grease, several large house jacks, or something else that didn't make it to a shelf. Every inch of space was used. Thank goodness the stairs were extra wide. Now don't let me forget the area above the stairs where there were several shelves that housed toilets of various styles and colors (some in the box and some out). There were also coils of electrical wire that were wider than the shelf they sat on, and always looked like they were about to fall off. Miraculously they never did. Oh yeah, on the opposite wall hung the three and four foot pipe wrenches that were occasionally needed. When you finally made it into the basement, the collection of plumbing paraphernalia didn't end. In addition to the large number of the bins that were filled, there were several long racks of empty baby food jars attached by their lids to the ceiling: their contents easily viewed by looking up. They contained everything from wing nuts, wire nuts, electrical nuts, flat washers, spit washers, star washers, cotter pins, brass screws, stainless steel screws, and a hell of a lot more. We also used a large number of old wooden Breakstone cream cheese boxes which made great storage containers for more items like bolts, wood screws, sheet metal screws, springs, very large washers, and by now I'm sure you get the picture. Yep, we had everything imaginable needed to fix anything we encountered. It was like living in a mini Home Depot.

We also made it a habit to save parts from prior jobs if we knew they were hard to come by. For instance, if we had to replace a complete toilet, we would often save the tank cover because tenants seemed to break them on a regular basis. It was cheaper to sell the colony owner a used tank lid especially if it was for some odd ball model. Although, if you noticed, most replacement toilet tank covers in the mountains never seemed to fit just right. In some colonies, after a tenant accidently broke a toilet tank cover, the owners would simply cut a piece of plywood that roughly covered the tank. Not to classy, but it did the job.

Now, if you visit any plumber's shop you're sure to see some interesting items and you might ask, "What is that thing? It looks like a piece of junk." The answer will always be, "Because it's hard to come by, I may need it someday." And sure as heck, the day you finally throw it out because it's been taking up space for the last ten years, and you've moved it five times, you wind up needing it the following week. I could never figure that out, but it seemed to happen so often. That's another reason why "stuff" stayed around the shop so long.

A portion of our basement was used as the business office. This was where we'd all meet after a hot summer day to cool off and go over the day's events. It was interesting that certain job tasks fell into a repetitive pattern all during the past week.

Let me give you an example. It was way into the season, and we were getting call after call that the propane gas hot water heaters were going off, or even worse started leaking, which meant they had to be replaced. I'm not talking one or two, but we were getting a call for them at least once every other day from different customers. Sometimes there were an excessive number of service calls for cleaning out the rust in a shower head as if there was an epidemic of shower *schmutz* taking over the mountains.

During this one particular summer, Barry and I noticed that we were working on an abnormal number of clogged sinks and stuffed toilets. How could so many tenants have the same problem? It had become such a daily occurrence that we started telling each other what we recovered that day. A stroke of genius hit Barry and that's when he came up with this brilliant idea! "Why don't we start collecting the junk we find while we're cleaning out the drains and toilets?" "Sure, I'm up for that," I responded enthusiastically already wondering what I was going to find on the next job.

So the job began of bringing home all the make-up dispensers, hairbrushes, combs, lip-sticks, rubber balls, kid's toys, forks, spoons, knives, an occasional key, broken jewelry pieces, toothbrushes, pens, pencils, and anything else we uncovered from the great plumbing abyss. We started attaching all the "treasures" we found to a piece of plywood that we kept in the garage. When we tried to bring our trophy board downstairs because we thought it was so cool, Irene yelled, "Don't you dare bring that crap into the basement!" As the summer progressed so did our collection since my dad had three separate crews working that season. When the first guys arrived home, if they had retrieved something, they got to attach their new found item very proudly on the trophy board.

There was one call that stood out from all the rest when we had to go to the Sun Valley Bungalow Colony in Monticello. The owner, Mollie, spoke to my mom about this critical situation, and when we arrived back at our house she instructed my dad to get over there right away. Hy didn't tell me much other than to get in the truck, we have an emergency call, and off we went. From the little bit that I overheard, I figured a valuable piece of jewelry went down someone's drain, not uncommon, and Mollie requested the "Mission Impossible Team". As we entered the tenant's bungalow, the wife was yelling at her husband," I always tell you not to keep them there but you never listen to me Harold!" She pointed to the bathroom, and as I looked in the toilet I saw that it was relatively clean water except for a big blob of toilet paper. "Thank God," I said to myself. We had been working on a sewer job all morning and this was a relief. The lady looked at my dad with a disgusted face and said, "My grandson went to *pish* in the toilet, he was fooling around, and somehow it fell in as he flushed. After Hy diagnosed the sick patient, we went to the truck to get our surgical instruments: rubber gloves, plunger, and an auger. When we returned to the bungalow, the lady was walking out of the operating room shaking her head and saying, "What am I going to do with you Harold?"

The bathroom was rather small, so my dad took the lead, walked in, and leaned over the bowl as I watched from behind. I could see his first attempt being made with some delicate plunging, and just let me say for the record that there is a specialized skill in how to use a plunger with finesse, but we'll go over that in Plumbing 101 at a later date. This was the recommended practice to start with, and as he kept up the steady pumping action to create a vacuum, the water remained very clean. There was hardly any movement of the blockage and nothing came up in the bowl. I still wasn't sure what we were trying to uncover, but I figured it was the old man's glasses. My dad turned to me, shook his head, gave me a look, and at that same moment we both knew what the problem was: "Roller Derby". The toilet paper holder was right next to the bowl allowing the young boy to feed the paper directly into the toilet as he flushed over and over. He watched with joy as it rapidly got sucked off the roll. Wait a minute, you never saw that done? I'll bet you'll try it after you finish this chapter!

It was apparent that there was a huge amount of clean tissue in the toilet, but surprisingly my dad wasn't making any progress. He opted for a more complicated surgical tool, the auger. Attention readers: Do not try this at home if you are not licensed. Side effects include nausea, shortness of breath, or one real messy bathroom. He set the end of the auger in position and with the skill of a master surgeon, he turned the handle several times, pulled on it with a good tug, and the lost item went flying out of the bowl as the water went down. There they were. Harold's false teeth. "So that's what the emergency was all about," I said with surprise. Hy washed them off, walked into the kitchen, went to hand them to Harold, who without missing a beat said," There's no way in hell that I'll ever be able to put them back in my mouth. Thanks anyway boys." And with that, we left his nagging wife berating him even further. "You know Harold, I could… "

I knew I was holding the best item ever recovered for the collection hands down. When we got home the other guys were showing off an intricate butter knife that they had pulled out of a sink that day. "Interesting boys," I said with a surprise up my sleeve. I starting walking away, turned and said, "Oh yeah, we found these beauties today." As I pulled the teeth out of my pocket they just *plotzed* from laughter. When my mom saw the teeth she took out an old blue ribbon that she had, and placed it on Harold's dentures. It was truly the winner that summer!

There were some real tuff times getting through all the hard work we had to do, so having some laughter thrown in helped us to get through it all. I think that coming from my artistic, out of the box way of thinking family, was another reason for the crazy collection of plumbing treasures. My grandfather, Sam, was an excellent oil painter, and my mother was an excellent artisan of all types of different media. They both taught Barry and I an important lesson. Your signature is a very important part of your art work. Any true artist will tell you that. Barry was doing fantastic weavings at the time, and took that lesson to the max as a plumber!

We were working at the Elm Shade Bungalow Colony on Route 42 in South Fallsburg for Chuck Freilich. He had hired my dad to do the plumbing on four duplex bungalows which had to be completed prior to the upcoming summer. Of course, this was in addition to all the other work we had to finish, but you grabbed what you could to make a living up here. I was walking back to the truck for something and as I passed my brother, who was working on his knees, I noticed he was holding a very shinny penny with a pair of pliers. He was in the process of soldering the copper coin to the pipes in close proximity of a shut off valve.

I said quite puzzled, "What's with the penny?"

"I want people to know that we did the work here, so I'm signing my plumbing sculpture with my personalized signature, a penny."

"What a great idea, Barry!"

I bent down to look under the bungalow, and the pipes were perfectly aligned with exact right angles and wiped solder joints. It truly was a work of art. The penny was quite appropriate, and made a definite statement. From that point on, the penny became the Frishman plumbing signature.

Let's jump ahead about 15 years. I'm now working as the building inspector in Fallsburg and just finished discussing a construction project at the Elm Shade with Chuck and his caretaker, Kenny. I just had to ask the question, "Hey Kenny. Did you ever notice any pennies that were soldered to the pipes near the shutoff valves?"

"Yeah, but how'd you know about them?" He didn't know that my dad was contracted to do the work there years earlier. I said, "Because my brother and I put them there. It became our signature." Ken said, "That's so cool! I always wondered who did that."

And to this day, as long as there are pennies around, and as long as I still do a plumbing job for someone, I place the Frishman signature on my work.

An interesting thing happened just recently when I mentioned to the new owner of the Elm Shade, Rabbi Horowitz, that I was writing this book about my past plumbing experiences. I asked if he knew about the pennies. He said he would ask his maintenance man to look for them, and just a few weeks later, as they were replacing a portion of plumbing under a unit, they found an attached penny. He brought in a "signature" piece of pipe to my office and said, "Does this look familiar, Allen?" I couldn't believe our signature was still around at the Elm Shade!

I'm still a collector, as anyone knows whose visited my house, but now the items have historical Catskill significance. One of those includes local vintage soda bottles, which I used to find under many of the bungalows while we were crawling underneath them. They were tossed there by individuals years ago who were too lazy to bring them to a garbage pail. So finding a Mission or Costa soda bottle was common. My collection has increased immensely, and recently I uncovered the mother-load of green glass, Circle A soda bottles at the old Fallsburg Bottling Plant. When I first started selling them on E-bay, because the plant was also a Doctor Pepper distributor at the time, which is imprinted on the bottom, the bottle went for $107.00 no kidding. What a score. I consider that hoard of bottles part of my retirement fund!

The $400.00 Free Bathtub

During the summer, the business ran non-stop from six o'clock in the morning until nine or ten o'clock at night. And that was on a slow day. One evening I had worked till midnight. Exhausted, I got into my truck, put it on automatic cruise and began my journey home. I was almost there when I saw the flashing lights in my rear view mirror. "Sh-t, what's the problem now?" I said to myself as the Trooper was getting out of his car. "Have you been drinking?" were the first words he spoke. Not, "How are you doing, or Where you heading?" I guess I was weaving all over the road, and he thought I was drunk. After I passed the breathalyzer test and told him I had been working steady since seven o'clock that morning, he said, "Go home and get some sleep." "That's where I am going, officer. My house is just down the road," I said in relief.

Because we were working at such a fast pace, keeping track of all the materials we used and how long we were on a job sometimes became a nightmare. When we finished a plumbing job we tried to immediately write down our material list, which at times could be quite long. The list had to include the time we worked and who was actually there; was it Hy, Benny, Larry, Barry, or myself?

This was critical when my brother and I were younger, because my dad couldn't charge full price for us until we were of age.

The information was usually scribbled on a piece of paper that was held on a clip board, along with various other lists, phone numbers, part numbers, schematics, or items that needed to be restocked in the truck. We didn't have a laptop back then. Oh yeah, neither did anybody else. If we ran out of paper the job list was written on a piece of cardboard that was torn off a toilet carton, or better yet, a 2x4 block of wood. We wrote on anything available to record the job before running off to the next emergency. If not, we could easily forget the materials used or the length of time we worked at the last job. This way of keeping track was not unlike the way grocers scribbled on brown paper bags. You used what was available to you in those days. Sometimes one of us would write the list from memory while the other drove. It didn't make for the neatest handwriting because of all the bumpy country roads.

And that's when my mom came into the picture. Remember, she was the company bookkeeper who had the task of trying to decipher our hieroglyphics. Sometimes Larry, with his dry wit, would describe a plumbing part by a different name. For example, on the material list he wrote two Rolaid valves. My mom would have to ask Larry, "What the heck is a Rolaid valve?" "A 'relief' valve, Irene, just like the commercial. What else?" he'd answer with a smile. Luckily, or maybe unlucky for us, the plumbing supply houses, which sold a huge amount of materials, used a more sophisticated and accurate billing system. At the end of one season, as my parents started going through the bills, they realized that my dad had installed an additional bathtub at one of the bungalow colonies, but couldn't remember which one it was! The plumbing supply house bill indicated nine bathtubs sold to my dad, but he could only account for eight installations.

Here's Hy catching a breather at the Monticello Supply House.
Check out those arms of steel. Who had the time and money to
go to the Gym? He worked out with wrenches every day.

My mom suggested that we send bills to a few of the colonies where we probably did the work. Either they would pay the bill and that will be the end of the confusion, or the owner would say it was a mistake and Hy would apologize.

About a week later a check arrived from the Pine Tree Bungalow colony. Great, problem solved. So we thought, until a second check came from Doctor Lockers, and a third check was received from Sun Valley. But after the fourth check came from White Rock, my dad realized the plan had backfired. The bungalow colony owners were so caught up in the summer's *tummel* that they also had trouble remembering how many tubs we had installed.

"What are we going to do, Hy?" my mom asked. Reluctantly, he responded, "Irene, return all the checks. It was our mistake and we'll have to eat it." That was the end of it. Somewhere, someone got a great deal that summer in the Catskills. Sometimes I wondered who was bathing in that tub free of charge.

Hy We Need Quarters, It`s an Emergency

Paul Mirsky, my ex-brother-in-law, who coincidentally was also a plumber, told me this tale about how he stored a considerable amount of cash after finishing a big job. It was Friday night and too late to get to the bank. The following morning he had to leave for a family trip, so he cleverly decided to hide the money in a Ziplock bag stuffed inside a frozen chicken. I thought that was ingenious, double protection! Well, upon his return from the trip he was extremely upset to see that someone had broken into his home through a back window. What made it worse was while the thief was in his house he must have said, "Hey, let's check out this guy's freezer." A few days later, still upset that the burglar stole his hard earned money, he turned to his wife, Ronnie, at dinner and said," I hope that bastard cooked that God Damm chicken, money and all."

Thank God that didn't happen to my parents who also hid money buried underneath the food in our large freezer chest. There was always an abundance of quarters because of the coin-operated washing machine business we owned. The freezer became my parent's personal bank and when my dad had to make a deposit he never had the time to defrost the money. The coins were always still cold to the touch, and when he'd hand a canvas bag to the teller they would always ask, "Hy, do you have cold cash in those bags?" To which he would always reply with a smile, "What do you think?"

After collecting the coins from all the washers and dryers, we then had the long and tedious chore of counting them out with our customers before giving them their cut. My Dad's business wasn't large enough to warrant a mechanical coin counter, so instead they were counted manually. We counted twenty quarters by sliding them off the edge of the table making five dollar piles and then stacked them carefully in neat rows of $100.00. We then gave the owner their due and took our portion home.

One evening my dad asked me to go along with him to Fialkoff's Bungalow Colony in Monticello. He had fallen behind in the scheduled collection that week and I was a fast counter and stacker. Fialkoff's, having three separate laundry rooms, was one of our biggest accounts and the haul would be over $800.00. I always helped my dad out when I could, but on that particular occasion I had *sphelkis* because I was going out with friends afterwards.

Before we counted we had to remove the marked coins which the owner used for their personal laundry. (Part of the deal for us to get their account was that they could use our laundry equipment for free. Their quarters were marked with red nail polish so they stood out). We had to count the money on Esther Fialkoffs' kitchen table, and I think we had about $500.00 neatly stacked when one of Esther's grandchildren came running into the kitchen and accidently bumped into the table. Can you imagine $500.00 worth of neatly stacked quarters spilling all over the place? I couldn't either until that night. We had to start all over which of course took more time making me even more upset having to be there. When I finally got back to my house the guys were waiting in the driveway for me. I looked at them and said "Don't even ask, but I'll tell ya there was a lot of money spilled in town tonight!" From that night on we set a new rule never to allow anyone near the counting table unless they could sit still.

Quite often, during a service call the ladies would walk into the laundry room and ask for change. Most of them didn't have cars to go to the bank, since their husbands used them to get back to the city for the week. We figured if our customers didn't have quarters for the washers and dryers we wouldn't get there business! So it was our pleasure to oblige. It was not unusual for an owner of a colony to call asking for an unscheduled collection because they needed change for their tenants. Even if it was for their own little grocery store, we tried to accommodate the owners the best we could.

But there was one phone call that was the winner. We had two phones lines in our house, 2236 was for family use, and 748 was the business line or "The Hot Line" as it was affectionately called. These were our telephone numbers even before we had dial tones. When 748 rang it meant you had better answer it, and in those days we didn't have the luxury of an answering machine to get our calls. So you made every effort to get to that phone. There were many times we'd be outside playing, the phone would ring, and my Mom would go running in the house in an effort to try and catch the call. This particular Saturday, my dad had a very long day and crashed about 10:00 pm. Thank God the day was over. But at about 11:00 pm, 748 rang. Irene answered, and the call went something like this. "Is Hy there?" "Just a minute, I'll get him." They were both already in bed sleeping, but the phone ringing woke up my dad. In his anticipation he said, "It must be an emergency plumbing problem to receive a call this late." She handed him the phone and my dad asked "Who is this?" The guy on the other end of the phone gave him his name but my father didn't recognize it at all.

"Hy, we have an emergency here."

"Where is here and what's the emergency?"

"Here, at Lewinter's."

"Why isn't Herman calling?"

"He's sleeping."

"So what's the emergency?"

"We need quarters desperately."

It seemed odd that someone else would be calling my dad besides Herman Lewinter, the owner.

My dad thought for a second and asked the guy, "Are there that many women doing laundry on a Saturday night?"

"No we're about to have a card game in the casino, and everyone forgot to pick up quarters so we could play!"

My dad was infuriated and said to the caller, "On a Saturday night, you call here at 11 o'clock for quarters because of your *facocta* card game? Drop dead!" And with that he slammed the phone in its cradle.

My father was getting busier and busier with the plumbing business which meant that I was running the washing machine enterprise practically on my own. When I graduated college and came home to make a living, my parents graciously allowed me to take over the coin-op business completely.

With my newfound college education I quickly set out to modernize the coin counting enterprise and purchased a tubular quarter counter which sped up the coin collection process. All I had to do was drop a handful of quarters in the tube, level off the top, slide a coin wrapper into the counter, and I could lay down a $10.00 roll onto the table. Plus, I no longer had to worry about "quarter spillage". It was great! What a time saver that little tool became.

At the White Rock Bungalow Colony in South Woods, Monticello, the owner's children were always intrigued with the number of quarters that I emptied into the canvas bank bags at collection time. Whenever I showed up, they'd come running into the laundry room and ask me, "Are you taking out the money today?" If I answered yes, they would stick around to hear the clacking of the quarters pouring into the coin bag as I emptied all the coin boxes. As the money bag would begin to fill the kids would comment, "Wow, that's like $4000.00 dollars!" I wish! They were all very young and didn't have a real sense of how much money there actually was, but off we went into Mrs. Mermelstein's unit to begin counting the coins on her table. Since they were so intrigued with all the collected coins I started a contest with them. We each had to guess the exact amount of money that was in the bag before I started counting. The one who was the closest got to keep it all. When we started the game, the kids would shout out "$5000.00, $6000.00." They really had no idea that the collection amounts were about $300.00 to $400.00 during a slow week or maybe $700.00 on a good week.

One night, after watching us play the game for several weeks, Mrs. Mermelstein took one of her sons in the other room and told him to say $430.00. He came back in and without me knowing about the tip off, and shouted out, "$430.00." Wow, where did that come from I thought. Alright my guess was $440.00. Now the pressure was on. Weeks had gone by and the kids never even came close, but the rule was if you guessed higher than the actual amount, you lost and they always lost. I made sure to always guess conservatively but this time I had to be right on. The quarter rolls were building up on the table. I was getting closer and closer to finishing what was left in the bag. And then it happened, $432.50. I lost for the first time and I could see his mom smiling in the back of the kitchen. Then I realized why he left the room for a few seconds. I had been taken by Bensey Mermelstein who came in closer than I did to the exact amount. He won the contest, but there was no way I was going to give a five year old my weeks-worth of hard earned cash. I conceded to giving him two dollars and said, "Games over kid." He was happy with the money, and even happier that he won, which gave us all a good laugh, especially his mom, Shashana.

The nine day observance of *Tisha B'av* always hurt the washing machine business in our religious accounts. During this solemn time, a minimal amount of laundry can be done. It was a slow-down period and became the time to overhaul our equipment in preparation for the mad rush when *Tisha B'av* ended. But, wait... figure you have a family with eight or nine children, and the laundry has built up like there's no tomorrow. *Tisha B'va* ends and the washing clock starts at sundown. Everybody wanted to wash at once, but there were only five or six washing machines. How did they handle that dilemma? They held a lottery. Everyone's name was put into a hat and you were picked by the luck of the draw. How's that for keeping things under control. The order of washing was posted in the laundry room. You'd be given a maximum of three loads to start. That was the way it was done. But God forbid if the machine you were using broke down, forget about it! It stopped the whole flow of this intricate balance of the washing machine lottery. This meant that we could get a call at any time of the night. Since they were washing straight through, 24/7, until they caught up, they figured we should be available to fix the machines 24/7.

When my son Chad was born during *Tisha B'av* in 1983 I still had the washing machine account at White Rock. Before the nine days ended, I delivered two extra washing machines that I had just rebuilt. There wasn't any more space inside the laundry room that already had 6 washers and 4 very large commercial dryers, so I placed them outside on wooden pallets hoping that this would help to alleviate the Ladies washing rush. Would you believe that three machines broke down the day after my son was born, which was the second day into the washing lottery. Just like my dad had taught me that those quarters got him through the long winter, I did what a man had to do, and off I went, right from the hospital to make the necessary repairs.

If we had a profitable season in the washing machine business it meant that it had been a rainy and cold season. The kids would get dirty much more often and that meant that the moms' were constantly washing and drying their clothes, since they couldn't hang them on the line in wet weather. The ladies had to keep putting in quarters and wait forever just to get a dry towel, but it wasn't the fault of the dryers. There was no place for the moisture to go. If I was having a bad summer, and some kids came into the laundry room I'd give them some advice. I'd say, "Hey you're in the country. Go out, have some fun, and play in the mud! That's why we have all these washing machines." If we were having a sunny hot summer, everyone just wore bathing suits, dried them over the rope cloths lines strung between the bungalows or if you had a porch, right over the railings, and you'd put them back on the next day to go swimming again. The business didn't do as well during those hot, dry summers.

In all those years of business there was one common complaint that we always heard from the bungalow colony tenants: "Your machines stink. Why can't you get us new ones"? The answer to that question was quite simple. The investment in purchasing new equipment would take a payback time of approximately four years. This was due to their limited two month seasonal use. By then, the equipment was really used. No, let me change that, abused.

To try and compensate for all their *kvetching*, we always made an attempt to upgrade our washing machines with used replacement equipment. My dad would always look for deals and buy used pieces from Laundromats in New York City. I was taught at an early age how to work on the coin-op machines and as soon as I finished my high school exams, I worked full time out of our garage making ten "new" machines out of 20 used clunkers. I would mechanically rebuild their insides and would spray them with fresh white paint to make them look like new. We only had about 6 weeks to get everything in place before our seasonal visitors would arrive, so there wasn't much time for dilly dallying. Unfortunately, no matter how hard we tried to satisfy our customers they knew they were old machines and still pestered us as to why we wouldn't go out and just purchase new equipment every year. We would try to educate them about the machines operating for only two months a year but they really didn't care at all about our problems. It was the rebuilding process that made our small business last as long as it did.

In the fall I would help my dad *schlep* a washer down the cellar stairs into the basement for a major overhaul. He would be underneath the machine holding back the weight and I would be on top guiding the hand truck, (dolly), step by step. And just like every new car is tested before it is released, it became Irene's job to "test drive" these rebuilt machines to make sure they were working properly. That meant coin slot and all. We had to be absolutely sure that they were going to run well in the up-coming season. In fact, we never ever had a domestic (non-coin operated), washer or dryer in our house while growing up. Why should we, the machines were better off running through the winter then standing still and we were always in the process of rebuilding and testing them. One summer we were having an abnormal amount of equipment breakdowns, and there was a little less than 2 weeks to go in the season. We just didn't have any spares left to replace what had broken, so Hy needed to take the coin-op washer that my mom was using right out of the basement. She wasn't happy, but she understood the situation. It had to be placed in a bungalow colony to get every quarter we could squeeze out of the season and not lose the account. It was going to be a long cold winter. There was no time to get the parts needed to completely rebuild another machine or to purchase a new one to collect money for only two weeks and then sit idle for the next ten months. That was unsound business.

I guess my mom and dad worked out an agreement because later that week, she handed my dad all the families' laundry in a multitude of plastic bags. On Saturday night when no one was washing clothes, since they were generally getting ready for the show in the casinos, he brought them all to Fialkoff's Bungalow Colony. There were nine washers and three commercial dryers in the main laundry room. In two hours he was able to get all the laundry done, plus he made lots of minor repairs that were badly needed but were pushed off during the season because we were so busy. He was also able to wash down all the soap that collected from the spillovers the past few weeks.

When it was time to replace a washing machine, we had a company ritual, which was looking for the money that was under that machine. If we were working as a team that day doing laundry room set ups, when a machine was placed on a dolly and moved, we would dive for the change that the tenants had lost as a result of coins dropping in between the washers or rolling under the machines during the past few seasons. Sometimes it could add up to a dollar or more, but it wasn't the amount it was the game that helped the job go by easier.

My dad only bought Speed Queen commercial washing machines. These were the Cadillac of commercial washers. There was one job that had to be performed on a yearly basis that we would do every spring. We had to remove the agitators to clean out the grit that would collect around the main post. After removing the agitators we would usually find coins and sometimes a piece of valuable jewelry which had been left in someone's pocket before they did their wash. One spring, while working with Benny Ortiz he hit a gold mine at Lewinter's. We must have missed that particular machine the prior year because he found almost $6.00 in coins and a solid gold chain. Now that's some booty!

It's funny that he found all that treasure at Lewinter's of all places. It probably belonged to the lady who always came running down to the laundry room when she saw my dad, and complained that the dryer didn't dry or the washing machine didn't rinse out properly. And I mean ALWAYS! It was absolutely impossible that the machines always broke when she used them, but sometimes he would return her money just so she would go away. It was a new season and I was now operating the business. Here she comes, running in and started her typical complaining. I had just gotten a face full of rust from an old washer hose and I looked her in the eyes and said," You know how you bugged my father every time we came in here. Well those days are over so "Gay cocken afen yum", and from that day on she knew her game was up. She never came asking for her fake refund ever again.

Another source of income that I engaged in was outside service work for other bungalow colonies that had their own commercial laundry equipment. One that used my services extensively was located in South Fallsburg on Pleasant Valley Road. This particular owner liked working with me, not only because I showed up rather promptly after he called, but because I would sell him used parts which meant a cheaper bill and that's all he cared about. After several long hours of repairing his equipment, I found the owner and told him, "I've got your old clinkers running one more time and with the parts and labor you owe me is $120.00", which was a very good price for all the time I had spent there. I was always fair with my customers, but he was just a cheap son of a bitch and he started yelling and screaming about how much I was charging him as he starting peeling off $20.00 bills from a roll that he pulled out of his pocket. He literally threw them at me one at a time which forced me to bend down and pick them up by my feet. His attitude was really uncalled for and I was going to start in with him, but I had a long day and was too exhausted. What I never told him was that he threw down an extra $20.00 by mistake. I didn't feel that I took him since I really worked fairly cheap, and on top of that I had to deal with his insult and his throwing the money at me. So you know what, the extra $20.00 was worth it. Thanks Sanford!

One of the great off shoots of being in the coin-op business was having a great coin collection, particularly quarters. My mom and I were always looking for the missing ones to fill the empty spots in our blue collector books. I had a few high school friends that were also collectors and one of them was Neil

Golivin. We had a ritual that on Friday nights, we'd borrow some money from our parents, go to the bank on Broadway, ask for several rolls of coins, walk across the street to his father's office in the Rhulen Insurance Company building, open up the rolls of coins, and search for the ones that we needed for our collections. This worked out great. We kept going back and forth with the re-rolled money and occasionally would find a coin that one of us was searching for. My friends would look through rolls of pennies, nickels, dimes, and quarters but I never bothered with the quarters since I had so many to sort through in my own house. For me, it was pennies and dimes. We had to make good use of our time, since the Friday night hours were 5:30 to 6:30. Every once in a while someone would yell out I found a such and such and would insert it into their collector books. But there was only one person in town who had a better quarter collection than mine and that was Jeffery Kaufman. Not because he came to the bank with us. It was because his father had a bigger coin-op business than my dad's. He even had some year round clients which meant that his source of quarters was much greater, which meant that his collection was complete. The one quarter that I never found was a rare 1932-S. One day I asked Jeffery if he had it. He brought his blue coin book holder into school and there it was without any openings, from 1930 and up. From that day on, I have repeatedly looked at all the quarters that I come in contact with or listen for the distinctive clink of silver currency in my change. I'm still hoping that one day I might find that 1932-S to complete my collection. As of this date it's not looking so good. So to all the readers, if you care to donate this quarter to completing my collection call me. I'm always home.

Benny and the Schleps and No Headphones for Harry

Getting the Catskills moving after the long cold winters took lots of time and hard work. Even though there was sometimes a break in the weather, we had to wait for many of the owners to return from their winter homes. Since the work ahead was too much for the family to do alone, my dad hired several helpers. One of them was Benny Ortiz Gonzalez, who remains a close friend of the family to this day. Benny was one of the hardest workers my dad ever hired, and he pushed us all to complete a job in one day, so that we wouldn't have to return. The colony owners definitely got their money's worth out of him.

The two of us would continue working after hours to make extra money as building contractors. Most of the jobs were constructing bedroom and porch additions at the White Rock Colony in South Woods. Since I had a background in architectural design, and could use a tape measure more efficiently, I was the "cutter." I laid out the job while Benny had the position of "nailer." He'd push me so fast and hard, that sometimes it caused a miscalculation in my cutting and would have to do it all over again. This resulted in wasted time which he hated. When we couldn't see the heads of the nails any longer (nail-guns were unheard of back then), we had to surrender to the darkness. Thank God, because after a full day of plumbing with my dad, and then the additional work with Benny, I was exhausted. A number of years later Benny left my dad to work full-time at Kutcher's Country Club where he remained a loyal employee for many more years.

He was also an outstanding tennis player, sought after by many of the guests. Because of his powerful arms, he had a wicked serve. One day at my dad's house, he was showing off his strength with a golf club and ball that someone found at a job that day. He proceeded to tee off at one end of the lawn and slammed the ball with all his might, expecting it to fly over our neighbor's house. Instead, it flew straight across the backyard and...Wham! Dad's storage shed got in its way and became Benny's unintentional target. Its walls were constructed of homosote, a composite-like material similar to cardboard. The ball lodged itself in the wall and became a monument to his strength, and it remained there for years. I forgot to mention that he missed the window by just few inches. Benny was just one of the memorable characters with whom we worked.

My brother Barry and I are moonlighting in NYC for our good friend Jerry Lerner. There was a hand rolled cigar store down the street, so why not? "What da mean you need a building permit and a license to work in the city!"

Louie Slamowitz's place was the conglomeration of several colonies on a large piece of property. As Louie got a little older, his son-in-law, Martin Greenberg, bought him an electric golf cart to be able to get around easier. You'd see the kids chasing Louie on what they nick-named the "Slamobile."

Now being one of the largest colonies meant having one of the largest crew of helpers. I called these guys "Louie's Army". Occasionally, Louie would find someone who had some real carpentry or plumbing skills. This was the case of Harry, one of his sergeant's. Harry was assigned to work with us because of his plumbing knowledge, and we could always use an extra hand in opening the water at the Ideal. But he did have one small problem. Harry couldn't hear too well, and communication with one another is very important when you're plumbing. We would sometimes be separated from a co-worker by a crawl-space and could be a hundred feet from a main valve. Quite often, we could be heard screaming, "Open the valve," or "Shut the valve off, quick!" It could take a few on and offs until we found all the leaks that needed repair.

To counter the frustrating dilemma of not hearing one another, my dad bought a set of wireless voice-operated hearing devices. They were extremely innovative at the time. All we had to do was speak into the small microphone that was strapped over our heads, and with the attached earpieces we could easily hear one another. The devices were particularly helpful when we were working at the larger bungalow colonies.

Now, here is where Harry comes in. We liked Harry a lot, but being one of Louie's "soldiers," meant hygiene wasn't one of his strong suits. In fact, I don't think the guy ever cleaned his ears, judging by the fact that he couldn't hear out of them too well, but maybe that's why? My dad suggested that we give a head set to Harry so he could hear us better, and that started our protest. We'd have to put the headphone sets on our own ears after Harry used them. We went ballistic. My brother yelled, "No way in hell is that going on Harry's head. We don't want any diseases that the guy might have!" We weren't going to let my dad give a set of headphones to Harry no matter what. So, Hy reluctantly agreed that it was no headphones for Harry. We just had to yell louder when we worked with him.

My dad always needed reliable help, and who better to serve him than his own boys. As I got a little older, my dad started charging the colony owners for the time I put in as a helper. He'd put me on the job after school and on weekends to assist with all the work he had. The owners *kvetched* that I was too young and that I didn't work like him. He would justify my expense by telling them that I could crawl under their bungalows easier and faster, thereby saving time, which translated into saving money. He'd often say to them, "Do you want me to stop what I'm doing to get something out of the truck? Allen can run and get it while I can keep working." They soon realized that my brother Barry and I were part of the crew and that was that.

By the time I reached the age of 16 my rock and roll band, The New Generation, was well established in the Mountains. Remember Norby, one of our professional *schlepers*? He became another one of my dad's helpers that summer. (Incidentally, years later, he started his own band with his family, The Rausch Brothers and has become very popular in our area).

We worked together that summer on an 8 to 5 schedule. Some nights we had gigs all over the mountains that could last until 1:00 or 1:30 in the morning. Then there was the packing up and the traveling home. Getting to bed at 3:00 a.m. wasn't unusual. The problem was getting up 4 hours later to go back to work, which, for my dad meant that we were going to be useless that day. But he taught us a very important lesson. We had to always look busy since the bungalow colony owner was paying for every minute of our time. He stressed that we should always carry a wrench so that we looked like we were working, even if we were just walking somewhere to "take" a leak (as opposed to "fixing" a leak). The other unofficial lesson we learned was that if we had to pass out from a lack of sleep, find a piece of cardboard from an old sink or better yet, a bathtub carton, throw it under a bungalow, close the crawlspace door, and grab a quick nap. One of Norby's attributes was his superior strength. He was great for breaking apart old pipe fittings, but when it came to threading new pipe, we always had to remind him, "Don't screw that joint too tight. Someday WE might have to loosen it."

Hy was at the plumbing supply house when the counter guys' were showing him a new type of nylon tape that was supposed to be indestructible. "Hy, you can't tear this tape without a knife. Go ahead, try it!" He was unsuccessful just like they said he would be. "Okay Joe, hook me up with a few rolls," he said. The following morning, when Norby showed up for work at my dad's house, he told Norby about this incredible tape. "You can't tear this stuff by hand," he said. Norby asked, "Can I try it, Hy?" "Sure." He unrolled the tape a little and started tearing the piece off with little effort. That's when my dad said, "Get in the truck, guys. We're going back to the supply house!" When we got there, my dad called the counter guys over and said, "Watch this." And without much effort, Norby proceeded to rip another piece of tape off the roll, as everyone's mouth dropped. He amazed the guys in the supply house. "You can keep your indestructible tape," Hy said, and with that they gave him a refund.

Larry Cardini was the last helper to work with my father until dad finally retired. They were working together in a small bungalow colony in White lake owned by a Russian couple. The wife basically ran the operation while her husband worked in New York City during the week. She was a rather large and *softik* woman who catered to a Russian clientele.

Larry and Hy were on the premises "jobbing". This meant fixing small items like a leaky faucet or cleaning out shower heads to get more pressure, not major plumbing jobs like opening water or installing a toilet, etc. Usually by the 3rd week of summer, when things started to slow down, it gave us time to catch up on all the smaller complaints. One of the tenants just happened to see Larry carrying a wrench and started yelling, "Mr. Plumber, Mr. Plumber, please come here for a minute." She complained that the water pressure in her kitchen sink was very slow and said, "The water tastes like sh-t!" To compensate for the bad taste, she had to buy bottled water. According to the tenant, she was the only one with this problem, while all her neighbors said their water tasted fine. She wasn't on the approved list of work locations that the owner gave them, so he told her he might be able to come back in a little while. A short time later, when Larry saw my dad walking on the grounds, he told him about the woman's lament.

Hy answered, "All right, let me talk to the owner." After finishing the work list he walked over to the owner's unit and said to her, "Natasha, Larry told me about the lady in bungalow 7. She doesn't have much water pressure in her kitchen sink, and she says her water tastes terrible." In a no nonsense tone, with her heavy Russian accent, she responded, "She's crazy. There's nuthing wrong mit her vater. Let's go. Ahl show you."

By now Larry caught up with them. They all proceeded to the tenant's bungalow. Upon arriving, the owner grabbed a glass from the drain board, opened the faucet, took a drink, and said, "See? Dares nuthing vrong mit your vater. It's in your head." She did admit that the pressure was a little sluggish, even with the faucet not having its aerator on. (We always removed them since it was a rust and *schmutz* collector that would decrease the faucet's pressure. If they were left on, the tenants would complain, "I don't have enough water pressure!" This would force us to spend time removing the aerator, cleaning them out, and to the owners this was considered a needless service call which would cost them money). In this case he figured a big chunk of rust got stuck behind the faucet spindle. That's why there was low pressure and was probably the reason for giving it that bad taste. But to see if the doctor's diagnosis was correct, the water had to be turned off to remove the spindle.

Larry looked under the sink to see if there were some cut off valves, but this was an older bungalow and valves added additional cost during the construction. Of course there weren't any. They're not for the customers, they're for the plumber's convenience, and anything was done to avoid spending extra money. But there was one thing in abundance under this sink: steel wool. This was the tenant's best weapon against mice from getting into their units. They would try and stuff every hole, especially around the plumbing pipes coming through the floor. (But the mice were smart and would just find another hole somewhere else to get in). The earlier bungalows didn't have insulation in their walls, so the mice found the next best thing. They would sometimes make their winter homes in the insulation of the walls of the kitchen stoves. What a nice warm comfortable place to settle in for the long cold winter. This worked great until that first day when the stove was turned on, and you could die from the mouse turds cooking. Okay, okay, let's get back to Larry and Hy.

It was decided that my dad would go under the unit to close the main water valve while Larry would work in the kitchen dismantling the faucet. Two hits on the faucet body meant close the valve, three hits meant open it up again. Hy heard the first signal, turned the water off, and waited patiently for the open signal. Larry started to dismantle the spout and saw an object lodged in the body of the faucet. "I think I found something," he said to both onlookers. Using his small needle nose pliers, and with the skill of a practiced surgeon, he carefully picked out a tiny object that was causing the restriction in pressure and probably the bad taste. "What is that?" the tenant asked inquisitively. "That's a small mouse that somehow got stuck in the faucet." Remembering the glass of water she just drank, the owner began screaming and jumping up and down. When my dad heard all of the noise, and saw the floor bouncing, he immediately came out from under the bungalow to see what all the commotion was about. Running into the kitchen he witnessed the owner still screaming and hopping all over the place, with her rather large bosom swinging in the breeze! It was a sight to see!

Larry held up his pliers with the tiny mouse still in it, and he and my dad couldn't hold in the laughter any longer. At that point they both lost it. The tenant started yelling at the owner, "I told you the water tasted like sh-t and you didn't believe me!" The owner was still screaming and started cursing in Russian at the mouse or maybe it was the tenant. The boys couldn't stop laughing as Larry put the faucet back together, turned to both women and said, "Have a nice day, ladies." That was one service call for the books! All right, just for this book.

Thank's for the Aggravation

My mother, Irene, was the bookkeeper, secretary, and receptionist of the family business. She worked in the trenches of the front line. There weren't any answering machines yet to take a message from an irate customer, of which there were plenty in the summer. So when the phone rang we had to answer as soon as we could. This meant not having a peaceful meal, because they always tried to catch my dad when they thought he was home.

We had a new customer one summer, Mr. & Mrs. R... who purchased the Pine Tree Bungalow Colony on Route 42. She and her husband owned a jewelry store in Brooklyn, and thought they could do well in the bungalow colony business (like everyone else who tried in the Catskills). A big influence in their decision to buy the Pine Tree was that her sister just happened to be Shirley Slamowitz who owned the Ideal Bungalow Colony directly across the street. Shirley explained to her that because we lived so close we could get there fast in an emergency. That was one of the main reasons for hiring my dad. The problem was she frantically called my Mom no matter how simple the plumbing problem was. In her mind, even a dripping faucet was an emergency.

One morning, Mrs. R... called the house at 8:15 and demanded, "Where's Hy? He promised me he would be here at 8 o'clock and that I was going to be his first customer!" My mom was very offended and replied curtly, "Why don't you look around the colony? He's already there!" The customer didn't even have the decency to check the grounds before she assumed that my dad had left her hanging. This gives you a little insight into the type of character she was. By summers end she must have realized how much *tzoris* she had given my mom, because she invited her to come to the colony for a small token of appreciation. At first, she refused. "Irene, please, it's just around the corner. I really want to meet you. Please." Her persistence persuaded my mom and dad to take a quick ride to the colony.

They arrived at the Pine Tree and Irene met the owners face to face for the first time. They apologized over and over for giving my mom such a rough time that summer. This was their first season operating a bungalow colony, and they were truly overwhelmed with all that was involved, especially with the tenants' issues. Mrs. R... had no idea what it was like to operate a colony with all the complaints and headaches that you had to deal with. It was nothing like the jewelry business that she was accustomed to. So, as an apology for her constant nagging, and being such a pain in the *tuchas* she placed a variety of jewelry pieces on her kitchen table and insisted that my mom pick something. Irene gave them a cursory look and quickly chose a pin.

My mother didn't wear much jewelry but knew she had to take something to make Mrs. R... happy. She had no intentions of wearing the item, and didn't even bother to look at it closely, figuring it was just a piece of costume jewelry. Being very polite she said thank you, and that was the end of the season. On their way home she coined the phrase "the aggravation pin" for all the aggravation Mrs. R... gave my mom that summer.

A few weeks later our cousin, Sam Cohen (he worked with the stripper at Sadownick's), came over for cake and coffee. During the evening's *schmoozing* she told him the story about the bungalow colony owner and her gesture to offer her some jewelry. She asked Sam, who was a jeweler, if he wouldn't mind looking at the pin which she assumed was a cheap item. He replied, "For you, Irene, anything." He looked at it and quickly said," You know, Irene, these are real stones. This is not a *schlock* piece of jewelry and it's probably worth about five hundred dollars." And with that she said, "It still wasn't worth the aggravation!"

Here is my beautiful mom holding her first born son, me, at Hemlock Grove. I was dressed to the nines back then.

Hey, It's the Movie Guy!

One of the biggest challenges that many of the bungalow colony owners faced was keeping the summer tenants satisfied so they would leave a deposit for the following year. As the area hotels started building swimming pools, the bungalow colonies followed suit. The "modern filtered swimming pool" became another added expense to keep the customers happy and they weren't cheap! Not all activities were costly. Something as simple as Bingo, played in the social hall, was exceedingly popular. But the one treat that everyone looked forward to was movie night.

Once a week, a recent movie was shown in the casino. Because this was a specialized service, there weren't too many companies to choose from. The company my family used, for as long as I could remember, was owned by Mr. Hecht from Woodbourne. In early spring he would send my grandmother Shirley the list of available films for the new summer season. She, along with my mom and my Aunt Rosalie, would choose what the tenants were going to watch that summer

."I loved Donald Sutherland in ... " someone remarked.

"Okay, we'll choose that one."

"How 'bout....?"No, that one's too racy. I don't need any complaints."

And, out of thirty movie possibilities, the list was whittled down to ten. One movie was chosen by our outstanding team of movie critics for each week of the summer.

The evening started with closing the wooden venetian blinds. This was followed by blankets spread out on the wooden floor. It was time for cartoons for the kids. The children quieted down as the grinding noise of the projector would begin.

Of course, there was always one boy who had to get in front of the projector light and make shadow puppets on the screen during the number count down. Try doing that when the adults were watching a movie and you might have been shot. The cartoons kept the kids occupied giving the moms' time to make dinner before the big show. There was no television in the summer. This was the "get outside and play" generation.

Movie night promised to be a profitable money maker for the resort owners since that meant the grocery store would be open and there was a captive audience of customers. Everyone wanted some type of snack like a Sugar Daddy, a box of Cracker-Jacks with a cool prize, a Doctor Brown's soda, a pack of Tops baseball cards with that delicious sheet of powered bubble gum (and if you got lucky you unwrapped a Mickey Mantle or a Willie Mays card), or maybe it was a Chocolate Mellow Roll that you had to slide onto a pointed stick and then remove the paper wrapper to get to the ice cream.

When the movie guy arrived, and God forbid he was late, he'd carry in the 16mm projector, the movie screen, and those indestructible protective cases that held the movies. A bomb could blow up next to one and it would survive. The projectionist was usually the "AV" guy (audio visual), from high school who knew how to thread the film through the sprockets of the projector and found his niche for making extra money in the summer in the Catskills.

Because my dad had experience using projectors, he sometimes helped out in the later part of the season and became the movie guy for the night. This was a savings for my grandparents since they didn't have to pay for Hecht's projectionist, plus it gave my dad a short respite from plumbing work. If I had behaved that day, and the movie was a comedy or something acceptable to watch as a kid, I could tag along with my dad. When I got to the colony, I played with my friends until the start of the main event. One particular film which caused a big stir was Alfred Hitchcock's block buster "The Birds". Everyone was talking about how scary it was, but a few of my young buddies at Sadownick's said, "I don't think it's that bad, it's just about a bunch a birds that land in this town."

When it was time for the main feature, Andrea Dinner, a good friend of mine, brought in a big blanket and laid it down in front of the wooden folding seats. The chairs were used exclusively by the adults who filled the casino on movie night, but some tenants got fancy and would bring in their own lounge chairs to get ultra-comfortable. When the birds came swooping down and started to attack the actors, we were so close to the screen it felt like they were coming for us. For the rest of the summer, when a flock of birds flew over-head, we all ran for cover. Okay, who said this wasn't a scary movie?

There was one small drawback when my dad ran the movie. Once in a while, without warning, the brittle 16mm film would snap and tear. This was not the typical changing of the reels at intermission. It always seemed to happen at the worst time. If it took my dad a few minutes to get things rolling again, the crowd would get anxious and someone would shot out, "Come on, Hy, we don't have all night." Boy, those comments really bothered me as if it was his fault. Eventually, things got rolling again, the movie ended and it was time to go home. I always fell asleep in the back seat of the car and was carried into my bed. Movie night was another one of those special events in the Country.

Come Closer, Closer Still

One of the more challenging places to work in the Catskills was in the Hasidic bungalow colonies. This wasn't due to the actual plumbing since all of the plumbing in the Mountains was *faklemp*, but rather the abundance of children. It wasn't just their multitude, it was their curiosity level. Their lifestyle did not allow television, media, or any outside influences from the *goyim*. So when we showed up, we were a totally new experience. The children would follow us around like we were the Pied Piper. If we had to work under a bungalow they would all peer in to see what we were doing. It got much worse if we entered a crawlspace and their bodies would fill up the entry door losing most of the natural light that shone in. It seemed like we were always chasing them away in order to get anything done.

We received a service call from the Crown Heights Bungalow Colony that was located on Fraser Road. The call came in one early Sunday morning from the owner who stated that the sewer line had clogged on Friday night during *Shabas*. There were no *goyim* at the colony to make an emergency phone call, and since the owner was very observant, he couldn't use the telephone to call my dad about the sewage back-up. Hy and I knew that the sewer line would be really loaded since it happened during *Shabas*. That meant all the husbands were up for the weekend increasing the population, which translates to an increase in toilet flushes, which translates into one really big mess!

Most of the waste lines used back then consisted of a black cheaply-made pipe known as Orangeburg. It was manufactured from tar and some sort of paper making it a very soft pipe. This made for easy access to the inside by carefully making a small hole using a sharp chisel so that the "snake head" could enter and perform its special function. This technique of perforating the pipe for a new access point was usually performed as a last ditch attempt if you were unsuccessful in unplugging the line from a clean-out location. It was already decided that the particular location where we had to enter the pipe was going to be punched in the middle of the main lawn of the colony. As soon as we pulled into the driveway the kids started gathering around the truck and closely followed behind us as usual. We kept telling them to *gay aveck*. Our request.... all right our demands... weren't working that well, since they would take four steps back, stop for a second, and when we turned away, they were still two steps behind us. My father had no other choice but to break these kids in with a real Catskill Mountain Plumber's experience.

This meant if you wanted to be a plumber, you had to get your hands dirty. Punching the hole in the pipe was about to begin, and in my dad's own special way, in Yiddish, he invited the kids to come closer to see what he was doing, "*Cuum, cuum,*" he said with a convincing voice. They immediately took his invitation and began huddling around us to see what we were doing. He carefully began chipping away making the outline of a small circle.

I had already stepped away, allowing more children to get a bird's eye view of what he was doing. Remember, the pipe was under tremendous pressure due to the back up of a few days' usage, and just as he gave it that one last tap, he stepped back as a six foot "fountain of sh-t" came gushing out of the hole. All the kids were caught by surprise as they were immediately covered with this awful mess. My dad and I burst out in total uncontrollable laughter. After the initial shock, all the kids started running to their respective bungalows, and as they entered their unit, you could hear each mom yelling, *Voz is doos, bist fill mit dreck*!

When the pressure stopped, we were able to snake the line, pack up the truck, and hightail it out of there. We made such a big impact on the kids that day, whenever we pulled into the driveway they now ran away from the truck.

They never ever bothered us again. I guess that's what a little poop can do to a young kid.

$300.00? Are You Crazy!

Winters used to be so much more severe while I was growing up. It was not uncommon for water main lines to freeze solid due to the extreme winter temperatures, and I'm talkin 10 degrees below zero for several days on end. On a rare occasion, if the pipes were accessible, they could be thawed with a large propane torch if you were lucky. However, if you couldn't melt the ice that formed inside them, it was a formidable task and a jack hammer was necessary to break up the frozen ground to get to the pipes. That was one hell of a job in the middle of a Catskill Winter.

If it was suspected that a whole water main froze, a large welding machine using its electrical current to thaw the pipes would have to be brought to the site. Without getting into the technical jargon, a cable would be connected to a fire hydrant, and another cable was laid out to a metal pipe in the house. When the welder was turned on, the resistance of the low voltage current created a heating reaction. After the welder had been left on for several hours, the pipes thawed and the ice blockage would finally break free. Even though this process could be costly, it was sometimes cheaper than having to dig up the ground to get to the source of the freeze-up.

After a night of constant winter winds and extremely low temperatures, my dad would inevitably receive a phone call from a customer who had tried using his bathroom that morning, and found out he had no running water. If my dad was unsuccessful in getting the water running, he'd subcontract his friend, Joe Sommers of Monticello, to help out. Joe was one of the few guys who owned a portable welding machine that was large enough to perform the thawing jobs.

Now picture this: You're the owner of one of the largest hotels in the mountains, and you're in the middle of Christmas vacation. You have a packed house, and you just lost your water supply because of a major freeze-up due to an extremely cold night.

That's exactly what happened in the winter of 1963 when Joe got a desperate phone call from the hotel's owner who frantically told him about his dilemma. His main business was repairing lawn mowers and the owner and Joe had a previous falling out regarding what he had charged for some earlier work. This set the tone for Joe's relucance to take the job. Unfortunately, there was nobody else around who could do this big a task.

Meyer Schachnovsky, who was also a local plumber, and Joe's son Seymour, just happened to be in the shop when he got the call. "Don't be stupid Joe. Let Seymour do the job so he can make some extra money," Meyer said.

"All right, get on the phone with him Seymour, and tell him you get paid $300 cash at the end of the job, no if's and's or but's! Got it?" Joe said emphatically.

After a brief conversation, the deal was made for $300, which wasn't chicken feed back then. The hotel owner really didn't have a choice, and stood to lose a lot more from his irate vacationers if he didn't get the water running soon. Seymour brought Meyer along to help *schlep* the welding cable out, set up the machine, and then wind the cables back.

Upon arriving at the hotel, Seymour checked in with the head of maintenance, determined where to locate the truck. Then, in the howling wind and cold temperature, the long cables were stretched out. When everything was finally connected to the plumbing source, Seymour watched for Meyer to wave his arms in the air giving him the signal to crank-up the big welder. Who had Walkie Talkies back then? Just the army, I guess. As I said, it was typically a waiting game until the blockage was defrosted, but surprisingly, after about ten minutes that the "Beast" had been running, Meyer gave the signal that the water was flowing. The kitchen reopened, and the toilets were flushing! Thank God the guests had water or this could have been a disaster for one of the hotel's busiest weekend. And let's not forget that refunding money was to be avoided at all costs since it was most likely ear-marked for paying other bills.

Everything was loaded on the truck and it was time for Seymour to get paid. He went to the owner's office and asked for the $300 that was previously agreed upon. The owner looked at his watch and shouted, "$300 bucks for forty-five minutes worth of work? (Joe actually expected the job to last much longer, but that was the set price). "Are you crazy? There's no way I'm paying you that kind of money." Seymour, in a calm voice said, "Okay," and started to leave the room. "Where the hell you going?" the owner asked suspiciously. Seymour turned to him and simply stated, "I'm reversing the current to re-freeze the pipes." The owner immediately shouted, "Okay, okay, here's your money," as he pulled out three one hundred dollar bills from his wallet in disgust. He feared the worst; the hotel not having water again. The funny thing was it was one big bluff. Once the water line was thawed out, there's no way to reverse the current and re-freeze the pipes, but the owner actually believed that Seymour had that ability. So, everyone was a winner that day. The hotel didn't have to close since the water was flowing, and Seymour got his money. Funny, what you don't know can sometimes cost you $300.

Bowling At Lefty's and Other Fine Establishments

I loved walking into Kiamesha Lanes, and hearing the sound of crashing bowling pins echoing throughout the building. The Bowling Alley was one of the more popular destinations for a camp activity, especially on rainy days. What else would you do with all your campers that otherwise would stay inside all day? Better to let them get out their frustrations smashing wooden pins instead of killing each other. Another cool thing about the bowling alley was their hot food vending machine. After purchasing your anticipated delectable hamburger, you'd place it in a small cubicle, which must have been some earlier form of a microwave. After you pushed the button and waited what seemed like seconds, "viola" your burger was piping hot and ready to eat. It wasn't the same as a great tasting burger you'd get from Char-Lou's, but it was cooked meat that was self-service, the beginning of the techno-age.

While we're on the subject of meat, let's talk about the best damn steak sandwich the Mountains had to offer, which was at Lefty's Charbroil. Everyone who came here remembers placing their order at the counter and waiting for their number to be called out when their food was ready for pick up. The smell from the cooking meat came wafting out of the huge exhaust fans that sent a delicious aroma throughout the neighborhood. Inside the restaurant were the well-kept potted plants that were strategically placed throughout the dining area. Because of Ida Herzog's green thumb they always flourished. How many people do you know who stole a cutting from them without asking?

In my case, I was allowed to go where no man goes: into the heartbeat of Lefty's, the central headquarters, the main frame, the kitchen. That's where it all began, the cutting, the slicing, the prepping, the cleaning, the stuffed-up sink. Yes, that's the reason my dad and I were called in.

It was a late summer afternoon and the place was packed. The stoppage in the main three-bay sink caused a disaster for Lefty. He called our house and nearly shouted, "This is an emergency, Hy! You gotta get here right away." My dad understood the urgency and asked if I wanted to help him on this service call. What person would say no to a grand opportunity like that? This was like being offered a trip to Disney World right here in Sullivan County. Of course he could have gone by himself, but he always preferred having a helper to make things go easier and faster. So, off we went. When we arrived and saw that the parking lot was packed, we could see why Lefty was stressing. We drove around back to the kitchen entrance, carried in some tools, and the kitchen help gave us a "hallelujah" before we even started working. Someone remarked, "The Messiah has arrived." They knew all would be fine by the time we left. Right next to the screen door I noticed a five gallon bucket of pickles. There was no air conditioning in the kitchen, even though it was running at full force in the dining room for the patrons' comfort at all times. Swarming around the uncovered pickle bucket were flies, and I mean lots of um. Every time I walked past the bucket, a little guy inside my head kept saying, "No more pickles." We fixed the sink, and since it was close to dinner time, we were offered some burgers. After graciously accepting, I quickly added, "And no pickles, please." It took several months until that guy in my head finally moved on so I could eat another pickle at Lefty's.

But I started telling you about the bowling alley before I drifted away and reminisced about my favorite subject, food. My dad and cousin Robby Bailin, who was living with us at the time, were called to the bowling alley because one of the toilets in the men's bathroom was not working. Not an uncommon phenomenon in a place of business like that. So off they went. When they arrived, they *schlepped* in the tools of the trade, which usually did the trick. But this time even the auger wasn't making a dent. It was one heavy duty blockage, no pun intended. Someone must have dropped something in the bowl and I don't mean what's supposed to be dropped. This meant removal of the bowl for an inside look. The water was turned off, the pipes were disconnected, and the whole toilet was temporarily placed in the middle of the bathroom. They looked in the bottom of the bowl and saw nothing. This meant something was lodged in the main waste line.

Both of them walked back into the stall with a drop light to investigate further. Seconds later, they heard the distinct sound of someone taking a leak. Now, of course you're saying to yourself, that's what you are supposed to hear in the men's room. But having trained ears for the sound of water, they both knew something was wrong from where the sound was emanating. As they opened the stall door they saw a young boy with his pants down peeing in the newly located bowl, the one they had just placed there moments earlier. Now, the normal reaction would have been to yell "Hey! What the hell are you doing peeing in there?" However, the right thing to do was to let him finish his business so it wouldn't cause any traumatic experiences that would haunt him for the rest of his life. Could you imagine the therapy this kid would have needed? The boy never knew he was using the wrong toilet, but both of the guys just stood there and had a good laugh.

My mom also had a money making venture with the bowling alley but it had nothing to do with the plumbing. She was an avid bowler, and while reading a bowling magazine, she came across a revolutionary product. When you massaged a little blob of it into both your hands, it would eliminate the dreaded problem of sweating hands which allowed for a better release of the ball. This could be great, she thought. We were already in the coin-op business and at a nickel a shot, she figured they'd line up at the pump. So for a minimal investment, she bought into the franchise.

A few weeks later, she received half a dozen, "bowling ball" dispensing machines and a few boxes that contained bags of what we called the "Magic Goop." The business really took off and people were extremely satisfied with the product. Actually, someone in her bowling league tried the magic goop and proceeded to bowl her highest game ever. She never reached that score again, but was hooked on the product. It seemed like a win-win situation since all that was needed was to refill the machines once a month, except for one problem, logistics. There weren't too many bowling alleys close to Monticello. Of course, we had the accounts in Kiamesha and Liberty, but we had to branch out into Port Jervis and Middletown.

During the busiest time of the year, making service calls for what might be a simple jammed coin was sometimes very difficult because of our already over loaded schedule. In the winter, the bad weather became a factor. After a point, my parents realized that a bucket of nickels just wasn't worth it. Remember the bowling alley had to get their cut of nickels, too. So, the magic goop business which looked like it would become an easy money maker almost became a money pit. Mom loaded the machines one last time, and emptied that "pot of gold" for the final hurrah.

My parents sold their home in Monticello in 2004, and while cleaning out the attic, I found an unused bowling ball goop machine. I couldn't believe that we still had one. (Oh yeah, we saved stuff). I brought it down for the family to see which brought back memories of the old business.

One of the coolest plumbing calls my dad ever received, at least that's what Larry Cardini, Hy's helper, and I felt, was having to go to the Pussy Cat lounge. That was the strip club that was a stones' throw away from the rear entrance of the Concord Hotel. The only details that were ever disclosed about the job were that my dad had to go there during business hours for what he said was an emergency. Not a bad "tip" for an easy service call, wouldn't you say!

But Your Honor

Everyone knew that the pace of the mountains slowed down considerably after Labor Day, the last day the Catskills officially ended for the season. This being the case, my grandfather Irving and my dad had to find more ways to generate a continuous income. The opportunity came their way to get into the propane gas business selling fuel. It seemed like a no brainer since it was so closely related to their already established plumbing business. It involved the sale and delivery of 100 lb. cylinders for cooking, hot water, and the necessary accompanying service work.

After a few hard years, a solid residential base was established. In addition, there were also some big commercial accounts. The biggest problem of the enterprise was that occasionally a customer would run out of gas.

When a business operator ran out, it was truly considered an emergency. Not having any hot water or the use of a cooking grill in a restaurant inevitably meant no business. My dad would try to accommodate the commercial customers as best he could, typically delivering an emergency 20 lb. cylinder (barbeque tank), too hold them over until a full delivery could be made by the gas company's bulk tank truck. (The Sullivan County Gas Company was contracted out to service the business accounts). Hy certainly did not want to be responsible for any business owner's financial loss. The homeowners were similarly prioritized if it meant they would not have heat. That was also considered an emergency.

The following tale involved a private Monticello homeowner, who was a former, I repeat former, long-time customer of my dad. One evening, this fellow who I will refer to as Larry, called our house at about 9:00 p.m. and said, "Hy, I run out of gas and I can't cook my dinner." It was late and my dad was exhausted from a long day's work, so he replied wearily, "I'll bring a tank over first thing in the morning." However, that wasn't good enough for Larry. He insisted that my dad come immediately.

"I need it now," he said.

"Well, you'll have to wait. You have hot water from your boiler, don't you?"

"Yeah..." he replied hesitantly.

My dad answered back, "You'll just have to wait until the morning."

Larry abruptly hung up on my dad. For the record, the customer had two tanks of gas with a flip gauge regulator, which would automatically switch the gas from the empty 100 lb. cylinder to the full cylinder. This would eliminate running out of gas by allowing the second tank to "take over". However, he never checked the regulator, where a red flag indicated that the first tank had been depleted. So he emptied his reserve tank and that's why he ran out of gas. This made my dad even more annoyed at Larry's irresponsibly.

Early the following morning my dad arrived at his house, as promised, to deliver two full cylinders. Surprisingly, before my dad had a chance to take a tank off the truck, Larry came out the front door in a huff and said, "Forget it, Hy. I don't like your service. I got someone else."

My dad replied, "No problem," and proceeded to pick up the two empty tanks. He figured that was the end of it.

He had no worries about losing this account, since he had plenty of others and would continue to get new ones. Besides, this customer was generally a pain in the *tuckas*. However, to my dad's surprise, he received a notice a few weeks later directing him to appear in Small Claims Court. Larry was suing him for the inconvenience of running out of cooking gas, and subsequently having to take his wife out to dinner. Remember, it was around 9:00 p.m. when he called. The total amount for the dinner came to $12.35. Yes, that's right, a grand total of $12.35! (Remember it was the 70's). My dad couldn't believe it. "Is he crazy taking me to Court?" he questioned.

Well, the big day finally arrived and my dad was prepared to be vindicated of his terrible crime. The judge picked up the paperwork, read the complaint, looked at our ex-customer, and said to him, "Larry, are you crazy? Stop wasting everyone's time!"

Larry jumped in with, "But, your honor."

The judge cut Larry off and abruptly said, "Get the HELL out of my courtroom!"

"But, your honor," he pleaded, only for the judge to repeat his command.

"I said get the HELL out of my courtroom NOW or I'll hold you in contempt!" It wasn't that my dad was surprised with the outcome of the so-called trial, it was the way in which the judge spoke so eloquently that day.

Hy's Dry

All the colony tenants presumed that the washing machine business was a huge money maker and that we were always ripping them off. Quite often we'd hear, "What's with your machines? It cost me fifty cents a load and the clothes still come out dirty." But after years and years of abuse, I closed the business in the mid-nineties. The Logan's, past owners of the Lantern Restaurant, were my last customer who also owned a small apartment building in Monticello. The cost then to wash a load was up to $1.50.

But let's get back to the 60's with all its mayhem. Most tenants were sure we were making millions... okay, thousands, especially if they saw us doing a collection as the money bags filled. They had no clue of the expenses involved in operating the business. There were the equipment purchases, whether it was new or used machines, all the different parts to keep everything running, time spent on service calls, the insurance, and lots more. Oh yeah, and a portion of the collected money had to go to the colony owners for their expenses.

If it was a rather large colony, which had the potential to be a good money maker, we wanted their business. So quite often there would be some haggling over the amount of their "cut". The owners would usually say, "You know, Hy, I checked with Kaufman's (our competition), and he's giving 25%, not 20%. Can't you do better?"

Occasionally, we had a different money problem when someone thought they were our partners and would pry open the coin boxes, which was fairly easy to accomplish on the earlier built machines. What a terrible feeling that was. Another source of money bleeding were those tenants who preferred to use copper slugs or a foreign coin that usually worked well as a substitute for a quarter. I thought it was funny that nobody *kvetch*ed to us if their phony money got stuck in the coin slot, and it jammed because their "slug" (the professional term), didn't fit just right.

In general, my dad was pretty fair on returns, and he could usually tell when someone was trying to scam him. But if someone complained while I was with him, and he knew they were trying to beat him, he'd put his hand on my shoulder and said to that customer, "I'm saving all these quarters for my son's college education. Do you want to take that away from him?" They'd look at me with my sad face, and most times walked away defeated.

Like I said earlier, there were always complaints from people about the machines not cleaning their clothes, but sometimes that was the result of the rusty or dirty water of the premises. You're probably saying, "Why didn't you put in a filter to avoid the headaches?" You know, one summer we tried that at Lewinter's. Our experiment resulted in getting a telephone call every other day that the machines weren't filling up with enough water because the filters plugged up so fast. Okay, back to the drawing board.

Many of our service calls were the result of constant overloading of the machines. Even though they were commercial washers, they had their limits, but the customers were always trying to get their money's worth and beyond.

One time at Silbert's Bungalow Colony, on the Awanana Road, we received a phone call from the owner telling us that a tenant was really upset. A washer had stopped with all of his laundry in it during the first cycle. The owner told him that we were on the way and that he should watch for us, so he would stop *kvetching*. The moment we pulled into the driveway he came running over complaining about how the machines were always breaking down, and his clothes never came out clean. It cost too much and he needed his clothes right away because he was going to the racetrack that night. Naturally, he wanted his money back! The guy wouldn't stop, and we hadn't even walked into the laundry room yet. Finally, my dad turned to the tenant and said, "Hold on a minute! Let me see what the problem is, all right?" We walked in, opened the service panel and tried to start the machine. Without going any further we could hear that the belt had snapped. Now it was time to see why. Hy opened the washer's lid, pulled out a pair of jeans and a large bath towel and plopped them on the adjoining washer. There were soap suds and water dripping all over the place, and there was still more laundry, LOTS of laundry in the washer. He proceeded to pull out two more pairs of jeans and six more bath towels and added it to the growing pile. We weren't sure how he stuffed it all into a top loading machine in the first place. The guy was still complaining when my dad turned to him and said,

"Do you have a washing machine at home in the city?"

"Yeah, I do. So what?"

"Would you put that much stuff in it?" my dad asked with anger.

"Of course not, I'd have to call a service man."

My father looked at me and he shook his head. I knew just what he was about to do. We picked up our tools and walked back to the truck. The guy was following us probably assuming we were going to get some parts. After we got into the truck and started to turn around, he yelled, "Aren't you going to fix the damn thing?" My dad looked at him and said in a disgusted voice, "No, go call your service man!"

We took off, and when the owner called our house a short time later, my dad told him what really happened. He remarked, "Just get back here when you can, Hy. He's a royal pain in the ass."

When my dad first started the washer business he was hungry for customers. He was asked to install a coin-op in a colony near Port Jervis, which was quite a *schlep* from our house, but you had to chase after the quarters back then. The early washers were made by Bendix and needed to be attached to a concrete base to prevent them from "taking off" during the spin cycle. It was a big deal to set up one of those babies. A few weeks into the season my dad received a call from the owner that the machine just stopped. Someone told him that after putting in her coins, nothing happened. Hy asked the owner if the machine was plugged in. Sometimes people unplugged the washers in the middle of the last spin cycle to avoid more potential wrinkling. The owner said, "I checked that." So off dad went. When he got there, almost twenty-five minutes later, of course the only problem was that it was unplugged. When the owner walked in my dad was in the process of disconnecting the washer from its base.

" Wow, I guess the machine is really shot if you have to take it away!"

"No it's not that at all. It was just unplugged, like I suspected. I asked you to check it so I wouldn't have to make this pain-in-the-ass trip."

"Then why are you taking it away?"

Hy looked him straight in the eyes and said, "Because I can imagine what else you'll be calling me for and I don't have the time to take a trip to Port Jervis every day!"

Over time, laundry equipment evolved. The Hy-Dry (not a spelling error), was the first heavy duty dryer that could handle double loads, and my dad was lucky enough to become the first distributor in the Mountains. They were manufactured by the Huebsch Company, and most likely named after some big wig in the company. The name Hy-Dry was prominently displayed on the front of every machine. Wherever we installed these new state of the art commercial dryers, our customers were quite sure that this was my dad's new company! Come on! Why else would his name appear on the equipment? To this day, I'm sure that there are people who still think that he's the owner of the Huebsch Manufacturing Company. I only wish!

Catskill Cash

One thing that was quite prevalent to the Catskills was the method many of the hotel and bungalow colony owners used to pay their service providers. If a colony owner had a lousy season, and didn't rent all of his bungalows, how were his vendors, who were responsible to the bank for their own loans, going to get paid?

The resort owners always had to provide all the basic amenities for their tenants, for example working electric (notice I didn't use the word safe here), plumbing (hey, you couldn't get electrocuted from a leaky sink), and maybe a dry roof over their heads when it wasn't raining. In most cases, the money needed to pay the service vendors to keep things flowing was never at hand. An owner could have had a bad season for any number of reasons. So, the signing of a promissory note became a customary practice. If the vendor had enough money he held the note for his customer, and collected interest plus the money that was loaned when the note was due. In most cases, the notes were given to the banks, the vendors were paid in full, and the banks collected the money due, plus the interest from the customer if all went as planned. This still put the onus on the vendor, who had to "cover" for the customer until the note was paid. Most times this practice worked quite well. It gave everyone some needed breathing time, but in this one particular case the system almost backfired.

My dad took a job in Fallsburg for a new customer that he didn't know well. (I'll bet you can almost guess what happened). It consisted of installing the plumbing for two new bungalows from start to finish. After the completion of the job, there was a balance due of $1200. When it was time to get paid the owner of the colony surprised my dad by saying, "Hy, I just don't have the money to finish paying you. You'll have to take a note for six months." Without having much of a choice, the note was signed by the owner. Hy took it to the local bank, he was given the $1200 and they assigned the note to the bungalow colony owner. However, my dad was ultimately responsible for the final payment. The bank stood to make the interest in the next six months.

Spring rolled around, and it came as no surprise that the bungalow colony owner didn't make his payment to the bank. They contacted my dad and said, "Hy, you need to make good on this note. It went into protest and it's overdue." After several attempts, he finally spoke to the owner, and angrily said, "I was just informed by the bank that you didn't pay off the note. What's the matter with you?" The customer tried to defend himself by saying, "You charged me too much for the work, and I'm not paying it. Sue me if you want to!" Unfortunately, this is not what Hy wanted to hear. The bank had no choice and had to deduct the $1200 from my dad's account, which really hurt since it was just before the season started when money was the tightest.

A few days later he stopped by the office of Marc Lerner, the owner of Fountain Pools, and coincidently walked in while Marc was having a discussion with his accountant regarding bank loans. The conversation ensued about my dad's defaulted note, and how the bank contacted him almost two weeks after the customer's failure to pay. Marc looked at my dad and stated, "Hy, I think the bank made an error in not informing you in a timely fashion. I'm going to a banker friend of mine in Newburgh today and I'll discuss the issue with him. You may not be responsible at all for their error." Later that day, Marc confirmed that my dad should have been informed immediately, but obviously the papers laid on somebody's desk till Hyin the bank for almost the entire duration of time prior to his notification. Hy immediately contacted his own lawyer, Carl Goldstein, and discussed the situation to see what could be done. Goldstein concurred with Marc and firmly stated, "Absolutely. In this case they had no right to take the money out of your account. It was their mistake." Carl contacted the bank, discussed their error, and they had no choice but to redeposit the money in my dad's account. Carl, who was also a very good friend of the family, asked for a small amount of money for his efforts which my dad gladly paid. He was very lucky that he didn't have to absorb the complete loss, after all.

Another means of payment that was commonly used was the oldest system known in the world, bartering. Occasionally, at the completion of a job, a customer would offer my dad some interesting items like building materials, tools, or maybe a riding lawnmower to settle their debt. Hy was always open to a good deal, and sometimes he knew this was going to be the quickest way to get paid. It was not uncommon to see him unloading some funky piece of equipment off the truck when he arrived home from a job. He acquired some great tools this way. For example, an electric pipe-threading machine that made life a lot easier on the job, or a professional Gravesly riding lawn mower that had been used on a golf course. Another score was enough oak parquet floor tiles to cover the floor in his bedroom and the kitchen in my house. You never knew what might come up as payment in lieu of money.

One of my dad's accounts was located on Fraser Road outside of Monticello. The property was owned by Geno Berger, a long-time plumbing customer of our family. He razed the old dilapidated units that were there and developed a new type of bungalow colony/community. The units were replaced with double wide mobile homes and sold to thirty individual families. They formed a co-op, which was a rather new concept in the area at that time. After we finished the entire infrastructure (water and sewer lines), for Geno, the new owners continued to use my dad as their plumber, and he provided service there for many years after. They were a group of Jewish conservative seniors, and one year, one of the big *machas* complained to my mom, after they received my dad's bill that he had charged them too much money for an emergency job.

What happened was the entire complex ran out of water early Friday afternoon while everyone was beginning to prepare for *Shabas*. This was a major disaster. Hy quickly determined that the pump had gone bad and had to coordinate the emergency work with Bill Getz, a water well mechanic, to pull the old pump out. They needed to get a replacement from the supply house, drop the new one down the well shaft, reconnect all the wiring and piping, and get the job done all before *Shabas* began. The timing was critical, because the rules state in the Jewish religion that you can't work once the Sabbath begins, period! The pressure was on and they worked their butts off to get the water running just in the nick of time.

Several days later the co-op was sent the bill for services rendered. That's when my mom received the call from the co-op President telling her the bill was too high. She told him that she didn't price the jobs, and with that he asked if they were entitled to a 10% senior discount. She thought for a second, "Hy is a senior, and he's given a break now and then. Maybe they're supposed to get one? No one ever asked." She said to him, "I'll have to talk to my husband about that." When Hy got home my mom told him of the conversation she had earlier, and he couldn't believe that after all of his effort, the customer was *kvetching* at all! They worked "beyond the call of duty" and this is what he gets! But after a brief discussion he said, "Why not? We'll make it up somehow." The owners were quite satisfied with the arrangement, and when it came time to close the water, he tacked on a few extra hours to make up for the 10% loss he incurred for that pump job. They felt they got a good deal, and Hy got what he initially deserved. More importantly, he kept a customer. That's what you did sometimes to make them feel that they were one up on you.

This was always the case with Louie Slamowitz, of the Ideal. When my dad handed Louie his first bill he started yelling and complaining about the amount. Hy saw the potential for a lot of work in the future, and he didn't want to lose Louie as a customer, so he dropped the price. The same exact thing happened again when he gave Louie his second bill, and once again he dropped. By the third time, Hy was wise to Louie's *schtick*, and from that point on, the bill was ALWAYS padded a little bit. This way, when he started with his whining my dad was ready to drop the price. Louie always felt he was getting a discount, and Hy knew he was getting properly paid for his work. My dad met Gene Mears, Louie's electrician, in the supply house one morning, and after a brief discussion they realized this was what Louie did to all his tradesmen.

In the bungalow colony business, occasionally there were irresponsible tenants who would drag out their final payment till the end of the season. Of course, the owners would *hock* them all summer long to pay, but they always had their excuses. Finally, on Labor Day the last payment for their summer's stay was made.

One year, my grandfather Irving received one such check in the amount of $100 from a tenant who made it known that he was not coming back the next summer to Sadownick's. My grandfather said to Shirley, "Great, that's the end of him. He was a lousy tenant and always *kevtched* about everything." Well, the check bounced, and when my grandfather got the call from the bank he was livid! The tenant must have figured," What the heck, it doesn't matter, I'm not coming back and those hicks won't come after me in the city." My grandfather called the tenant who immediately started complaining that this was bad, that was bad, and that's why he stiffed him. Irving then phoned his close friend, next door neighbor, and his lawyer, Carl Goldstein. When Carl heard what happened, his immediate reaction was, "Does this guy really think he can get away with this sort of thing? He's in for a real surprise."

Carl called Albee Rosenblatt's father, who was a local processor. Albee's dad knew a New York State Trooper very well, and together they went to Brooklyn to bring this criminal to justice. They located the defendant in the middle of the night, woke him up, which scared him to death, and served him papers to appear in Monticello Justice Court. The court date was set for late September. Carl said, "Let's have some fun with this guy for trying to mess around with the locals. We'll teach him a lesson." The tenant drove up from Brooklyn, arrived at court on the scheduled date only to find that the case had been adjourned. Carl arranged for a second last minute adjournment. After the third time, the tenant realized that the locals were standing together. When he finally had his day in court, he was glad to pay the $100 and all the legal fees. He realized there was no way he was going to win. It was costing him triple the amount that he initially owed just between of his loss of work in addition to his travel time.

Word got around in the city amongst some of the summer residents regarding this incident. Most bungalow colony owners wouldn't have bothered to go to the extreme that Irving went through. But, because of Irving's connections, and winning the court case, there was less stiffing of the colony owners at the end of the season, at least for a few years. It was also a lesson for my grandfather to never wait until Labor Day to get the final payment.

Good Water, No Water, Fun Water

What visitor to the Catskills would not be enticed by the cold, clear and delicious water of the mountains? This valuable commodity was occasionally hyped up at some resorts, like the small hotel in Loch Sheldrake known as Ehrennrich's Playrest Hotel. (Don't you just love that name?) Advertisements for this hotel emphasized the pure spring water that ran continuously right on the premises.

Mr. Ehrennrich, being a smart business man, knew how to capitalize on his spring. Right in the middle of the lobby was a pipe from which water continuously flowed for his guests to enjoy. The sign above the fountain proclaimed, "Icy cold water from our very own spring." And when the vacationers tasted it, they'd all remark, "Oy, this is a *machaya*. It was true that this Catskill nectar came from a good tasting well, but what the guests didn't know was that the water first passed through a coil of pipe inside a refrigerator behind the wall. The guests were absolutely sure that it was coming directly from a natural spring right under the building. Hey, an extra dose of chilling never hurt.

One of the most important lessons that my dad constantly reminded me and my brother was never to drink water that had been lying dormant all winter. Due to the antiquated plumbing of the area which consisted of galvanized iron pipe, it most often contained fowl tasting water full of dirt and rust. When tenants first arrived at their summer lodgings they would often complain that the water looked brown, at which point we would explain that they needed to run the water for a while to clear out the rust.

Working on those old iron pipes was always a real challenge because quite often they'd snap under pressure, leaving no threads to screw on a new piece of pipe. You had to know your stuff to be a plumber back then as there were no plastic pipes or adjustable rubber couplings for fast fixes like there are today.

Finally, in the early sixties, the "new kid on the block arrived" which was copper pipe. It was fantastic! There was no more threading pipes, repairs could be made much faster, and a person with half a brain could be taught to be a plumber's assistant in no time! There was only one drawback. It cost a lot more, and with the expense came the new phenomenon of copper thieving. The pipe was sometimes stolen and resold as scrap metal during the off season. What a drag it was when we'd go to open up a unit and water would come gushing out of the crawlspace. "Hell, it's another break in the pipes," I'd say to myself, even though I knew I took out that hard-to-reach plug last fall to prevent any breaks. Then I would bend down only to see the worst. All of the pipes stolen! Frustrated, I would yell out to dad, "Ah sh-t. Someone stole the copper!"

The copper thieves had no class and would just hit and run bending the pipes off flush with the floor. This left us no connection to which we could attach the new replacement pipes. Of course, they didn't care at all. This some-times meant opening a wall upstairs to perform some major surgery. Having to take more time than we had planned for, eventually translated to costing the owners an extra buck or two... or three. Unfortunately, there were some places that were easy targets, like Sun Valley on Route 42 in Monticello. They seemed to get hit on a regular basis. Let's face it, the colony was empty, it was out of view from the main road, Christmas was right around the corner, and there was no snow on the ground for footprints that could be tracked. So, just before hunting season in late fall it became known as "Copper season." Finally though, with the advent of new plastic pipes introduced into the industry, we could install this type of pipe in the "high crime" areas thereby eliminating the sometimes yearly theft.

One very cold spring day, my dad was demonstrating this new plastic P.V.C. pipe to Louie Slamowitz. He said to Louie, "It's much cheaper, we can install it faster, and you'll save money!" And with that, my dad grabbed a piece of 2 inch pipe and said with confidence, "Louie, look how strong this stuff is!" He lifted the pipe above his head and with a powerful swing he smacked it against the ground. My dad's jaw dropped when the pipe shattered into a million pieces.

"What kind of *dreck* are you trying to sell me?" Louie barked. My dad, although still in shock, quickly answered, "The pipe's frozen. It was in the back of the truck all night. This never happened before, and you don't hit it against the ground like I did!" Despite this catastrophic demonstration, Louie finally agreed that the plastic pipe was the way to go.

The following season Louie called my dad and said he wanted to come up early. He asked Hy to get the main house ready, but upon my dad's arrival he noticed something odd. There was an unusual number of crawl space doors left opened, and as he started checking underneath the reason became apparent. The Ideal got hit, the largest colony in the mountains. But we're not talking a few bungalows. Almost 70 % of the copper piping was stolen. That's huge, so huge that Louie decided to put the job out to bid. It seemed like an insult to my dad who had worked for Louie for the past 30 years, and to further add insult to injury, we didn't get the job.

"I've had enough of all of his *schtik*. Let someone else deal with his *mishagas*," Hy said. He wasn't getting any younger and was starting to scale down his business since his retirement was soon approaching. This was going to be one big job and he didn't have a big crew to work with. My dad wasn't sure if he could truly handle it plus getting all of his regular plumbing work completed for the upcoming season. Besides, from having worked on his knees for so long he started to develop a plumbers' disease known as "kneesals". You know Irene, it was *beshart* that we didn't get the job," he said to her with relief.

Quite often, it became quite a challenge for us to get under a tight bungalow. They weren't designed with the plumbers in mind, and being built so poorly, they continued to sink into the ground. So, crawling into a confined space was not unusual. As my dad got older he put on a few pounds which made it more difficult for him to get back into those tight spaces. That's when he had to call the "Mission Impossible Crew", which was my brother in this particular case.

It was at the Friendship Bungalow Colony in South Fallsburg. Barry had to crawl in about six feet to fix a pipe that had burst. There was just enough space between the ground and the floor for him to shimmy in on his belly, and with a flashlight in one hand and some tools in the other, he began his journey into the bungalow abyss. It was slow moving, plus there were plenty of webs (not web sites, but spider webs), that needed to be knocked away to keep them off his face. Oh the joys of being a plumber! Barry was in about four feet when my dad asked," Is everything okay?" "So far so good, Hy," he responded confidently. He continued to turn and twist his body, making un-hurried progress. His whole body was out of my dad's sight except for his work shoes when suddenly a loud cry came out from under the bungalow. "Get me outta here! Pull me out, pull me out now! Fast!" My dad was kneel-ing next to the crawl space in anticipation if Barry needed something when he hastily reached down, grabbed him by his boots, and with one swift pull he was outside in the real world again. My brother jumped up and yelled, "Somethin's livin under there! I pointed the flashlight upward to find the bro-ken pipe, and all I saw were these two shiny eyes looking right into my face! There's no way I'm goin' back in there!"

The repair still had to be made so they had to cut a large hole in the floor, and constructed a trap door that was used from that point on. Of course, it cost the customer a lot more money to make the repair, and when he asked my dad why the bill was so high, he answered him by saying, "You know, you had some tenants that moved in early this summer." "What the hell are you talking about, Hy?" And that's when he proceeded to tell the owner about Barry's close encounter.

Several years later, when my son Chad was about seven years old, I took him on his first service call involving a laundry room set up at the Country Park Cottages Bungalow Colony in Mountaindale. This just happened to be one of my dad's last plumbing accounts. It was the start of another season, and Chad's job was to clean the washing machines of the winter's dirt and left-over soap scum from the previous summer. The water had already been turned on a few days earlier by my dad and Larry Cardini his helper at the time. As I opened some of the valves in the laundry room for the first time, it appeared to be good water, but I knew that at any moment a chunk of dirt, rust, or who knows what else, could come shooting out of the pipes. It was the perfect time to give Chad his first lesson about drinking bungalow water, just like my dad gave to both of his sons. After working for about an hour or so, he said that he was thirsty so I suggested that we walk over to the owner's unit to ask for a drink.

"Come on in, boys, come in," Mrs. Fink said warmly.

"My son Chad is thirsty" I explained, "but we can't drink the water in the laundry room yet because it's still too dirty."

"Please sit down for a minute. You've both been working real hard."

She walked over to the refrigerator, took out a glass bottle, and graciously poured Chad and myself two cold glasses of water. I assumed that my dad had run the water in her house for a while so it was safe to drink. "So how was your winter, Allen?" she asked. And at that same moment Chad spit a mouthful of water out across the table. I whipped my head around towards him with a "What the hell was that all about," look! She immediately realized what had happened, profusely apologizing for not running the water long enough.

You see, the water in some wells has to be "shocked" every year to kill any bacteria that can form since it sits all winter long and stagnates. A gallon of Clorox is all that is needed to disinfect the water supply. It's generally poured directly into the well and is dissipated as the water runs continuously for several hours. Apparently, she forgot to run the water for a while after she poured in the Clorox. It was immediately evident to her why Chad spit out the water. I picked up my glass, put my nose to it, and could smell the trace of the Clorox. She just kept apologizing over and over for her mistake, and offered Chad some lollipops and other candy to get that awful chlorine taste out of his mouth. It took him a long time after that before he trusted anybody enough to drink water from their faucet. Could you blame him?

Four generations of Catskill Plumbers, L to R: Me, my son Chad (at 5 years old), Grandpa Sadownick-the master plumber, and my dad, Hy. That truck was a real workhorse.

Everyone that was in the resort business prayed for a hot dry summer. This meant a lot of pool time, sun tanning, outdoor sports, and lots more contented weekend guests who had come to escape the cities extreme heat. But sometimes you can get what you wish for. One summer, in the mid-fifties, what began as a very hot summer, turned into a very serious drought. It was so severe that wells were starting to dry up. The Village had to place water restrictions on the residents, and at one point even the Laundromat in Monticello was forced to close, to help maintain the Village's water supply.

The resorts that were located on the Old Liberty Road around Sadownicks, were Feits, Treibers, Kassimows, Schifferins, and the Delano Hotel, all had deep wells. As a result of the drought, the wells in this area were beginning to run dry rather early in the season. This was turning out to be a disaster, as some tenants in the other colonies started leaving the mountains. You couldn't keep your customers if there wasn't enough water.

The water level of Kiamesha Lake, the water supply of Monticello, was showing a depletion as the shore line was never that visible. It was imperative that my grandfather provide his tenants with water. Otherwise he would be refunding their money due to their shorten stay. He still owned his private home on Smith Street in Monticello which remains standing today right behind the court house. With his quick thinking in time of crisis, he bought two 275-gallon steel fuel oil tanks and had them delivered to the house. Since they were brand new and easy to clean, they could be used for non-potable (non-drinking) purposes. He put them on the back of his old Diamond T pick-up truck, used a hose to fill them both from his house, and now had 500 gallons of water that he delivered to the bungalow colony.

My grandmother, upon Irving's arrival, made an announcement on the loudspeaker system that there was water available for the tenants' use. They came down with large pots or glass jars and placed them under a spigot for their rationed supply. At least they now had water for their bare necessities. Remember, in those days buying bottled water in a store was unheard of.

At one point, somebody from one of the adjoining colonies actually came over when they heard the announcement and asked my grandfather if she could have some water. Feeling sorry for her he filled her container, but insisted that she not tell the rest of her friends where she got it. After a few days and a few trips back and forth to the house for tank refills, they got through the rest of summer as the water supply was replenished by natural forces. It finally rained like hell!

I've always preferred a good cold glass of water instead of soda, and the best tasting water that I ever had, hands down, came from my grandmother's kitchen faucet at Hemlock Grove. There was definitely a distinctive taste in the water. My dad always said, "Its great taste comes from the combination of the minerals in the water and the two handled brass faucet mounted on the large cast iron sink."

Let me digress for a moment to tell you about those old cast iron sinks. After the *kuchaleins* started disappearing, and the tenants now requested their own kitchens, every new bungalow had heavy cast iron sinks installed. Most had the side drain board surfaces built right in that added to their weight. They were usually installed on top of a white metal cabinet that matched the wall cabinets. I can't tell you how many of these sinks were eventually removed from bungalows to be replaced with a modern wooden cabinet and an inexpensive lightweight steel sink. I'm glad I was young during the cast iron sink install period, since they were a killer to move around because of their weight. Cast iron is really, really heavy.

Getting back to the water at Hemlock Grove, anyone who did taste this miracle of nature always said, "You should bottle this stuff. You could make a fortune." Unfortunately, we didn't take anyone's advice and now all you see is everybody drinking bottled water. Much of it coming made from municipal water supplies. What a great rip-off.

An alternate source of water was the creek where a small swimming hole had been formed by removing some rocks from the bottom of the stream-bed. This reservoir of water had to be pumped up hill to the boiler room. This was typical for making hot water in many colonies with stream access, and was a pre-cursor to the individual propane hot water heaters that were later installed for each bungalow. An old Gould "one lunger" was the pump of choice at that time because of its unsurpassed reliability. Plus, they had the power to draw water from distant cisterns or small streams, as was the case at Hemlock Grove.

My job as building inspector occasionally took me into the woods to perform a site investigation for a future development. Occasionally, I would come across one of these old work horses rusting away, but still standing proud on its foundation. The electric lines needed to service these pumps were generally hung from trees. "What, are you kidding? I'm gonna buy electric poles when there's plenty of trees along the way?"

Believe it or not, there are lots of things buried in the Mountains, but I'm not referring to valuable treasures. We were working at the Sunken Meadows Bungalow Colony on Dillon Road in Monticello. (Even the name sounds like lost treasure). Our work there wasn't completed when my mom reached us on the CB radio to say that she had gotten an emergency sewer call from Louie, and we had better get over there right away. "Great, I just love working on a sewer pump on a hot summer day," I said sarcastically to my dad, but a job's a job and we had to go there immediately before it got worse. We jumped in our truck, and my dad started pulling a head on the grassy driveway when out of nowhere the front of the truck took a nose dive!

"What the hell was that?" I shouted out.

"I got a gut feeling we just found one of the old septic tanks," Hy replied.

"In the middle of the driveway?"

"They've probably been driving over it with light cars, not like the weight of our truck," my dad said with disgust.

By now some tenants had gathered to investigate our misfortune, followed by the new owner, who came out of his place to see what all the *tummel* was. "Hy, what happened," he asked? "You know that septic tank that you couldn't find? Well, I think I did!" My dad responded.

We made a call to the Kapito Brothers, our local mechanics, to pull us out of the hole. The old owners of the colony never told the new owner where a lot of things were located, and he'd have to find things by accident, but this became our accident. By the time the tow operator from Kapito's arrived, the smell in the vicinity was getting pretty foul. He pulled up to our truck and said, "Looks like you got yourselves in a real sh-tty situation!" How could you respond to that? It was a fairly easy tow job, thank God, and we rushed to get over to Louie's. We arrived about an hour and a half after his last phone call to my mom asking her where we were, and pulled right up to the sewer pump station. Louie came walking over to the truck to give Hy a hard time about getting to his place so late. I got out of the truck, could still smell the lingering odor from our last mishap and said to him, "Louie we got stuck in sh-t!" He didn't say a word after I pointed to the front of the truck where there were still some remnants clinging to the vehicle from our previous encounter.

For a while after that septic tank incident, the standard joke was, "Hey, let's see if we can sink or stink at Sunken Meadows."

Okay, what do you think about this crappy story? We were working at a religious bungalow colony on a sewer pump. It was a hot day in the middle of July and our job was to lift this heavy pump out of a sewer pit. Not fun on ANY day of the year. This was going to be a messy task to say the least. We set up a tripod with a pulley to make the job go a bit easier. After disconnecting the pipes we began pulling on the heavy rope, and just as the pump was starting to see daylight a few of the *bookum* came over to see what we were doing. They're first question was, "Gentlemen, did you put *Tefilin* on today?" The pump was about half way out by now dripping of the pits contents. My dad looked over to the boys and said, "Not yet, but if you help us finish pulling the pump out, sure we'll put um on with you." I guess they couldn't take the smell which had become unbearable even for a trained plumber's nose. Or maybe it was the sight of all the mess. They just turned and walked away rather quickly.

Now here's one last tale involving "fun water". My dad was working in one of Fialkoff's laundry rooms in Monticello, when one of Esther Fialkoff's grandchildren came running in soaked from head to toe. He'd been in a squirt gun battle when his gun broke. After recognizing my dad he asked him for his help. He thought for a minute and said, "I've got something for you".

There were always empty plastic detergent bottles in the laundry room garbage pails. He rinsed out a jug, poked a small hole in the lid with a nail, filled it up with a half a gallon of water, and said, "Watch this, kid"! And with a steady squeeze of the bottle, a stream of water shot out about 12 feet across the laundry. Off that kid ran with the original super soaker squirt gun to conquer the day. About a half hour later he walked back into the laundry room with a victorious smile to thank my dad for his help. Hy would always help somebody if he could, even if it was just a kid. I think he inherited that trait from his dad.

You know, most visitors to the Catskills had no clue what was really involved in opening the water in a summer resort after it had been closed for 10 months. I think they figured a valve was opened and "voila", the water simply flowed. But as you NOW know, there was much more to it than that!

Hey, Where'd that Bungalow Go?

A common way to expand a bungalow colony was to purchase units from another one that was closing. It was not difficult to move the purchased units to the new site since there were hardly any restrictions on the public highways and the building codes were practically non-existent in those early years.

I think a little Catskill construction background is necessary for the reader at this point. All the main houses, often the original farm houses, were built on old laid up stone foundations. The bungalows, however, were simply set on large flat rocks, which were plentiful and free. As a result, many of the bungalows would physically lift, twist, and turn due to the frost heave that they were subject to every winter. Who had money to invest in an expensive foundation? So, just like any project in life, if you don't have a good foundation, you won't have a good finished project.

Sometimes, there were units that did survive and were very easy to move because of the non-attachment to a foundation. Once two steel girders were skillfully slid under the bungalows, the unit was jacked up a few feet for clearance. Specially made wheels were attached to the girders, a transport vehicle was connected, and the bungalow was then moved to its new location. How easy was that? Here is a tale of a bungalow that almost didn't make it to its new destination.

Whenever a unit was to be relocated, the mover had to carefully measure any encumbrances along its route, like the height of the electric or telephone lines, tree limbs or any other obstacles that might cause interference with the transport. Sometimes a "slip stick" was put on the top peak of the bungalow so the utility lines could gently slide along the peak edge of the roof until they dropped off the other end.

This particular moving job was different from all the rest. There weren't many height restrictions to worry about along the way. Instead, there was a width restriction regarding the old iron bridge that spanned the Neversink River in Woodbourne. The mover, Steve Jacobs and his brothers, Eddie and Howie, carefully measured the width of the bridge and calculated that there was about 10 inches of clearance on each side. Not much, for an amateur, but more than enough room for these guys who were seasoned house movers. The tedious job of lifting the unit off the ground, and getting it ready for transport were all completed. It as was ready to roll.

It was a picture perfect day in Woodbourne as the bungalow traveled down Route 42, heading towards the bridge. What a sight that must have been if you were sitting in Malman's Luncheonette having an egg cream, and looked out the window to see this bungalow creeping down the road. A short distance away, was the crossing of the bridge that added to the challenge of this move. He slowly entered the old steel structure with the tow vehicle and maneuvered to get the unit exactly in the center of the bridge's opening. Very slowly, he proceeded to execute the crossing, but when he got about half way through, something unexpected began happening. The clearance of ten inches on either side was gradually reducing and when his brothers started yelling, Steve realized something was wrong, real wrong.

He stopped the truck to see what the problem was. One of the boys yelled, "We're down to about 3" of clearance!" He answered back, "That's impossible. I measured the bridge." He couldn't open the doors to squeeze out of the truck, so he told one of the boys, "Go measure the other side." That's when the impossible became a reality. The other end of the bridge was built narrower by about ten inches. Now, his challenge became a crisis. The bungalow was partially within the bridge's framework, making it impossible to back up. He just shouted, "We're gonna squeeze this son of a bitch through the bridge and whatever happens, happens!" Being that the bungalow was relatively light, and his truck was an Army Tank Retrieval Vehicle that had tremendous strength, he was praying that the bungalow would stay on the two steel rails and not get wedged in the middle of the bridge.

As he restarted the diesel engine, a big black plume of smoke belched out of the exhaust stack, and rose between the bridge's top truss members. He slowly began moving again, but now had attracted an army of curious on lookers. As the clearance to the outside edges of the roof diminished to zero, the eves started ripping into the steel bridge structure. You could hear the splintering of the wood as the bungalow was being dragged through the narrow part of the bridge. The bridge's steel uprights were starting to vibrate from the building's pressure against them. After several more crunches and screeches, all the noise stopped. Except for the running of the engine there was a strange silence in the air. The bungalow started to mysteriously pass through the bridge's steel work without any problems. He now yelled to his brothers, "What the hell is happening now?" They re-measured the bungalow and realized that it was not constructed squarely either. It was built so that the rear half of the bungalow was actually narrower than the front half by a few inches, the exact opposite of the way the bridge was built. Now, for a bungalow it was quite typical, but who would have thought that this was also the way the bridge was built? The reduction from the breakage of the front half of the bungalow was enough to squeeze it through to the other side, and the unit was delivered to its new location without any more incidents.

You know that saying, "If only the walls could talk?" Well, if you rented this old bungalow for the summer, it could tell you how it almost got stuck during its adventurous river crossing. It was only a few years later that the bridge was replaced making that the last bungalow to cross over the Neversink on the 100 year old structure.

While discussing the writing of this book, I had a discussion with Steve and his brother Eddie, and they told me another tale in regards to that same location. While the State was working on the replacement, a temporary plank bridge was constructed right along-side of the old one to allow traffic to continue traveling across the river. Steve was hired to move a large unit from a hotel that was closing, to Camp Belz, located outside of Woodridge. Before moving day, Steve checked with the foreman of the construction crew to make sure the temporary bridge could handle the weight of the truck, the moving trailer used to haul the structure, and the actual weight of the building. He needed to know if he could transport the building using this route, which would save him several miles of travel. The foreman said to him, "No problem Steve. You just need to take it slow."

On the day of the move he approached the bridge cautiously and started over the river. There was no problem with the actual superstructure of the bridge, but the fact that it was not anchored to the ground on its ends with any permanence caused it to "walk". The bridge was actually shaking back and forth. The State guys all stepped way back, expecting the worst, as they held their breath praying that the temporary structure wouldn't collapse from this unanticipated movement. No one considered this situation before hand. The boys were too far along to turn back (now, there's a déjà vu), and just kept going with the rig. As the last of the wheels touched solid ground, the bridge crew applauded, knowing full well how lucky everything went that day.

When Steve and Eddie came to my office at the building department, I asked them to review that last story. Somehow, the subject of the Aladdin Hotel came up, and they told me about this rather "moving" tale.

Carrie Komito was the longtime owner of the Aladdin Hotel in Woodbourne, and wanted to expand her facility with more rental units. Richmond's, a small bungalow colony owned by Irwin Richmond's family, (author of several Catskill Mountain books), was located on Route 42 in Woodbourne. Irwin's family was getting out of the rental business, and a deal was made between both parties. It seemed like a no brainer since they were almost adjacent properties; all except for one small item, the Neversink River. Because the summer had been rather dry, it made the river a viable route instead of having to *schlep* the units all around Woodbourne. Steve prepared the bungalows as they were made ready for the trip. Only one small glitch stood in the way. Somehow, the Department of Environmental Conservation found out that they wanted to transport them across the river and began monitoring the situation on a daily basis. It was definitely a "no-no" to drive through the river, especially with a bungalow in tow.

Steve decided to take the chance, ticket or no ticket. The crew was ready, his monster truck was started and the first unit began to roll. The D.E.C. officer was no-where in sight. Oh yeah, I forgot to tell you, it was nine o'clock at night. With the full moon shining brightly Steve entered the bank of the river with one small bungalow right behind him. He was proceeding cautiously, and things were going well till he hit the other river bank. And then, seemingly out of nowhere, he hit a soft spot as the truck began to lose traction in the mud and stopped right there. At least the bungalow was still sitting upright on its rails in the river. Luckily for him, he anticipated the worst, and had hired Carl Hartman, who owned a tremendous bulldozer, and was waiting on that side in case some extra horsepower was needed. They chained up the dozer to Steve's truck, put all the equipment in low, low, gear, and gave it all they had. There was a massive show of strength as both vehicles worked in tandem pulling the bungalow out of the river. They were successful with that first unit and several others as they worked through the night. When the D.E.C. arrived the next morning to see what Steve was up to, there were no more units at Richmond's.

Because there was time for the water to clear itself from any mud discoloration, and the officer hadn't actually witnessed the move, there were no citations that could be issued to Steve and the crew. The job was a success and everyone came out a winner, except for the D.E.C. of course, but hey, you can't ALWAYS get your man!

The Whip and My Cousin, the Elevator King

Many people may think that the most important piece of equipment that a plumber owns is his wrench. Well they're wrong. It's really his truck. It's much more than a vehicle to get to a location. The plumber's truck is his workshop on wheels. Our truck contained a plethora of pipe, fittings, torches, specialty tools, valves, electrical parts, an assortment of nails, screws, hand cleaner, graham crackers, and most importantly, toilet paper. (Do you see how the last three items go hand in hand?) I could give you a list a mile long of the items contained in our truck. The reason for having so much stock at hand was to be able to fix almost anything encountered without having to go to the (plumbing) supply house or back to the shop, which costs time, and in turn, costs the customer money. Not that taking a ride was such a bad thing, especially on a hot day. This gave us a breather or maybe even a cat nap from all the *tummel* if we weren't doing the driving. Besides having bins, shelves, racks, and lots of containers for the vast assortment of supplies, we also kept lots of items on the dashboard, and always joked about putting in a glass shelf for more stuff. Space was such a premium, so why not in the front window?

We had a new item added to our pick-up truck that made *schlepping* the washing machines and gas tanks a heck of a lot easier. It was a hydraulic lift gate. Finally, we didn't have to lift the old clunkers onto the truck anymore and worry about getting a *killa*. We could have never guessed that the lift gate was going to become an amusement ride. Please let me explain. Any child who stayed at a bungalow colony in the mountains, remembers "The Whip". This was the doubled seated ride that traveled along an oval track in the rear of a caged truck. With music blaring from the cheap, tinny-sounding loud speaker, the seats would enter the turn at the end of the oval, and snap or whip your "car" around the track, thus the name The Whip. It was the Catskills' premier portable amusement ride of the 50's.

You're probably wondering what this had to do with our work truck. Well, at the end of some jobs, if we had a few moments, we would give the kids at the colony a ride. Yep, just going up and down for a distance of four feet wasn't much, but if you're starved for something to do, that was the ticket! We loved to watch the look on their faces as it started to lift off the ground, and they would grab each other to hold on. This thrill-seeking adventure left a strong impression in some of the kids' minds.

About ten years ago, a young lady came to my office to ask me a question regarding a clothing store that she wanted to open in South Fallsburg. She saw some of my collection of Catskill memorabilia on the wall, and for some reason asked if I was related to the plumber who had the "elevator truck". It took me a few seconds to figure out what she was talking about, and then it hit me. I said to her, "Possibly. What colony did you stay at?" She said, "My family owned Lasky's Bungalows that was located on Rubin Road outside of Monticello." She continued to tell me how her cousins always ran to the truck before it left in order to try and catch a ride. I lifted some papers off my desk, pointed to my nameplate and she said, "Oh my God! Was your father Hy Frishman?" "Yes", I replied. And then she said, "You're not gonna believe this, but one of those cousins works for an elevator company now." Who would have guessed?

The last plumbing truck we owned was a heavy duty van that we custom built for our needs, and believe it or not one of the best items we used for storage were plastic milk crates. Even after the summer ended, there were always lots of them lying around the colony groceries not having been picked up by the milk distributors. We used them to store all of our plastic P.V.C. fittings. They stacked quite easily taking up a minimal amount of space. Unfortunately, we didn't read the fine print on the sides of the crates which clearly read, "Property of Golden Flow Dairies." We never gave it that much thought till one day while working at the White Rock Bungalow Colony, a company truck from the Golden Dairies was delivering products to the grocery. The driver saw "his crates" in our truck, came running over, and started yelling, "You can't use those crates, they're mine! Empty um right now or I'll call the cops!" Then he pointed to the fine print and said, "Hey, guys, I'm not kidding!" We didn't want to argue with the guy. It was easier to dump all the fittings in the back of the van and give him back his *facockta* crates. We replaced them with cardboard boxes, but they didn't hold up or stack well. Several weeks later at a different colony we found some other brands of crates, replaced the cardboard boxes, and never got hassled again. Thank you, Sealtest and Dellwood!

Miscellaneous Parts

Darf Bed Gavant

Before there were calling cards, before there was dialing AT&T for collect calls, even before there were push button telephones, there was person-to-person telephone calls. For those of you who are too young to know what that was, the caller picked up the telephone and dialed zero. No one asked if you wanted English or Spanish, but a live operator would cheerfully answer to accommodate your request. You would give the operator a phone number and the name of the party you were trying to reach on the other line. She would call that telephone number, and when someone answered she'd ask for that person. If they were not available, and they never were, you weren't charged for anything. Many families would employ this tactic to prevent being billed by the telephone company, and would use specific names for various messages. Many times a signal word let the other party know they had arrived home safely. Typically, a husband traveling from the country back to the city would place a person-to-person call with the operator, and would ask for himself by name. When his wife answered she immediately knew that he had made the trip back home. She would not accept the call for that person (her husband), for whom the operator was asking. She would say, "I'm sorry he's not in right now," and there would be no charges incurred by either party.

One of the best stories I have ever heard incorporating this money-saving trick was when one of my uncles arrived at Hemlock Grove, in Mountaindale, to stay for Passover. In that particular year the holiday fell very early in April, and along with the holiday came a surprise cold front that dropped the temperatures drastically. My grandparents didn't have enough heavy blankets for everyone who had already arrived. My cousins knew better than to keep clothing or blankets in their bungalow dresser drawers through the winter because the mice would build a condominium inside them.

There is a *bubamicea* that the use of moth balls will keep the mice away, but if that is true, then Catskill Mountain mice must be some mutant form of the species. Moth balls never worked well at all, especially in those bungalows where they were strewn all over the floors. In many instances drawers were also filled to prevent occupancy by any critters. All they ever did was stink the place up and the mice didn't care. Actually, when our plumbing crew was closing water in the colonies and we entered one of those "moth ball factories," we made sure to crush every ball that our work shoes came in contact with. We hated them!

To further prove their ineffectiveness, my mom told me this little tale. She was helping my grandmother, Shirley unpack her belongings from her return trip from Florida. She opened one of the dresser drawers and saw several little pink balls mixed in with the moth balls she had placed in the drawer last fall. She asked her mom what the pink balls were and when my grandmother looked in the drawer she yelled, "*Oy vey*. They're baby *miceala!*" This was scientific proof of how well those stinking mothballs didn't work.

Let's get back to the story of the cold-spell. My uncle came up with a brilliant idea. He knew that another member of the family was arriving early the next day, which necessitated an emergency telephone call for more blankets. Of course, the call was made person-to-person in order to save a few dollars on my grandparent's phone bill. My uncle spoke to the operator and requested a person-to-person call for "*Darf Bed Gavant.*" The operator wasn't sure what she heard and asked him, "What was that name sir?" "*Darf Bed Gavant,*" he replied. She then asked him, "How do you spell that please?" And right on cue, he came back with, "His first name is Darfbed. That's D, A, R, F, B, E, D, and his last name is Gavant spelled G, A, V, A, N, T". The operator then spoke to my cousin in the city with perfect pronunciation. "I have a person-to-person phone call for Darfbed Gavant. Will you accept the charge? My cousin imme-diately understood the message, which translated to, "We need bedding." He knew right away why he was calling since he was aware of the unexpected cold front. Sounding a little disappointed he quickly responded by saying, "I'm sorry Operator. Darfbed just stepped out." "Thank you sir," was her answer.

The signal call went through, the blankets arrived the next day via the Short Line Bus Company and everyone slept well the next few nights. But the best part about it was that a few dollars were saved and they didn't have to give it to Ma Bell. Now wasn't that one of the best bedtime stories you ever read?

Jewish Lightning

Remember earlier in the book I mentioned "Jewish Lighting"? Now I can't say I personally experienced this unusual phenomenon, but I was told this poem not too long ago that gives you an idea of what it means.

> Once I had a candy store and business was doing bad.
> I went to the Rabbi and this is what he said,
> "Take a little kerosene and spill it on the floor,
> Then take a match and make a scratch, and poof,
> No more candy store."

You might be asking yourself, "What does this have to do with the Catskills' prosperous hotel and bungalow industry?" Well, with all of the huge hotel buildings that were present throughout the mountains, it was truly a miracle of God that there were hardly ever any major fires that included loss of life. All of the old buildings were wood frame construction and if a fire started somewhere in the structure, it usually meant total devastation. It did seem strange that many of these spectacular fires occurred right after the high holidays in late September. (Notice how the owners would squeeze in one last renting of rooms to make a buck before the "lightning" struck). So let us get to the financial aspect of Jewish Lightning. Say a hotel owner didn't rent well that summer because of very poor weather conditions like excessive rain which discouraged some customers from not showing up at all. Most owners were already so far in debt they couldn't borrow any more money to get through another financial crisis. It was time to cash in the chips on an insurance policy. The worst buildings were usually chosen for their demise. Remember, that wasn't the cause of every fire in the mountains, but let me repeat a story that was told by Moshe Ratner, a resident and longtime fireman of Mountaindale.

While in attendance of our monthly fire company meeting, of which I was President that same year, Moshe described in vivid detail a fire call that came in two days after Yom Kippur. A local fireman was alerted by a passerby that there was a huge fire burning at a hotel outside of the Hamlet of Mountaindale. Notifying the fire company became a feat in itself since there weren't many telephones in the area yet. There was only a big iron ring, standing almost 4 feet in diameter that was repeatedly hammered to get the attention of the surrounding residents. Soon there were enough firemen hastily making their way to the hotel. When they arrived, they found the hotel owner seated firmly in the entrance driveway with a disgusted look and a shotgun. Before the firemen could even get out of the truck, he stated in no uncertain terms, "If anyone puts a drop of water on that building, I'll blow your ass right off this property." Everyone knew what was happening. They turned the trucks around and headed back to the firehouse. They let that building burn to the ground. Yes, the fire company report started that the fire was started by lightning, but that day there was a perfectly clear sky. It was the strange phenomenon of "Jewish Lightning."

We'll jump ahead to a certain character that shall be referred to as the Hippie Rabbi. One of my grandfather Sam's attributes was that he always tried to help people, no matter what the situation. He might be trying to capture someone's runaway horse, helping someone who felt ill, (the great Dr. Frishman, see Pop Frishman), or assisting with a small plumbing job for a neighboring property owner. Such was the case with the Hippie Rabbi who purchased a rooming house near my grandparent's bungalow colony. My family nicknamed him the Hippie Rabbi, since they met him in the mid-sixties and his ways just didn't seem to be in keeping with a traditional Rabbi, even a reformed one.

My first encounter with the Hippie Rabbi occurred when my grandfather asked if I wanted to tag along with him while he was going to fix some plumbing leaks for his new neighbor. Of course, I jumped at the opportunity to be with Pop and hopped right into his car. Up the hill we went, but before we got out, he warned me of some of the Rabbi's peculiarities. I remember him saying, "Whatever you see, don't ask me any questions in front of him, and stay close." I was puzzled with what my grandfather said, but he insisted, "You'll see!"

After knocking on the door, we were greeted warmly as the Rabbi enthusiastically blessed my grandfather for coming to his aid. I was also given a quick "koshering". As he led us down a long hallway, I noticed a peculiar smell. What the heck was it? Moments later the strange odor revealed itself. There, in one of the rooms, were several goats. This was a little too much for me not to stop dead in my tracks. I just stared in the room for a few seconds. Could this really be here, right inside his house? Okay, I could understand a room with a dog or two, or a few cats or birds, but goats? I saw that my grandfather had continued walking with the Rabbi to where he was having the plumbing problem. After catching up to them, I took a few more steps, turned my head to look in another room, and once again was dumbfounded by what I saw. There, in front of my eyes was a small horse. The Rabbi turned back at me and simply asked, "So, Allen, what do you think?" In an effort to save himself from being embarrassed by his grandson, Pop gave me a look as if to say, "It's okay. He's a little cuckoo." I just replied with one word, "Nice." That was enough for me to become the Hippie Rabbi's friend. Well, the plumbing job didn't take too long, and we hurried back to the colony for dinner. As we ate our sandwiches of tuna fish on challah bread, I told my family the bizarre story of where the Hippie Rabbi kept his animals. It became one laugh after another at the table.

I hadn't seen the Rabbi for a number of years, when by coincidence I bumped into him at a local gas station after work. I was gassing up my truck to get back to Mountaindale when I saw him filing up one-gallon empty plastic milk containers with kerosene. I'm talking LOTS of milk containers! Enough to fill his entire station wagon with the rear seat down. I walked over to say hello and in the conversation asked why all the kero? He told me he purchased chickens and was raising them in some of the old coops that were on his property, but he ran out of fuel for the heaters. Just like my grandfather, I offered him my assistance if the need should arise and gave him my business card. He commented on how much I was just like my grandfather. I thanked him for the compliment and told him how well-loved my grandfather was because of his giving nature. He *schmoozed* with me for a few more minutes, shook my hand, made sure to bless me, and said goodbye. I thought that was the end of our brief encounter. But, I was wrong, way wrong.

My phone rang very early the next morning, about 2:30 a.m. I grabbed it and muttered, "Hello." On the other end I heard, "Allen, I'm really in a jam, and I need your help." I was a little more awake now and realized it was the Hippie Rabbi calling. *This can't be for real*, I thought. I said "Rabbi, why are you calling me in the middle of the night? I don't feel well and you just woke me up." (I had a bad head cold, and the disruption was incredibly annoying). He quickly answered, "I have a flat tire on my car and my bumper jack broke." Impatiently, I said, "You're calling me in the middle of the night for a jack? Are you crazy?" I knew the answer to my own question. He continued, "Please, Allen. I have a helper with me who's sick and I have to get him to the hospital right away. I know this is a big inconvenience and I am willing to pay you $20.00." Now, $20.00 might not seem like a lot to get out of bed in the middle of the night with a head cold, but at that time in my life it was more money than I had in my wallet. I agreed to meet him in ten minutes, and the blessings started before I hung up the phone. I threw some clothes on, and grabbed my ten ton house lifting jack out of the basement. I didn't want to encounter any problems with a missing bumper or something else that would keep me there all night. I met the Rabbi in the garage and quickly jumped out to lift his car and put on the spare tire. Curiously I asked, "Where's your sick helper?" There was only one small light bulb that illuminated the garage. The Hippie Rabbi pointed to a man standing in the corner of the darkened shadows. The man didn't look too sick, but who cared.

The tire change was completed in no time, and I was promptly paid $20.00 as agreed. He blessed me one more time and we all got into our vehicles. As I began to turn my truck around, he sped past me in an obvious hurry, taking a turn onto a road that eventually became a four-wheel drive trail. There was no way that he was going to get to the hospital using this route, but I said, "Forget it. He's lost. I'm exhausted, it's the middle of the night and I have to go to work in the morning. When he sees the road's going to disappear, he'll turn around." I figured he knew better since he was familiar with the roads in his immediate area. I got back home and passed right out with a little help from Mr. Nyquil. I must have had a really good sleep, because I heard nothing for the rest of the night: no trucks, no sirens, not a thing. I got up a few minutes late for work and struggled to get dressed and out the door.

Driving to Monticello, there was a strange smell in the air. Further up the road, I turned a curve and thought I was hallucinating. The garage where I had just changed the Rabbi's tire was gone, as well as two of the large chicken coops. Getting out of my truck I shook my head in disbelief. I saw one of the local firemen and said, "I was just here like five hours ago. What da hell happened?" He got my abbreviated story of the previous evening and a few weeks later I was retelling my story in great detail to the BCI (Bureau of Criminal Investigation), when they came for a visit. I told them the whole story, from soup to nuts and surmised they were done with me.

About three years later while working at my dad's house, a black car pulled into the driveway and two "suits" came out, badged me, and asked if I was Allen Frishman. My heart dropped since at that time I was involved in several indiscretions. (See "The Green Thumb and Magic Tomatoes"). I thought I was being busted at my dad's house! They explained how I was needed to testify in federal Court for a fire that occurred in Mountaindale several years earlier. I knew right away what they were talking about. I immediately said, "I'll help you anyway I can gentlemen." They handed me a subpoena and boy was I relieved!

A few weeks later, before the trial began, the lawyers made it clear that I was their key witness, since I saw the defendant just before the fire. As I entered the courtroom and walked by the Rabbi, he blessed me with his usual enthusiasm. The courts justice shooed me away as I said, "I'm tellin them the truth Rabbi." Not surprisingly, he lost the case, and had to serve some time.

The craziest part of the story was that years later he came in to my office while I was still working as the Chief Building Inspector, and would you believe with no hard feelings he blessed me. He then reminded me how good a man my grandfather was and that I was just like him.

Unfortunately, several years after that incident, there was another serious arson case in Mountaindale that wasn't Jewish Lighting. This one really hit home. I was Assistant Fire Chief along with William Hutchinson, the first black Fire Chief in Sullivan County. Things were actually slow as far as fire calls, which was fine for the both of us. All that changed upon the arrival of a new fireman, John. Apparently he needed more action and decided to "torch" the main house at Hemlock Grove. It was a disastrous fire that destroyed a large portion of the beautiful building.

Incidentally, in one of the upper rooms there was several hundred pounds, okay, 2,200 to be exact, of paraffin wax and candle making equipment. Wax is used as an accelerant in many arson cases. It belonged to my cousin Steve (he was much older now so Stevie doesn't cut it), who was going to begin a custom candle making business the following summer. By the time the fireman arrived, and it does take more time in a volunteer company, the building was already fully engulfed in flames, but the wax helped the fire to burn even more intensely. I'm sure the torch man couldn't have wished for anything better being present in the building.

Now you're probably asking why we thought it was John? Suspicion arose when several firemen, including the past District Attorney Steve Lungen, witnessed the new member's peculiar behavior at the fire scene. A few months later, after several more suspicious fires, John called in a false alarm and used my home as the location. That took some real *batesum*. The call came over the fire company pagers as a structure fire with a garage on Quiat Road. Holy smokes, I thought to myself (no pun intended), my house was the only one with a garage on the entire block. It was about 11:30 at night when I heard the dispatcher, and I remember running outside in my pajamas to see if my house was on fire. There was absolutely no sign of smoke or flames anywhere. I rushed back in, put some clothes on, jumped into my truck, and drove around the neighborhood to see if someone else's house was on fire. I figured maybe the call came in with the wrong location, but after a rather quick investigation, there was nothing anywhere to be found. As I returned to my house the other firemen were beginning to arrive, and here comes our suspected torch man in the lead truck.

I had a conversation with the D.A. and said, "Things are really getting out of hand. I want to listen to the control centers tape of the incoming call." And sure as hell, I recognized John's voice immediately. After a police investigation, he admitted to all the false alarms, which were becoming a real nuisance, but never to the other serious fire calls for which he was a strong suspect. Interesting though, after he plead guilty, paid his fines, and left town, all of the suspicious fires ended. It was a miracle that no one ever got hurt during his reign of terror. But The Lord does work in mysterious ways. One of our local firemen found out that John was killed several months later in a hit and run car accident.

Here's one more final tale involving the Egg-U egg farm in Glen Wild. This was a large fire that was caused by a malfunctioning heating unit. There was nothing "dirty" about this one. There were many surrounding fire companies present that evening and where able to save most of the structures. The loss of chickens was kept to a minimum compared to what could have been. I was no longer a fireman, but in my capacity as Code Enforcement Officer, I was called to the fire scene.

Little did I know that the spicy Mexican dinner I had earlier would make its presence known at the fire scene. During some of the conversations with the guys, my flatulence level went to a new high. Boy was I ripe as the odor encompassed the entire group that I was standing with. "What the hell is that smell!" Someone said, "Holy sh-t that's awful!" Even though I was quick in telling them that the stench was coming from the coops, everywhere I went the smell followed. It was one hell of a stinky fire and every one of those guys bought into my story. I would never have gotten away with that at any other fire call, or they would have thrown me off the fire scene for causing a disturbance!

The Birth of Electric & the Death of a Cold

It was early 1941 when my grandparents, Sam and Celia Frishman, bought Hemlock Grove. Because of the war, many supplies and services were simply unavailable or in limited quantities, and the luxury of steady electricity didn't exist at the farm yet. This was partly due to its rural location, and because the electric company was experiencing a lack of resources due to the war effort. All the available copper was being used to manufacture bullets instead of wire for electric lines.

This meant that there was no refrigeration so ice had to be cut from the lake in the winter months for cold storage of food for the rest of the year. The large ice blocks were packed in sawdust, which provided insulation, and were kept inside the ice house for the rest of the year. It was located in close proximity to the lake for ease of transporting the heavy blocks. There was also the large cluster of huge hemlock trees that provided a perfect canopy of shade helping to keep the ice house nice and cool during the summer's heat. It was truly amazing that this primitive system worked as well as it did, and that there was always a supply of ice on hand. This was an integral part of survival in the Mountains in those early days which were really tough.

Unfortunately, just before the war began, electric poles that were planned for installation had to be left on the ground by the lineman crews due to the

Country's immediate need for soldiers. So, to supply electricity for the few boarders who were staying at the farm, my grandfather purchased a generator that ran on kerosene fuel. It was my father's job to make sure the generator was turned on every evening for several hours to supply light in the boarder's rooms. The manufacturer of this valuable equipment was the Delco Generator Company, and the family nicknamed it "The Delco".

One summer afternoon some of my dad's friends came by and asked if he'd like to go swimming with them. Not only was it hot out, but there were several young ladies in the car! He had already finished all of his chores, and had some time on his hands. How could he refuse? So off they went, and what a great day it was. His problem began when he returned home and it was already dark. He was having so much fun with the ladies that he forgot about his primary responsibility, operating the Delco. And trust me, there was no good excuse! The tenants were already complaining to my grandmother, "How come we don't have any light? We can't see anything!" My grandmother Celia had no answer for them, but she had a real good one for her son. She was waiting for him…Okay, she was actually pacing the floor in the kitchen with a stick. Luckily, just at the moment he arrived, his Aunt Tonta saw him and warned him, "Don't go near your mother or she'll kill you." He knew he was in big trouble, but things got even worse when he went to start the Delco and the battery was dead. His favorite hobby was building model airplanes so, instead of panicking, he went to the barn to find his tool kit. In it were a small glow plug and a coil that he used to start the model airplane engines. He figured this would work to get the Delco started, and thank God it did. He saved the day, well at least the night, sort of. He was still in plenty of hot water with his mom. He hid in Tonta's bungalow for the night until my grandmother had some time to cool down. (He's still flying his model airplanes at age 89).

Jumping ahead, the war was finally coming to an end, and there were roughly 350 people on a waiting list to receive electricity from the power company. This would eliminate the task of running the Delco. Just the thought of having electric 24/7 back then was an almost unimaginable extravagance, which we so often take for granted today. My grandparent's farm was not high on the waiting list for receiving this valuable commodity, since they weren't on the main run. So their expectations were still rather low.

During a pre-summer visit by my cousins Dave and Ceil Bailin their young son, Robby, who would eventually design Mendel's Mansion, caught a pretty bad cold. The local town doctor was contacted to examine him at the farm, but he had a busy schedule that day. He told my cousin Dave that he couldn't get there until evening to see Robby. (If you're old enough to remember, in those days the doctor's made house calls).

It was quite late when the doctor finally arrived and walked into the room where Robby was staying. The room was dimly lit because of the low voltage lighting system provided by the Delco. He started complaining to my grandfather that he was having trouble examining his patient because of the poor lighting. Pop explained to him that their only electrical source was the Delco generator. After completing the examination, the doctor who was a friend of the family, said to my grandfather, "Sam I want you to meet me at the electric company in Monticello tomorrow and follow my lead."

They met the next day and spoke to the electric company representative who happened to be the doctor's good friend. He explained that he was having difficulty caring for his young patient due to the inadequate lighting that was supplied by the generator. It was absolutely imperative that the company install the overhead electric lines that were so badly needed at the farm. A week later the line crews began working, and soon there was bright light in every room. This was all due to cousin Robby getting sick. Who would have figured that a bad cold would pay off with such big returns?

Always On Empty

Pop Frishman's life in Poland made him an extremely resourceful and frugal person. It was quite evident when it came to gasoline as he always seemed to get from place to place with the gas gauge on empty. Remember, fuel cost money and that was something he didn't have a lot of. We were all sure that his car ran on fumes.

Hemlock Grove was located on top of the mountain outside the hamlet of Mountaindale. One of Pop's cost saving tricks would be to put the vehicle in neutral and coast as far as he could going into town. I can vividly remember when I was with Pop and my cousin Ricky as the car went silently traveling down "Snake Hill" (Church Road). He seemed very comfortable as he began to pick up speed. My cousin and I prepared for the final right hand turn as we simultaneously exaggerated leaning to the side. I guess we were experienced co-pilots by that time and knew what we had to do.

One weekend before the summer officially began my cousin, Stevie Frishman, was staying at the bungalow colony with his good friend Howie Mintzer. A friend of theirs, Steve Rosen, was living in Treasure Lake which is a short distance from Mountaindale. My cousin asked Grandpa if he would take them to Steve's friends' house, and without hesitation he replied, "Of course," because he could never say no. Steve got in the front with him, and before Howie had a chance to close the rear door, Pop took off like a rocket. He was traveling rather fast towards Rock Hill, and Howie's face turned white. He had no idea that Grandpa always drove like this on the back roads. Pop had the reputation of being a very fast driver, and if he happened to be a passenger and the driver was going rather slowly he'd always say, "Hurry up. The soup's getting cold."

After traveling for a few minutes, Pop hit a bump when simultaneously the wind blew a sign into Howie's lap that said Student Driver. "I'm a dead man!" Howie thought to himself. Actually, the sign was used by my grandfather when he took my Aunt Helen and other relatives out to practice their driving skills in preparation for getting their licenses.

When they arrived in Rock Hill and got out of the car, Howie looked like he had seen a ghost. Steve asked if he was okay. "There is no way in hell I'm getting back in the car with that crazy man. He's just a student driver and he drives like one. Why didn't you tell me?" Howie said agitatedly. Steve didn't say a word.

When it was time to leave Steve Rosen's house, another friend offered them a ride back to the colony. Boy was Howie relieved. What a hell of a ride he had that country morning.

Grandpa Frishman is working on one of his earlier cars. The engine's missing but he still has a smile. Do you see what the car rack is made of: milk crates and planks! Definitely not OSHA approved. Boy, I wish I had that car now!

On another occasion my grandfather was in charge of the team's transportation for the Hemlock Grove vs. Mirth Bungalow Colony baseball game located on Taylor Road. It was a long, gentle, uphill ride from Hemlock Grove, which meant Pop could coast back home. After the game ended, he packed all the kids in like sardines, since naturally he was only going to make one trip. He started out the driveway and after picking up a little speed, he put the car in neutral. It was on automatic cruise all the way back to Hemlock Grove. "Just 100 feet more," he said to himself as he turned back onto Church Road. And just as he had planned, he drifted right into the driveway saving a few more pennies on gasoline.

A few times every summer, Grandpa loaded up a bunch of kids in the old trailer with the wooden stake sides. Off they went to the Lyceum Movie Theater in Woodridge where he would drop them off for the evening. If the trailer happened to be overloaded, some of the kids would have to ride inside the car, which was a bummer because all the fun was riding in the trailer. The best part of the ride was when one of the girls had to sit on your lap because it was so crowded. The jostling ride with your laughing companions and the magical Catskill air all made for unforgettable summer memories.

Country roads seemed to call out to all potential new drivers, "TEST DRIVE HERE"! But before heading out on the road, there was no better place to start then the ballfield at Hemlock Grove. Whether you stepped on the gas or the brake, you had plenty of distance to correct yourself. The only thing that Pop would insist on was that the ballfield was dry, so the tires wouldn't cause ruts in the soil making it difficult to play baseball.

My cousin, Freddy Bailin was trying to get his license, and after practicing with Pop a whole summer he was ready to take his test. He returned to the city where he proceeded to fail three times in a row. When my mom found out she called him and said, "Listen Freddy. When you get up here next summer, I'll teach you how to drive."

When summer arrived she took him to the Rutherford Elementary School practically every day. Freddy's driving skills were excellent and she couldn't understand why he kept failing. She thought perhaps his nerves were getting the best of him. The day arrived and she took him to the Department of Motor Vehicles in Monticello to sign up for the driver's test. While he was filling out the application my mom just happened to look over his shoulder. She saw that he checked off the box for chauffeur's license which has much more stringent requirements. My mom asked him, "Why are you checking off chauffer's license?

Freddy turned to her and replied in total seriousness, "When I get my license, I figure I'll be driving the family up to the mountains." My mother laughed and replied, "No, that's only if you're hired to be a *hack*!" She had him correct his application and he passed the test with flying colors. He thanked my mom over and over again for helping him practice and especially for looking over his shoulder that fateful day. Who knows, he still could have been taking driving tests to this day!

Frishman Versus Fishman

In the late 70's, many of the hotels and bungalow colonies that were still in operation were beginning to change hands. The owners were getting on in years and they had succeeded in achieving one of their most important goals: sending their children to college. They had become doctors, lawyers, and other professionals foreign to the resort industry. The owners wished for a better life for their children, and their dreams were coming true. The children were no longer interested in operating a family run hotel or colony as they had witnessed their parent's struggle. In some instances one of the life-long partners became ill, as in the case of my grandparents, the Sadownicks. Shirley had succumbed to a debilitating illness making it impossible for my grandfather to carry on the business by himself. The colony needed to be sold as quickly as possible. But who was willing to buy the old resort? Not my parents. They had enough of the bungalow colony business.

The children of the prior bungalow generation had become affluent Jews, and were now taking their vacations all over the world or staying in their Long Island homes for the summer. They no longer needed the fresh air of the Catskills. There were buyers for the resorts who were still Jews, but of a more religious persuasion. The future of Sadownick's Bungalow Colony rested in the hands of a gentleman by the name of Mr. Fishman (not Frishman), who purchased the property.

Because of the similarity in our names, there was a rumor going around Monticello that my grandfather sold the colony to his son-in-law. At first this was not an issue, but that changed when my mom received a telephone call from the Monticello Water Department. The clerk in the billing department said to my mom, "Irene, we haven't received your payment yet for your water bill."

Puzzled, she replied, "What are you talking about? I sent you a check over a month ago."

"Well there's a bill of $3,693.00 that hasn't been paid yet and I didn't want you to incur any late charges."

"My bills are never that high! That must be for the bungalow colony!"

"Yeah, of course it is."

"Irving doesn't own it anymore. It was sold to the Fishman's, not the Frishman's. Take the "r" out."

"Okay, sorry for the confusion, Irene, but we didn't receive the new records and I was told that you and Hy bought the colony from your parents. Because the names sound the same I guess the new owners didn't get their bill yet," said the town clerk apologetically.

It took quite a while for people to get used to the fact that my family no longer had further ties to Sadownick's Bungalow Colony. All that remained was the Sadownick's Bungalow Colony sign on the casino for the first year of the Fishman's ownership, for identification purposes. Some of the locals still believed it was sold to my dad, and they were keeping the family name.

The financial transaction was further complicated by the fact that the Fishman's were quite impressed with my grandfather's attorney, Carl Goldstein. Being unfamiliar with any of the local lawyers, they requested that he act as their attorney too. That added some mayhem in Carl's office because of the name similarities and the assumption that Irving sold the colony to his daughter.

People in the community were not surprised to see a *machetzah* built around the swimming pool, which is needed in the religious communities. But it wasn't built using the typical black plastic sheeting that had become a standard at so many newly-converted religious colonies. It was quite different. This one was made using wood, was appropriately painted, and didn't have that *schlocky* look. One afternoon, while shopping in Daitch Shopwell, the supermarket that was located on Jefferson Street, a local doctor who knew my mom said to her, "I'm really glad to see you took the time to construct an attractive pool fence instead of the *schlocky* ones that other owners have put up.

She answered him by saying, "We had nothing to do with that. There's a new owner operating the colony whose last name is Fishman."

Before he could finish saying "I thought Irving sold..."

She cut him off with, "I know, I know. Lots of people think we bought it. But the new owners are doing a good job, aren't they?"

Interestingly, this similarity in names almost repeated itself in my family's colony in Mountaindale. About twelve years ago my dad's side of the family, who owned Hemlock Grove, collectively sold the colony to Joyce David, an attorney from New York City. Ms. David's plan was to have the colony occupied by many of her family members, just like we did for so many years. To celebrate her ownership of the property, she hung a sign near the road that read "Camp David". This was a reference to the famous Camp David where President Carter would stay and was also her last name. No problem, right?

Well about a year before the change of ownership, while I was still assistant Fire Chief in the Mountaindale Fire Department, we had to respond to a rather large structure fire on the outskirts of the hamlet. The building's distance from a good water source and its antiquated construction resulted in a total loss, even with all of our attempts to save it. Ironically, the owners were actually in the process of remodeling the structure with the intention of developing a drug rehabilitation facility. That summer they had brought up a small group of troubled kids from New York City to get a needed change from their environment. There was a great deal of negativity towards this proposed project at the town meetings as a result of the lack of respect the kids were already giving the residents in town. The church group named the property "Camp David", a biblical reference. Because of the destruction of the building, the plans of the organization never came to fruition.

Less than a year later, a new "Camp David" sign appeared at my family's previously owned bungalow colony. The locals in Mountaindale knew the family had been trying to sell the property for several years. Now the story that was circulating was that we sold to the same group that wanted to open the rehab facility that had been on the other side of town. There was a renewed fear that the juveniles were coming back to Mountaindale. I had to quickly put that rumor to rest by explaining that a very nice woman whose last name was David bought the property. She had no intentions of running an institution of any kind, but just wanted a good old Catskill resort for her family. I always thought that it was ironic that the situation of name similarities occurred after the sale of both of my family's bungalow colonies.

And here's one more tale about the Frishman name that confused a store owner during the course of my job. While serving as the Building Inspector, the office received an anonymous complaint about an electrical hazard in one of the stores in Woodbourne that shall remain nameless, but they made good pizza. The next day I went to see what the complaint was all about. As I entered the store I checked my wallet for my card and realized that I had given out my last one that morning. I introduced myself to the manager saying, "Hi, I'm Allen Frishman, Building Inspector of the Town of Fallsburg. The manager immediately responded, "I know why you're here. He had an electrician in last night to correct the violation before you had a chance to come back. I'm surprised that you didn't point out the problem to the owner last week when you were here." I finally had the chance to say, "I don't know what you are talking about. This is the first time I've been in your store this season." He told me to wait a minute for him to get the card I had left. In a flash he came back with the card of another inspector with the name Melvin Fishman. Suddenly understanding, I said, "That's not me. Mr. Fishman is an inspector who works for the New York State Agricultural Markets and has nothing to do with the Building Department. His job is to inspect your fresh food products. That`s his jurisdiction, but he must of seen something that was really glaring in his face and pointed it out to your boss."

And from that day on, my assistants, whenever they entered a store that was selling food products, would always ask, "Was Mr. Frishman or Mr. Fishman here to see you?"

Mad Cow

At the magical age of 13, when a Jewish boy has his Bar Mitzvah, he has supposedly reached manhood. That's why at Hemlock Grove, as well as many other colonies, parents felt that their children now earned the privilege to attend the activities in the casino on Saturday nights.

The weekends were a time when the husbands were all up from the city, and left their worries behind. It was a time to have fun, maybe get a little drunk, perform a mock marriage, and in many places it became the night for adult entertainment of all sorts. But what do you do with the children who were left behind? Some of the older children baby sat for the younger ones, since they were more interested in making money then attending Saturday nights' festivities.

Twelve year old Richie Abraham wasn't old enough to attend the *tummel*, but was able to spend the night by himself in his bungalow. This was not the first night he had been left alone. Plus, in the 50's, parents didn't have to worry about any intruders or child abductors. He was fine in the country, and it was as safe as could be. So his parents kissed him goodnight and off they went to have fun. What Richie didn't know was that this particular night was going to be just a little bit different from all the rest.

It was a quiet evening in the country, the air was still, and the chirping sounds of the crickets and the cicadas were starting to lull Richie to sleep. In the background there were the comforting sounds of laughter and music and syncopated clapping coming from the casino. But there in the darkness, while lying in bed, he started hearing some strange noises. At first he figured it might be a bird or a small animal. However, the noise kept getting louder and louder and closer and closer to the bedroom window.

Richie's fear was increasing with every second, and his imagination was running wild. He kept asking himself, "Should I hide under the blankets or see what sort of monster is lurking outside?" His curiosity got the best of him as he quietly walked over to the window, grabbed the string to the wooden venetian blind, slowly pulled it up, and there, right in his face, were two large brown eyes staring back at him. Richie's heart skipped a beat, when all of a sudden there was a horrific sound that came blaring into his bedroom. What sort of monster could this be?

What Richie hadn't known was that there was an unannounced visitor on the premises that evening. It was one of Adee Budd's cows who broke out of his pasture and meandered up to the colony in search of apples. It was late in the summer when the first fruits began to fall. She could smell the apples from a quarter mile away which were a definite treat over the plain grass that the cows had to eat in their not-so-secured pastures. As the apples lay on the ground, they would begin to ferment, and occasionally an escapee cow would get to the orchard and consume a large number of these tasty treats. Resulting from this unauthorized consumption, the cows actually became a bit tipsy as if they had been drinking applejack or hard cider! That's where the saying "Mad Cows" came from. But hey, could you blame them? It's a cow's life! They instinctively knew where the apple orchard was and always tried to make a break for it. Pop never had a problem with them visiting because what they left behind was like money in the bank. Well, more like crap (fertilizer), on the ground.

At that moment Richie had no clue that he was looking face to face at one of Adee's cows. The frightening moo was not as loud as the scream that came out of Richie's mouth. And with all of his twelve years of strength, he yelled, "M-O-M, M-O-M!" and froze dead in his tracks! Even above all of the excitement and noise in the casino his mom distinctly recognized her son's shrill piercing scream and took off running to their bungalow. Everybody else heard it too, and followed her to see what had happened to Richie. Was there a bat flying around the room as was so common in the old bungalows? Was it a snake crawling around the floor that Richie had seen out of the corner of his eye? Whatever it was, it was his mother's duty to save him from this grave peril.

She ran inside, picked him up, and after the crying finally stopped, he began telling her about the monster he saw that was just outside the window. After Richie's scream, the cow simply meandered to the back of the bungalow where there were plenty more apples to feast on. She wasn't going to stop enjoying the food fest because of a little noise! Someone walked around the bungalow to see what animal had the nerve to disturb him, and there in the darkness, they spotted the bovine. They walked back in the bungalow and said to Richie's mom, "Thank God the Mad Cow Monster didn't eat him alive. That would have been just awful."

Where Did This "Sheet" Come From?

Does the name "Sporty" ring any bells? Probably not, unless you're a member of my family or you listened to the Molly Goldberg Radio Show. My grandmother Celia, adored Molly's show. So it seemed appropriate that the first dog to take up residence at Hemlock Grove was affectionately called Sporty named after Mollie's dog.

Sporty became the protector of all the children in the colony and was always watchful of their doings. He lived a pretty good life, and it was quite a blow to the family when he passed away. But soon a replacement dog was found, and to carry on the tradition, he too, was named Sporty. And so was Sporty #3.

While my brother and I were growing up in Monticello my parents permitted us, after some persistent nagging, to get our first dog: a cocker spaniel to be exact. I'll give you one guess what we named him. Did you get it? Yep, Sporty. He was with us for a while, but soon after his passing, my mom wanted the companionship of a less demanding animal. So the first cat that was allowed into our household came with one stipulation. And if you were paying attention, that one stipulation was that he had to have the name Sporty. Why change names if you don't have to, right?

My brother Barry and cousin Mikey Frishman with Sporty #1 in front of my grandmother's house at Hemlock Grove. From the dog to a cat and now to a turtle, the name lives on. He started a tradition in the family.

Luckily, all of our Sportys had permanent homes, but this brings up the sad subject of "summer rental" animals. I'm referring to the small animals that the vacationing tenants would acquire at the beginning of the season. Cats were the number one choice and were typically left behind when the vacationers had to return to the city. According to their leases, they couldn't have cats in their city apartments. They couldn't flush them down the toilet like a gold fish, so they were usually dropped off at the nearby farms for the locals to deal with. One thing that the farmers could count on every fall was a new "mouser" to have to feed in September.

Early one Fall, an unexpected surprise came to Sadownick's when a young cat magically appeared at the colony. Realizing that the only life remaining at the place was at my grandmother's apartment, she started meowing at Shirley's front door to get her attention. When she opened it the cat immediately start-ed rubbing against her legs for comfort and affection. Shirley took to her the same way, and an instant bond was formed. I guess you could say it was "love at first rub." Since this animal was not on my father's side of the family, the traditional name of Sporty was finally dropped and a new name, "Tinky", was born.

Tinky was a very talented "hunter" and held the mouse population down at the colony, making her a part of the official working crew. Quite often a dead mouse or mole was left in front of the door of my grandmother's apartment as a gift.

My Aunt Sheila Needleman was renting an apartment in the main house and had just started to cook dinner for her two kids. As she went to light the stove she jumped 5 feet in the air and suddenly ran out of her apartment waving her hands, yelling and screaming. Upon hearing this commotion, all the nearby tenants rushed out of their apartments to see what was wrong. What could have happened? Did she burn herself, did she see a ghost? "Shelia, what's wrong?" they all kept asking. She wasn't making any sense until someone told her to slow down so they could figure out why she was so *fatummeled*. She finally blurted out that when she went to light the burner on the stove, (and you had to use a match in those days), a mouse jumped out, ran right across her frying pan, and snuck back into the stove through another burner. She wasn't going back in there come hell or high water. Someone ran downstairs to get Irving and told him of Sheila's dilemma. My grandfather, whose nature was to conquer any challenge that he faced, found Tinky sleeping on my grandmother's side of the bed. He gentle picked her up during her late afternoon nap and tucked her under his arm. He walked to Shelia's apartment and spoke to Tinky in a very gentle voice telling her what her job was going to be. As he opened the apartment door he caught a glimpse of the mouse scurrying back into the stove. He walked over to the stove, opened the oven door, took out the oven rack, carefully placed Tinky inside, and quickly closed the door behind her. The mouse's fate was sealed. He walked outside and schmoozed with some of the tenants for a few minutes while waiting for Tinky to pay for her keep. About five minutes later, he walked back in, opened the oven door, and there she was triumphantly holding the mouse in her mouth. He opened the apartment door and she ran out with her new "playmate" ending the unwanted tenant's stay at Sadownick's. Irving commented to my Aunt Sheila, who was waiting outside on the porch, "Nobody stays at Sadownick's, if they don't pay the rent!"

My grandmother Shirley, loved her cat, but she was never, ever fond of dogs. Because of that she did not allow anyone to have them at the bungalow colony, except for the Boker family. Shirley Boker told me this wonderful story about my grandmother at the Sadownick's reunion in Florida. Their dog was extremely well trained and the Bokers made a promise to my grandmother that she'd never see any dog poop on the property, which was my grandmother's main concern. The dog was always taken to the woods to do his daily constitution. Well, one day Shirley Boker asked one of her kids to take the dog for his walk, but he didn't make it to the woods in time, and pooped on the front lawn right near the sidewalk. The kids brought the dog back to their bungalow, didn't say a word to their mom, and thought nothing of the deposit he had just left in the worst spot. Moments later, my grandmother, while walking across the lawn, spotted the fresh pile in the middle of the just-cut green grass. Without missing a beat, she went into the office, gave a little *bloz* into the microphone making sure she'd be heard, and this is what came out next: "Whoever's "sheet" (sh-t) is on the front lawn, better come and pick up that "sheet" right now. If not, you'll be leaving with the dog and the "sheet" he left behind." Of course grandma knew where the dog's "sheet" came from, which was removed immediately. Shirley Boker yelled at her kids for not picking up the mess, but without any confrontation, my grandmother took care of the matter and it worked extremely well. From that day on there was never any more "sheet" left on the front lawn.

Here's some more helpful advice TIP #5- When you get a new puppy add some rubber bands to their diet. This way, when they poop, you'll have little handles to pick up their land mines. Kids, don't try that at home!

Pack the Van Guys, We're Going to Woodstock!

Of all the big name acts in the local hotels, and the concerts held in New York City in places like the Filmore East, there were none that came close to the Aquarian Exposition: the actual name of the concert/festival that became known as Woodstock. I was very fortunate to have grown up in the Catskill Mountains, but I never would have guessed that the biggest and greatest rock concert in the world was going to be held in my own backyard in Bethel, New York.

Since we lived so close to the Woodstock site, we saw what was happening for weeks in advance. My friends and I would take a daily trip to the site to see the progress that was being made and to scope out the area. As the festival grew closer to August 14th people started rolling in and began setting up camp sites in close proximity to the main stage.

It was about this time that I learned I had the coolest parents in the world. Not only did they give me permission to go to the festival, but they also allowed my younger brother Barry, who was only thirteen at the time, and his friend Joe Lorino to tag along. Arlene Kaminsky and Sandy Speigleman, "groupies" and good friends of the band, had Arlene's mother call my mom to ask if she and Sandy could hang with us. My mother said, "I have all the boys. It's no problem for me. You have the girls." Finally we all set out for Woodstock, along with the band's bimmies, Jeffrey Karasik and Steve Moss.

Two days before it was to begin, we all went to reserve a spot close enough to where the action was going to be: by the stage. We packed our band's van, "The New Generation", which was brightly painted with our logo on both sides. It was packed with blankets, pillows, canned goods, flashlights, large rolls of plastic, rope, a first aid kit, and anything else that might be needed for a camping trip. You name it we had it in the van. My mom drove it to the Woodstock site since most of the band members couldn't drive a standard shift yet! Traffic on Route 17B was already sluggish with the continuous flow of incoming cars. She took the back roads and some of us followed in her car. We weren't ready to stay there yet, but wanted to reserve a great spot before the festival began.

The New Generation van a few days before leaving for the Woodstock Festival. L to R: Glenn Vandervoort, Me, Guy Lagerway, Jeffery Karasik, Steve Moss, Barry Frishman, and Mark Streifer. In the van is Marlene Greenspan, (my girlfriend at the time) and neighbor, Hildy Rosenberg.

When we arrived at the festival site, there was already a steady stream of people picking out locations in all the fields nearest the stage. After finding a great spot on a hill looking down at all the excitement, we cordoned off the area with rope and parked the van right in the middle. While setting up camp, my mom took it upon herself to direct traffic in the field in order to help more people park as organized and efficiently as possible. Somebody official came over to her and said, "Lady, if you plan on leaving you had better do it soon or risk getting stuck at the festival site with the rest of us." She wasn't too worried, knowing that she could leave using the lesser known back roads towards Black Lake.

Our next step was to set up a marker to locate the van, since we knew we were going to be in this incredible sea of people. We attached a twenty foot high pipe to the bumper that had a yellow construction blinker on top that continuously flashed throughout the concert. For daytime reference my old Cub Scout flag blew proudly in the breeze (or sometimes in the rain). How appropriate was the motto "Be prepared"! Now that everything was set up, our plan was to return in two days but we left our bass player, Guy Lagerway, to reign over and watch our reserved spot.

Those two days were shortened by one day as more and more people were traveling to the festival way beyond anyone's wildest expectations. The writing was on the wall and with our tickets in hand. It was time to get to Woodstock. (Didn't someone write a song with that phrase)? Otherwise our van and Guy would be attending the festival without us, and we weren't going to let that happen! My mom drove us all back to the festival as close as she could, and off we went to experience the most incredible concert of all time. She made sure to tell me, "Watch your brother and Joe." To which I answered, "Of course Mom." When we reached our campsite I said to them, "See the marker? Don't get into trouble, meet back here for dinner and have a good time." I knew they were both responsible boys, and would be in good hands hanging out at the Hog Farm, which was the California based Hippie help station.

We were now camping in what seemed like a small town. We pitched our tents for our female guests, and opened up the roll of plastic and constructed a large tent-like structure for Barry and Joe. We were ready for absolutely anything that came our way and we were there a day ahead of the music actually starting. How cool was that!

That first night was unbelievable. There were people walking everywhere, and it turned out that our twenty foot tall marker was extremely useful to a LOT of people. They wouldn't have known where the heck they were going if it hadn't been for that yellow flashing light.

At about 10:00 p.m. that evening we all heard a pounding sound that was coming from up the road. Glenn and I had to investigate to see what was going on. There were about forty people banging on a very large metal tank that was supposed to have been filled with water, but obviously the tanker truck couldn't get into the site to make its delivery. Instead, it became the community drum that was used by all who passed by. I still remember seeing a guy passed out lying right below the tank. This guy must have had some headache when he woke up!

The following day, because we had a great site, we were able to get very close to the front of the stage. The opening ceremony consisted of a blessing from a famous Guru, whose ashram was located in Texas. I didn't know this Guru from Adam, but who did I see sitting right next to him up on the stage? My cousin Ricky! Yes, my courageous cousin who rode the homemade go-cart with me down Snake Hill. He had been studying with this Guru who was asked to open the festival. What were the odds that I would see my cousin, especially on stage, amongst hundreds and thousands of people? I figured the odds to be about 300,000 to 1. I asked my friends to help me yell his name out, and at the top of our lungs we started yelling, "Ricky, Ricky." Astonishingly, amongst that sea of people, he heard our voices and spotted me waving my arms furiously in the air. I could see the look of surprise upon his face as he waved back. Now that was entertainment!

The festival was in its second day and I was getting a little restless. I needed something to do, and wanted to help out. So I took a walk to the Hog Farm where Barry and Joe had been hanging out most of the time and saying how cool it was. The Farm was providing people with free food and help if someone was coming down from a bad LSD trip. I asked someone in charge what I could do and his response was, "Go around with these large plastic bags and just have people throw in their garbage. That would really help." I wasn't afraid of a little trash. Hell, I was working as a plumber. So off I went with my back pockets stuffed with as many bags as they would hold, and that became my job for the afternoon: an official Woodstock festival garbage man. I distinctly remember walking through the festival site while Canned Heat was playing on stage and I was asking people to give me a hand and fill the bags with their trash. Everyone was very appreciative of my efforts. Not one person refused.

While we were all attending the festival, there were many people back in Monticello trying to deliver food to the site to help feed all of the unexpected hungry kids who showed up. One of these people was Gloria Winarick, one of the owners of the Concord Hotel. She had been collecting donated food from some of the Catskill hotels, including her own, and was working on transporting it all to the site. My dad happened to be at the right place at the right time, when a friend of his, Victor Gordon, said, "Hy, Gloria and I are going to deliver food to the festival site. Wanna give us a hand?" My dad responded quickly, "Sure, Vic, both of my kids are there. Maybe I'll run into them." They met at the Concord and started loading the vehicle with all the needed food items. Unfortunately, dad wasn't as lucky bumping in to me as I was in seeing my cousin.

There was truly a concerted effort by so many locals to help with the masses at hand, but in any situation where a buck can be made, some people will take advantage. As they were traveling to the site she spotted one of those individuals, and to make matters worse, she thought she recognized him as an employee of her hotel. Your probably wondering what he was doing? He was selling water at a ridiculously inflated price. Gloria was infuriated and told Victor to stop the truck immediately. She jumped out and said to the water salesman, "Don't you work at the Concord?" Realizing who she was, he sheepishly replied, "Yes, I do." Her reaction was, "Good. Then if you have the nerve to sell water to these kids, especially at that ridiculous price, then you don't need to work for me anymore!" And that was it. She fired him on the spot. You go girl!

By the second evening of the festival, which was actually our third day there and Guy's fourth, a mutual agreement was made. We were having the most incredible time of our lives, but we all were absolutely exhausted. It was time to go home. Somehow I was able to find a payphone that was connected (remember, there were no cell phones back then), and called home asking if we could get picked. Our meeting spot was going to be up the road near Reinshagen's Farm. When the limo (our station wagon), arrived we all piled in. We left the festival site and our van behind, but not before giving away all the remaining food and supplies that we had. After the concert had been over for a day or so, Irene said to me, "We need to go back and get the van."

Arriving back at the site seemed so strange and dreamlike with all the festival attendees having just been there. The site was now transformed from the largest amount of people to gather to the largest amount of trash I had ever seen in one spot in my whole life! There were literally tons of stuff like wet clothes, torn sleeping bags, food wrappers, sneakers, backpacks, and who knows what else was strewn all over the mountainside and beyond.

We walked through the festival site with all the rubbish around us. Mom would point to something on the ground, maybe a program that was still in perfect condition and say, "Pick it up. We're going to keep that." There was a hand-painted wooden directional sign that somebody had torn off a tree that she pointed to. "Grab it. That's beautiful," she remarked. This sign was shown in Life Magazine when they did an article on Woodstock a week later. Who knew? Her watchful eye gave me a great collection of authentic Woodstock memorabilia which I still own today. But the best part of the collection came years later, when I was visiting with her one night in Monticello. She pulled out that old Cub Scout flag which we used as our day time marker. I looked at her in amazement and said, "I can't believe you still have the flag!" She replied coolly, "Do you really think I could throw something like that out. You know I save everything!"

Special People

Pop Frishman and the Colony

My grandpa Sam, or as some of my relatives liked to call him, Pop, was truly the most loving, easy going, resourceful person I ever knew. This was not only my opinion, but all who knew him described him similarly. This chapter is about some of the extraordinary things that he did.

I don't know who set up the rules at Hemlock Grove, but certain individuals had specific job duties when it came to injuries or illnesses. My aunt, Mary Fox, was the official "Nurse" for removing splinters. She had been assigned that task, and if you got a splinter you went to her bungalow for the necessary delicate surgery. First, she would pour a little Bactine out of the green bottle onto a cotton ball and would gently clean the wound. As the tears started forming, some words of encouragement were always given to the patient. Step two was sterilizing a sewing needle with a match, and in the later years, when there was a pilot light, she'd use one of the burners on the stove. After some pricking and prodding, the splinter was removed, with one final step to go; the application of the scary poison. You know, the little brown bottle with the skull and crossbones, the "burning red paint" as some of us called it, iodine. There was, thankfully, one thing her patients could look forward to. She always rewarded the brave child with a cookie for being so well-behaved. And off they went.

On this one particular night, a patient had a very serious condition, and needed much more expertise. Pop had one incredible trait. He knew a little about almost everything, including how to make you feel better if you were ill. It was about two o'clock in the morning when someone was frantically knocking on the door of the grocery, where my grandparents resided upstairs in the summer time. My grandmother practically jumped out of bed, ran down stairs, and upon opening the door, saw that one of the tenants was in tears. She told my grandmother that her husband was very sick and that she didn't know what to do. By now, Pop was awake from all the commotion and heard the lady's dilemma. He jumped into his clothes, grabbed some items from the bathroom cabinet, and followed the woman back to her bungalow. As he entered the bedroom he saw his patient in agony rocking on the bed. After talking to him for a few minutes, Pop assessed the situation and told the gentleman that he needed an enema treatment immediately. The tenant gave him a strange look regarding Pop's prescription, but was in such a dire need of relief, he would have agreed to anything. The enema was administered to the patient, and Pop left to resume what remained of a much needed night's sleep. The next morning the patient came to my grandfather's house to thank him for his amazing medical expertise. From that fateful night on, Pop became known as "Dr. Frishman" around the colony.

Another of Pop's outstanding talents was playing the mandolin. One of his greatest joys was performing for all who would listen, which lead to his joining the Miami Beach Mandolin Orchestra. There were mandolin players of all calibers, but what set him apart from the rest of the members was the amazing fact that he performed on his own hand-made mandolin. In his basement, he would meticulously bend wood using his homemade jigs. The bridge, which lifts the strings off the neck, was carved from a piece of beef bone that worked perfectly. Believe it or not, his hand crafted mandolins were envied by many of the members of the orchestra because of the rich sound they produced. Every season he'd return to Florida with a new model, and was constantly asked if he wanted to sell any of his early ones. Even with all the fancy, expensive mandolins that the members owned, they desired one of his. He never sold any of them, and he once said to me, "Why should I buy one if I can build it!"

When Pop started dabbling in oil painting, he didn't have any extra money to buy brushes, so he made them from real horse hair. He would drive down to Adee Budd's farm, cut some fresh horse hair from the tail of one of his horses, attach the hairs to a well-balanced brush handle with nylon fishing string, glue these components all together, and voila! Another excellent paint brush was added to his collection. Adee never minded at all, and come to think of it, neither did his horses. But wait... a painter needs a surface to paint on, and there was no way that he was going to spend any money to purchase a canvas at an art store! No, instead he would recycle, and that word wasn't even popular back then, some of Mom's used table cloths. Years ago they were also referred to as 'oil cloths.' He would stretch the table cloth across a wooden frame that he constructed, with the rear side of the cloth facing forward. This made a perfect surface on which he could put his base paint and go to town! The texture was similar to painting on canvas. To this day, if you flip some of his earlier paintings over you can still see the colorful pattern of the original table cloth.

Pop had been painting for several years when my mom asked him why all his pictures had a similar pallet of muted color. His answer was, "These are the colors of oil paint that I use to paint the bungalows." Soon after that conversation she gave him his first real oil painting set with a variety of colors and some good canvas boards. "Oy, what a *michaya*. This is so much better," he said to her with great love. His whole painting style changed since he wasn't restricted any longer to the few colors that he had been using in the past. Now he had choices of so many different shades of green or blue, etc.

Very often, after receiving a complaint from one of his tenants that the walls inside their unit needed painting, he would use his rope technique to create a fresh look. He'd pour a little paint into a shallow pan, and dipped in some bunched up rope which he then pressed against the wall to create new abstract designs within a very plain room. It made the space look entirely different, and upon the tenants' arrival in summer, they would thank my grandfather for the new paint job. It hardly took any time and paint which saved him money but more importantly, it kept the customers happy.

While performing my duties as Fallsburg's Building Inspector, I was making preparations for the removal of an unsafe building that was located up the road from Hemlock Grove. A written report with photographs was needed for the town board before it could be legally removed. As I entered one of the upstairs bedrooms to get a photograph, there, on the decrepit plaster walls, was Pop's undeniable style of painting.

One of Pop's most ingenious methods of painting was used on the three story main house. He made the longest extension pole possible using a twenty one foot long metal ½" pipe. Don't get excited, I'm sure you've seen long roller handles. His ingenuity was in the special rollers he used on the end. He could have easily purchased some very good fluffy rollers to paint the clapboard siding, but they were way too expensive. Well, I don't know what was going through his mind that day, but he looked into the clothes closet and said, "That stuff is perfect. I can make fantastic rollers from that, they'll be great." And without hesitation, he took the bottom portion of my grandmother's Mouton coat and cut the fabric into what became the best damn rollers in the world. (Mouton is similar to mink, and was very popular in the 40's). You couldn't buy a roller anywhere that came close to that texture. Now he was able to paint the main house in half the time using the extend-a-pole and his custom-made mouton rollers.

Unfortunately, there was one small glitch with his innovative painting system. Grandma didn't know that he borrowed part of her fancy coat. That's right. He figured they didn't go out too often, she'd never miss it, and he had put it to good use. He was wrong this time because the day finally arrived when she went looking for the coat. "Sam, where's my coat? Did you see it? I know it didn't walk away," she said to him.

Did I mention that Pop was also a very resourceful negotiator? He really used his talents that eventful day, because Grandma didn't divorce him, or throw him out of the house. He knew that the style of coats at that time were getting shorter, so he hemmed the shortened new edge, and Grandma was left with a beautiful, stylish mouton coat. Not only had Pop saved money and time and given her a fashionable new coat, but he justified his deed by saying, "Celia, you don't like when I climb ladders, and if I fall who would get the work done?" Now, could you even imagine taking something similar that belonged to your spouse to use for a house project? I don't think so. Grandma Frishman was also an amazing woman, and made an excellent partner for my grandfather, the "Doctor".

There were other items recycled besides oil cloth and mouton coats. Pop collected used motor oil from Carnise's garage at the four corners, which they happily gave him. One weekend, when I was staying with my grandparents, Pop informed me that we needed to replace the floor in the laundry room. He took rough cut planks off the wood rack and handed me a paint brush. We were going to use the recycled motor oil as a protectorate by covering the rough cut planks. It worked great, lasted for years and most all of it was free!

One day, Pop noticed his 1964 Ford Falcon was beginning to show its age and wanted to protect it from any further rusting. People in the late 60's were not accustomed to having the option of their cars being rust proofed. Even if it was available Pop wasn't going to spend any money to have it done. So he used the best paint possible to get the job completed; the paint that he had on hand. Now, you don't think he used ordinary house paint, do you? Of course not! Left over that spring was an almost full, five gallon bucket of very expensive swimming pool paint. The paint was made to resist chemicals, sunlight, rust, and general wear and tear that a steel pool was subjected to. This paint was supreme! He figured, "What could be better?" as he carefully brushed it on (yes, brushed, not sprayed), being extremely careful not to let it streak. The paint job came out wonderful, plus you could easily spot the car in any parking lot! The color, aqua marine blue, was the standard of all swimming pools, not cars. It turned heads when he drove down the road. Even after the car was taken off the road, it lasted for years without any further rusting. It was just like he planned it. He was no dummy!

It was an early spring day when my dad took me for a ride to the colony. When we arrived I saw a bunch of buckets hanging from the trees in the front yard. I raced into his house to ask my grandfather what he was doing to the trees. "*Boychical* come with me", he said. We walked back outside to one of the buckets and he told me to taste what's inside. I dipped my finger into the cool liquid, licked it quickly, and tasted sweet nectar. He said to me, "I started making maple syrup by tapping the maple trees for the sap. Then I boil it down and finish it in the house. To make a gallon takes almost forty buckets." That was hard for me to imagine as young as I was.

Pop took my hand and we went back to the house. Inside, he took a small glass jar out of the fridge, dipped a spoon into the caramel-colored liquid and said "Try this, and tell me what you think." It was fantastic. This was the first time I ever had real maple syrup and not Log Cabin or Mrs. Buttersworth. I was instantly hooked on the *goodtah*.

About 20 years later, when I was living by myself in the bungalow colony, I took a shot at making my own maple delicacy, which was a lot harder than I had anticipated. Using the canning process to store the "finished" liquid one quart jar at a time, I began pouring the hot syrup into a canning jar when I heard a crack! Looking down I saw the bottom edge had snapped all around. The syrup began slowly oozing out of the newly formed crack and starting running down into the gas stove. What a mess! There was absolutely nothing that I could do about it since it was boiling hot. So, I waited till all the syrup ran into the stove and finally cooled off. What a waste of effort. The only ones who benefitted from that disaster were the carpenter ants. They shared the bungalow with me in the summer and I already had way too many. That spring when they woke up from their winters sleep, they had a real heyday with the syrup remains that had seeped into all the nooks and crannies of the stove and the old wooden floor. (I hated linoleum, which was standard bungalow flooring. I immediately removed the stuff when I moved in). I thought about what he always said when the woodchucks got into the garden, "Even the animals have to eat, so if they share some food, its ok." I tried to use that same philosophy in that case, but it was really hard with the worst ant infestation I ever had.

Another one of Pop's specialties was making homemade wine. Every August, when the huckleberries ripened, a one-gallon glass jar was filled with just the right amount of sugar, huckleberries, and water, and was left to ferment. This concoction eventually lead to the most exquisite homemade wine money could buy. Pop had a few special friends who would come by to share and enjoy the fruits of his labor.

These were just some examples of some of my grandfather's creativity and resourcefulness. Nothing stopped him, whether it was making beer in the basement or creating custom hats, he did it all with great confidence and the will to try anything. That was my Grandpa.

Helpful Tip #7- Never leave your wife's fancy coat near the table when your kids are doing Arts and Crafts projects.

Here's another day in paradise at Hemlock Grove, swimming in the lake. I'm standing next to my Aunt, Helen Harris, while Sporty is crossing the bridge over the falls. The pathway continues up to the baseball field. The lake was the main reason Grandpa decided to buy the old Andrew's Farm: the resource of running water.

Jerry Weiss Meets Johnny Carson & Other Characters of the Mountains

In the process of gathering information for this book, friends would sometimes share a special story with me regarding their own Catskills experiences. I wanted to include a few of these gems in my book. I think you'll agree that they're priceless!

My mother-in-law, Gloria Blank, is a very gracious and giving woman. During the holiday season, she invites individuals for dinner who may not have family of their own. This is how I met Jerry Weiss, who was the talent manager of Grossinger's Hotel for nearly forty years. At a Thanksgiving dinner at Gloria's, he told me the following humorous tale.

Jerry had met a tremendous number of famous individuals while working at Grossinger's. It was a Saturday night, after the performance of a certain up-and-coming singer, who we'll call Steve, when Jerry happened to be passing through the lobby. A crowd of guests were gathered around the performer. As soon as Steve spotted Jerry he yelled out, "Get over here, Jerry. You're the one who booked me for this job!" Photographers were on hand to snap a few shots when Steve put his arm around Jerry. Eventually the hub-bub died down, and both Steve and Jerry went on their separate ways.

Several months later, Steve's continuing popularity landed him an appearance on the Johnny Carson show. As planned ahead of time, the interview focused on Steve working in the Catskill Mountains, specifically performing at Grossinger's Hotel where his professional career started to take off. Carson held up a few black and white photographs of Steve that were taken after the show afore mentioned performance at Grossinger's. The last picture was one of Steve with his arm around the waist of an unknown individual. Johnny asked curiously, "Who's that gentleman standing next to you?" Steve quickly remarked, "That's Jerry Weiss, who was the entertainment director at the Hotel, but he recently passed away."

It was not more than two minutes after the Carson show that Jerry received a telephone call from a friend asking him if he was ok. He answered, "I was fine until you woke me up!" The caller said to him, "Steve was just on the Tonight Show. They showed a picture of you and him together and Steve said you were dead!"

After a moment of silence, Jerry said, "As far as I know, I'm still here!"

Jerry received several more telephone calls in the next few days all inquiring if he was okay. Unfortunately, Jerry did pass away in the spring of 2008, but up until then was comfortably enjoying the holiday dinners at my mother-in-law's house.

—m—

A few years ago, I was invited to a breakfast club at Poppy's Restaurant in Del-Ray Beach, Florida by Ted Drew. If you're taking notes, he contributed the well-known song, "The Nasso Hotel." Okay, so maybe it's not such a popular song, but let me relay the story that was told by Dudi Kessler who was in attendance, and was a long-time resident and butcher in Woodridge.

One day Kessler found himself in need of another butcher. As luck would have it, the union was able to immediately provide a fellow who was said to be an A-1 butcher. This was true, Dudi stated, as long as the fellow was working, but he had one small problem. He made too many trips to the bathroom, which took place almost once an hour. "How often could a guy have to take a leak?" Dudi wondered.

The hourly excursions continued until Dudi's kids, who had decided to investigate, found that the medicine cabinet was packed with mini whiskey bottles. When Dudi's kids told their dad what they found, he figured it was time to play a little game with the new butcher on the block. Early the next morning, before the work day began, the kids added castor oil to all the tiny bottles. Soon after arriving that next morning, the butcher began his hourly retreats like clockwork. By mid-day, he was starting to feel the results of the additive in his booze. He couldn't take it any longer and finally approached Dudi, who knew exactly what was going on. The butcher blurted out, "I gotta get the hell out of here. I can't stop sh-ttin'!" And with that he barreled out of the store. Everyone else just broke out in laughter.

—⁂—

Jack Degraw, a long-time resident of Fallsburg, told me this great tale about a union painter who made his complainant known at a Union meeting. He felt that he wasn't getting any of the good jobs like the other guys which might have been a result of not being Jewish like everyone else in the organization. He couldn't take it any longer and at the next meeting he stood up and declared, "I'm tired of getting the worst jobs because I am not Jewish. As far as you guys are concerned, my last name is no longer Smile. From this night on, it's Smilowitz!" We don't know whether if it was due to his outburst or if it was his name change, but from that day forward he always got better jobs.

—⁂—

Friday afternoons were always busy in the mountains because of the upcoming weekend and having to prepare for *Shabas*. The kosher butchers, of which there were many, were no exception. Lashinsky's, which was located on Broadway in Monticello, was overflowing with customers one Friday. So much so, that there were patrons congregated outside the store waiting to hear their names called.

One of the local year-round customers came by to place an order for his standard Friday night meal. When he saw all the *tummel*, he squeezed in the store and grabbed Leon, one of the owners, and said, "Leon, save me a Bar-b-que chicken and I'll pick it up before you close down." Leon's hands were soiled from just cutting some meat so he told the customer he would have Ethel, his wife, write it down for him. It was such a crazy afternoon that Leon forgot all about it.

Several hours went by and it was almost *Shabas*. The blinds in front of the shop were dropped down, signaling the store was closed. The Lashinsky boys (of which there were three), were exhausted from this exceptionally busy Friday. Just then, the local customer returned to pick up his order. As soon he walked into the store, Leon realized that he had forgotten to put aside a chicken. He immediately apologized profusely to the customer and offered to give him one of the fried chickens that he was taking home for his own family meal.

"Fried chicken, who eats fried chicken for a *Shabas* meal?" the customer complained. "That's all I have left, what can I tell ya." Leon said with a shrug. And with that, he took out one of the chickens from his own bag, placed it on the counter to cut it up, weighed it, re-bagged it, and announced, "The chicken costs $6.25." The customer reached in his pocket and placed $6.00 on the counter. "That chicken's only worth six bucks," he said.

Without missing a beat Leon reached back in the bag, pulled out a drum stick, took a nice big bite, put it right back in, and justifiably said "NOW it's worth $6.00. Have a good *Shabas*."

The customer didn't say a word, turned around with his bag of fried chicken, and left the store. Leon looked at one of his brothers and said, "And there goes another satisfied customer."

You know how when it's really bright outside, you walk into a dark room, and can't see that well for the first few minutes? Well, that's exactly what happened to Harold Gold when he entered the kitchen of the Astor Hotel in South Fallsburg back in the 50's. The owner of the hotel was renting the facility for a summer to Benny S. Harold was there to try and collect money for an outstanding propane gas bill. The kitchen had an open ceiling with exposed rafters, and was lit with just a small wattage light bulb hanging on a wire from the ceiling. As he entered the room, he could hardly see anything. Coincidently, Benny's wife, who was a rather large woman, was standing right there as he walked in. After exchanging greetings he asked, "Do you know where your husband is? We need to settle an outstanding gas bill for this past summer." She quickly replied with this excuse, "I haven't seen him all morning." But as Harold's eyes began to dilate, he could see a small figure standing directly behind her which turned out to be Benny S. He'd been hiding behind his wife the whole time. "You know Benny, you still owe me that money...

If you have a great story to share, I would love to hear it. If you would like, please submit them to me using my email address, mtdaleboy@gmail.com. Maybe there can be a sequel entitled, "Tales of a Catskill Mountain Plumber's Friends."

Helpful Tip #5 - If someone says, "I heard you died!" Tell them it was a rumor started by Johnny Carson. He's the one who's dead.

Ruby the Knish Man & the P.A. System

Possibly at some point while enjoying the book, your cell phone rang. Perhaps a special ring tone alerted you to the caller's identity....your family, a friend or a business associate. Without leaving the comfort of the couch, you reached for the phone and began chatting.

Now, let's go back to 1955 when there was only one phone in your house. Do you remember picking up the receiver and the operator would say, "Number please," and you waited till the connection was made? What a slow process that was, but even that simple luxury was lost in the Mountains. No one had a phone in their bungalow. There was only a payphone centrally located in the bungalow colony usually housed in a hand built phone booth by the owner out of wood. If you were lucky, it had a front door with a multi-pane window with one or two panes of glass that were usually missing. The telephone company charged extra money to have one of their fancy, schmancy phone booths installed, and who needed to pay for that when you could build your own?

Quite often, the owner had a P.A. system in their house. When a call came in it was announced over the loud speaker. First came the traditional double *bloze*, and then someone's name was spoken twice to avoid confusion over similar names like Friedberg or Greenburg. If it was your name blasting through those 2 foot mega-phone speakers you went running for the call. Even if it was raining, you had to get to Ma Bells money maker to speak with the caller. Now, if you wanted to make a call you had better have a pocketful of change. That is, if you wanted to speak for a while. Otherwise, your call would be interrupted repeatedly with the operator telling you to deposit another coin. Then you would have to wonder how long she had been listening to you talking!

In some of the smaller colonies, when the public phone was not located in the main house, because the owner didn't want to bother, it would ring and ring and ring until someone answered. It then became someone's unofficial duty to make the announcement for the caller. Usually, the kids enjoyed answered the phone because they it gave them an excuse to use the microphone. The problem was their annoying antics following the person's name.

After teenagers met at neighboring colonies, sometimes a budding romance would develop. The daily announcements would begin, "Andrea Dinner, you have a telephone call (and once more of course), Andrea Dinner you have a telephone call." In some cases it became a contest to see who was getting the most calls from their respective boyfriends.

Every phone booth had a local phone book, but it was much more convenient to write down the numbers that were called most often right on the walls. You might see the phone numbers for Singers Restaurant, the Kiamesha Bowling Alley, Mendel's Taxi or maybe another popular colony that was down the road. Why bother looking it up repeatedly when you could have it readily available? The walls were covered in some cases. Personally, I believe the most significant use of the phone booth was after dark when it became the Kissing Booth for the younger kids. Sometimes when we played games on the front lawn, the phone booth became the spot where a rewarding kiss was received from a young lady. Where else could you get a little privacy!

In the early days at Hemlock Grove, my grandparents had a less costly telephone system. Shared with the neighbors, it was known as a party line and trust me, it was no party. For the younger readers, sharing a phone with neighbors is hard to believe, isn't it? Of course, the party line didn't allow for privacy, but that's all that the phone company offered in some rural areas because of the limited line availability. You always had to be careful what you said on the phone, especially if you didn't get along with your neighbors, since they could be listening to every word! Each home had its own ring pattern. In our case one ring was for the neighbor and two quick rings meant the call was for my grandparents.

It could be quite frustrating if you had to make an important call while your neighbor was on the line. You had to keep picking up the receiver to check if the line was open, and you couldn't yell at him like you would if you kids were hogging the phone. Once in a while though, things could get a little testy with your neighbor if he wasn't off in a reasonable amount of time.

The P.A. system was used to make other announcements besides phone calls. When we were working at the Ideal, a tenant would come into Louie's office complaining of a plumbing problem and the next thing you'd hear would be an announcement. In Louie's low gravelly voice, blasting out of those big gray megaphone speakers, you'd hear throughout the colony, and of course way beyond the premises, "HY, DA PLUMBER, GO TO BUNGALOW 47. THE TOILET'S STUFFED. HY, DA PLUMBER, GO TO BUNGALOW 47. THE TOILETS STUFFED." Yes, only in the Catskills could you hear such poetic words echoing through the hills.

On more serious occasions the P.A. might be used to find a lost child. For instance, "Leon Steven Schwartz, this is your mother speaking. (Notice the use of the middle name-this indicated that Leon's mother was really serious). If you are not home in exactly five minutes you can forget about going to Fun Fare tomorrow!" Boy, I'm glad I'm not Leon. With an announcement like that, it only had to be said once. Between Leon and his friends, someone definitely heard it, and believe me, Leon didn't waste any time getting home.

But the most exciting announcements were made when the vendors arrived. These traveling salesman went from colony to colony selling their various products: the fruit and vegetable man, The Chow Chow Cup, (Chinese food made in a truck. It tasted just like it sounds), Dugan's or Madnick's Bakery, or maybe it was the Blouse Man. One time while my dad was working at the Ideal in Monticello, a salesman pulled into the parking lot in a Rolls Royce, that's right. He opened the trunk and began selling ladies clothes. Now that was a strange sight to see. What a convenience these salesmen were since most of the women didn't have cars.

There was one customary policy of the Catskills. The vendors knew that the owners needed their cut, and my grandmother made sure she got hers. They always gave her something; linen, clothing or a Black & White Cookie… but always something for allowing them to sell their wares on her premises. That was the deal.

The blouse man had a seemingly lax policy, where the ladies would come down to the parking lot, take a blouse or a pair of pants off the rack, and try them on in their bungalows. Maybe they thought he wouldn't remember that they had his apparel, because prior to him leaving, he would always have to go to the office and make the announcement, "Bungalow 22, it's time to return the pants. Bungalow 22, I need to leave. Please return the pants."

There was one individual who was smarter than the rest of the vendors because he came with his own P.A. system, and that was Ruby the Knish Man. He traveled around the mountains in a car with a charcoal heated rack built right into the trunk keeping the knishes hot all the time. Upon his arrival at a bungalow colony, he would get on his own microphone and make the most enticing announcements about his one-of-a-kind Jewish delights. "Ruby the Knish Man is in the driveway. Ruby's here. Come and get your hot, tasty, fresh knishes. We got kasha, we got potato. Ruby's here." Not only did Ruby make the best knishes, he was one of the best showmen and was loved by all the people who stayed here. The unique fried knish recipe was his wife's creation. Of course after making your purchase, you'd grab the handle of the slightly dented aluminum dispenser and shake a little *saltz* in the brown paper bag that made them taste just perfect.

Ruby visited Sadownick's quite often and became a true friend of the family. There were times when he arrived with something broken on his knish car, and if my dad just happened to be there, he`d ask Hy if he could please fix it. Maybe it was a hinge that broke on the heater door. If my dad had the part on his plumbing truck, which was a traveling hardware store, he always made an effort to help Ruby out. This was the kind of relationship we had with Ruby.

I remember finding a small toy car in Davco, the big toy store on Broadway in Monticello. It was about two inches long and looked almost identical to the car that Ruby drove. I cut out a small portion in the trunk and inserted a small wooden cube painted silver to look like the knish heater. When it was finished, it looked just like his vehicle. I attached a string to the hood so he could hang it from his mirror. The following day, upon his arrival, I ran to the driveway and said, "Ruby, I made something for you." I had it cupped in my hands. As he looked down from his tall stature to see what I was holding, a huge smile appeared on his face. "I made it for you because you're my good friend," I said. And with that, tears came to his eyes. He was so touched by the fact that here was a young boy who cared so much for him. He gave me a big hug. And even though there was a long line of customers, he stopped to hang it from the mirror where it hung for as long as he drove that car. Many years later, I met his daughter who remembered the little car and said it was one of the nicest gifts he had ever received.

Helpful Tip # 6- For you knish connoisseurs, did you know that the same famous recipe is still available at Izzy's Knishes in Loch Sheldrake? Listen, I'm just letting you know where to get a delicious nosh.

Labor Day, It's Finally Over

While my family was eating bananas and cream for lunch in the big kitchen (the summer kitchen in the main house at Hemlock Grove), under the heavily covered strip of fly paper, someone came running to the door and shouted," The Rosenblatt's are leaving!" That was the signal for my grandmother to grab the cowbell on the counter and run outside. I quickly followed as all the leaves were beginning to show a slight tinge of yellow and red, and the hot summer days were gone. It was Labor Day and the summer exodus was in progress. The tenants were all packing their cars, or their "hack's" cars, to leave the Mountains and return to the city.

As the families gave one last hug and a kiss to my grandparents, the children began crying knowing they were leaving paradise. The summer residents got in their cars and headed out the driveway while the traditional send-off began with my grandmother ringing the cowbell. For the tenants that hadn't left yet, they joined in and started chanting, "See you in the city!" It was quite sad to see them driving out of the colony with their belongings strapped to the roof, and overflowing from the trunks. When the last family drove away, many of whom were my relatives, I was left alone in the mountains; the "lucky one," which is what everyone said to me. With the departure of my two closest cousins, Ricky and Marty, I too, started crying. I'd often wondered to myself, "Why can't I go to the city so we can play together like we did all summer?" I knew I would have to wait till Thanksgiving to see them again. I felt so bad especially after the see you in the city send off, which to me meant they were all going to be together with one another but not with me. How was a young kid going to understand?

In addition to all my family members leaving me, both of my girlfriends (that's right, I had one at Hemlock Grove and one at Sadownick's), had to return home. Hey, listen, I took advantage of a situation: I had won two rings in the Playland Arcade in Monticello.

Florence Balch, composer of many Hemlock Grove parodies, is getting ready to leave the mountains as she begins *schlepping* stuff to her car.

For my grandparents, it was a time of extreme relief; no more complaints, no more grocery to operate, no more summer *tummel*. But, there was still plenty of work that had to be completed before winter set in. The first job at

Hemlock Grove was gathering all the Adirondack chairs and tables, and moving them under the covered porch of the main house for protection from the winter's snow. There were always newly carved initials in the wooden arms of the chairs and I'd try to identify who they belonged to.

At Sadownick's, my grandmother Shirley was busy cleaning out the bungalows and apartments, especially the ones that would have to be rented next summer to a new customer. She had a habit of saving many of the items that had been left behind, and it meant nothing for her to store it in the in the huge attic of the main house. When the colony was sold, my mom and I had the dubious task of cleaning out what seemed like a warehouse. As we got into all the nooks and crannies of the attic, we discovered more and more great old items that she had put aside years ago which we later sold at a local auction hall. I saw a sealed carton inside a large closet and when I opened the box I yelled out, "You're not gonna believe what I just found Mom, come here!" What a shock it was in finding a huge number of Golden Age comic books, like Batman, Detective, and Superman in mint condition. We found two more boxes with those vintage contents. Shirley had no idea that what she was saving would become a future fortune. "God Bless you Grandma. We're raking it in on E-Bay!"

After the exodus to the city, Adee Budd's cows were allowed to pay a scheduled visit to Hemlock Grove, leaving behind their invaluable dung as they grazed on the front lawn, or what was left of it. This would jump start the grass growing again in the spring like a professional baseball field. My grandmother would also take advantage of this fantastic fertilizer and bring some down to the garden. Not bad for a freebie!

The first job of closing the water was emptying the swimming pool. As the main valve was opened, a steady stream of water would run into the woods for hours. It was depressing to see the water level dropping in the pool. The water pipes were the next operation of business. The plugs were removed and then the toilets had to be pumped in each and every bungalow. This was the job that I was given as I got a little older. Great huh?

After the season, my grandparents, like most of the other resort owners, had to decide if the construction of a new bungalow was in order. Did they make enough money to afford a new unit after all the bills were paid? Usually not, but many places had to expand and modernize in order to keep up with the "Joneses". In some cases, before leaving the colony, a tenant would leave a bigger deposit to reserve the newly proposed unit for next summer. It was my grandparent's expectation that the older unit would be rented come spring.

If it was decided to go ahead with this new venture, preparations had to be made to start construction before the cold weather set in. As long as the shell was completed with a shingled roof and the windows were set, you could keep working through the winter. On the very cold days, we'd work with the intense roar of a kerosene salamander (industrial heater), in order to try to stay warm. There was no such thing as insulation in the bungalow walls, so the heat never seemed to warm up the space. Sometimes we'd stand right in front of the salamander until we felt like our clothes were almost on fire, and after cooking for a minute, we could get back to work for a little while. When those heaters were finally turned off at days end, there was always a sigh of relief from the elimination of the constant roar.

Even though the place was officially closed for the summer, instead of renting out the casino like Irving did at Sadownick's, there was still one more season to make a last buck before winter. My grandparents Sam and Celia had moved out of the un-winterized main house and back into their winter home which they rented out every summer. During the season they had to live above the grocery store. After the old barn succumbed to the lightning fire, they rebuilt their new home with an additional winterized apartment. This translated to a rental for the city guys who wanted to come up in November for hunting season. They came every fall and had a warm place to stay, plenty of land to hunt (the property was 78 acres), and a good home cooked meal that my grandmother would make for them every evening. It wasn't a bad deal for both parties as it brought in some extra cash before the long cold stretch ahead.

Another drain that had to be opened was located right below the dam by the lake. (It was really a small pond by its size, but it sounded so much more grandiose when it was called the "lake"). At the opposite end of the dam was a portion of the lake referred to as the "crib". It was built by my grandfather, and had a hard concrete surface that allowed you to enter the lake without walking right on the muddy bottom. There were some upright pipes set into the concrete and a rope that was strung around the crib to keep the little ones in this shallow area. That's how it got that name.

I'm in my tube in the "crib" at Hemlock Grove with my cousins, L to R, front row, me and Marty Fox. Rear row Freddy Bailin and Robby Bailin.

By summer's end, lots of silt from up-stream had floated into the lake. It was easily removed by opening the large twelve inch valve at the bottom of the falls as the lake would need to be drained. When the rainy season ended in late spring, and the sediment was washed away, my grandfather was able to enlarge the crib from year to year. He would hand mix more cement and add scrap pieces of old galvanized pipe or bed springs that acted as reinforcing rods, a common Catskill practice.

Before the big valve was opened, my grandfather would place a large metal screen-like cage in front of the valve. This prevented the fish like Pickerel, Trout, and Sunnies from heading downstream. What a great supper after an easy day's catch! Once it was time to refill the lake, the big valve was closed and it would fill up in just a few days.

Most of the vegetables in the garden had already been picked by the time we were closing up for the season, but before the first frost, there were always some green tomatoes that hadn't ripened yet. My grandmother Celia used them for making her sour tomatoes. Once they were done fermenting, you took a bite out of one of those babies, and they'd kick your butt. Those were truly sour tomatoes!

The acorns and the hickory nuts were starting to drop off the trees that dotted the property along Church Road, and you could hear them falling as they hit the asphalt; a sure sign cold weather was on the way. When I moved into my newly-renovated winterized bungalow after graduating college, I took my cues from the neighborhood squirrels that were collecting those nuts. I started gathering firewood for the long winter ahead, and picked the apples from our orchard to make dried apple slices over the woodstove. We worked hard, knowing the first snow was right around the corner.

Ruby the Knishman was no longer making his amusing announcements. He returned to Brooklyn, followed by the Chow Chow Cup, Dugan's Bakery and all the other great vendors. The bungalow bunnies were gone, and there was hardly any traffic on Route 42. You could go shopping again and not have to wait on any long lines.

Even though I was aware of the beauty of fall in the Catskill's, for me, it was just a time of endings. I never did like the fall even though "we got back the country", but as I grew older I understood and came to appreciate what that meant.

A New Beginning

Before getting into A New Beginning, this would be a good time for a little history lesson on how the wonderful hotel/bungalow era ended.

After World War II, the Catskill Mountains grew at an almost alarming rate. Many of the returning Jewish service men wanted to get out of New York City to escape the summer's heat and to have a safe haven for their children. Thus began a transformation as never before seen in the Catskills. Any building at the Jewish owned farms and homesteads were being converted to rental units for the influx of Jewish clientele. There was no road without a bungalow colony and the number was staggering at about one thousand. Hotels were also growing and numbered about eight hundred at its peak. This was the vacation mecca of the whole country that was spread throughout the Catskill's. All the property owners were experiencing prosperous years.

But that was years ago and those who recently returned to the Catskill Mountains of their youth were quite saddened by the striking change that had occurred. They often ask me, "Where are all the people who used to hang out on Broadway, and what happened to the Playland Arcade in Monticello? Where's Joey Messina's Crossways Restaurant that was next to the 'Falls' in Fallsburg?" And, "What happened to the ..... where I stayed at when I was a kid?" Even the original Concord Hotel site was completely cleared with the dream of a new upscale hotel/spa. For now, all that remains are huge piles of concrete and steel from the demolition of the landmark buildings, and hundreds of concrete footings sticking out of the ground along the landscape where the most famous hotel of the Catskills once stood.

As the next generation of Jews became more affluent they said, "Why do we have to keep going to those nasty old bungalows that our parents vacationed in?" By this time they really had become nasty old bungalows. During the late 60's and 70's, the "regular" clientele of the Borscht Belt slowly stopped coming, and for some started dying.

Some of the major reasons for the demise of the area were the development of the three A's; automobiles, airplanes, and air conditioning. Cars were much more reliable so you could drive longer distances without breaking down as easily, and taking a flight to Europe or California had become more reasonably priced for a great family vacation. And let's not forget Vegas with its established Casinos.

Most of the clientele who had been coming to the mountains came to enjoy the cool fresh air, and to seek relief from the hot sweltering temperatures of the city. But now, all that was needed was an air conditioner to beat the heat. A person could stay in their apartment and remain cool and comfortable. The affluent newer generation of Jewish children started building their own homes in long Island where they enjoyed central air, "*Hoo Ha*" and cooling dips in their private swimming pools. Air conditioning was an amazing invention; the impact on society was huge but it really helped put the final nail in the coffin for the Mountains.

A last critical reason for the decline of the Catskill's was due to the strong Jewish cultural ethic of striving for higher education. The resort owners put their kids through college hoping it would result in an easier life then they had. After their children graduated and became doctors, lawyers, or other professionals, there was no way they were coming home to run the family hotel or bungalow colony. The owners' wishes came to fruition, but it eventually put them out of business, since there was no one left to run their facility. Many of the old hotels and bungalows that dotted the landscape were abandoned and left to decay.

Strangely enough, it became my job 28 years ago to start with the forced removal and clean-up of those dilapidated structures of a sweeter time. They were truly everywhere. Through the efforts of many Code Enforcement Offices in Sullivan County, the tedious job began one building at a time. Ironically, many of the old Catskill relics were removed by having their remains burned by a local fire company as a practice drill, and then a local contractor would bury the remaining debris on site. What an appropriate way to perform *kadish* for what once was.

But there's a new beginning in the Catskill Mountains; a recycling of the older vacation sites. The bungalow days, as we knew them, are over. Only a handful of places are left where a dated, otherwise obsolete unit can still be rented. Many of the affluent Orthodox and Hasidim Jews have bought old bungalow/hotel sites because of their valuable infrastructure of water and sewer. For instance, where the old Shady Nook Hotel once stood in Loch Sheldrake, a "modern bungalow colony" was developed in the mid-eighties called White House Estates. It consists of several clusters of newly constructed duplex units. There was no need to drill new wells and the sewer system only needed some upgrading.

In some instances a developer cleared everything that was left behind of an abandoned summer establishment and built whole new condominium communities. The new housing complexes have their own Synagogues, *Mikvas,* and two swimming pools, one for men and one for women. Each one is surrounded by a *machetza*, which is an indication of the newer sects of Jews who have come to the mountains. Years ago, the sight of a pool enclosure was uncommon, and were cheaply made usually consisting of black plastic sheets. They quickly became eyesores as the plastic ripped and flapped in the breeze. Today, because of all the towns zoning regulations, they're constructed of wood or corrugated metal.

And lets' not forget the day camps for all of the young children, which was a major Catskill draw. Every new development still has one, but many are now located in the lower levels of the shuls. They no longer have them in the old *schlocky* buildings of the past. They have clean tile floors, air-conditioning, and multiple bathrooms. Yes, this is the current trend in towns of Sullivan County, like Fallsburg, Liberty, Bethel, and Thompson. It's a true resurgence of the Jews coming back to the Catskill's but many are investing in their own properties, and they don't have to listen to the colony owner complain why it cost so much to fix this or that.

An old hotel or bungalow colony that was still breathing was occasionally purchased by a Jewish Orthodox or Hasidic group from Brooklyn, and now serves as a summer learning retreat for its students. Some examples are Yeshiva Viznitz in S. Fallsburg, once the Nemerson Hotel or Sherith Haplata that was owned by the Damasek family in Woodbourne. Gradually, many of the older buildings at these sites have been replaced. Antiquated hotel kitchens for example, were torn down and replaced with an upgraded facility that also incorporates an attached well-lit dining room. New dormitories have replaced many of the old main buildings where the students were housed. This transformation occurred mostly when the money became available through donations.

All the new modernized units that have been recently built meet a whole new building standard. The revised New York State Building Code changed the construction practice in the past decade, making those old-style bungalows unlawful to build. There are no more un-insulated, poorly wired, single pane weighted windows, no-foundation "wooden boxes". Where there was once an old hotel or colony, now stand new units ranging from 1400, 1800 to 2000 square feet. Four to six bedrooms have become the norm. Within the units are amenities like double-sink kitchens, two dishwashers, one for meat and one for dairy (for kosher purposes), oak hardwood flooring, and ceramic tile work throughout the bathrooms that would make you *kvel* if you saw them. Interestingly enough, when I ask these new owner/vacationers what draws them to the Catskill Mountains it's no different from the last four generations of Jews: fresh air, trees, openness and the overall beauty of the country. These are the "modern" bungalow colonies, a condominium of 60 to 70 families still enjoying the Catskills, but without having to light their gas stoves on a cold night in August or sealing in the holes around the bathroom shower stall handles with steel wool to keep the mice out. All right, some places still have a mouse appear now and then, but at least the owners aren't sharing their units with "families" of them. No, the bungalow colonies are not what they used to be.

The new clientele come up for Passover and stay for the High Holidays, making the season last much longer. There are also times throughout the winter when the new homeowners visit on weekends knowing they will have enough men for a *minion* in their synagogues. How nice it is to see the lights on in a development from time to time, as compared to the dark, desolate properties of yesteryear.

Another example of what has happened in the Mountains occurred at Hemlock Grove. After many years of struggling to make ends meet, my grandparents were approached by a religious group to ask if they were interested in renting their colony for the summer. Even though it was already rented to mostly family members, it was still a business, and my grandparents had to accept the group's offer since there was a lot more money, almost double, that could be made. It was no easy task. There was a great deal of initial work that had to be completed before reopening, like adding and moving beds for instance. During the summer the grocery store became a huge responsibility with so much more work in ordering food for *shabas* for all the tenants. But at summer's end it paid off.

Even though it worked out quite well, my family members were extremely upset with the situation. When they came up for a weekend visit to stay with my grandparents in the main house, they couldn't cope with seeing the "new crowd" using the place. The *machetza* around the pool, and the restrictions on *shabas* were too much for some of them to handle. This was the place where many of them first learned to swim, played baseball, or first kissed. How could it be overrun with so many kids wearing *yalmakas*? After two years of renting to that group, a unique arrangement unfolded. The family approached my grandparents and asked if they could buy the colony as a co-operative. It was a wonderful concept which allowed the family to "take back" Hemlock Grove from the intruders. The agreement was written amongst ten family members, all becoming share-holders of Hemlock Grove Estates Inc. My grandparents' were given living rights to their unit until they died.

This arrangement worked out to everyone's benefit since maintaining the property had become too much for my grandparents to do alone. We were one of the earliest colonies to form this type of ownership, but since then it has become a trend. Other places like Lansman's in Woodbourne or Skopps in Fallsburg, which were privately owned by the Lansman and Fisher families respectively have become co-ops with many of the new owners having been past renters. The prior tenants wanted a piece of the Catskills to call their own. The old style rental arrangement kept them from improving "their" units. But now that they owned shares in the corporation, they felt confident in spending money on their summer homes. This in turn resulted in an explosion of building activity in some places where owners have constructed bedroom additions, cathedral ceilings in the enlarged kitchens, large decks, and of course personal laundry rooms with shelves and excellent fluorescent lighting. In most cases, the same base bungalow unit was used, but with an extreme makeover inside and out. This is the direction that is taking place in the new Catskill Mountains.

There is also an appeal to year round middle class professionals, who can't afford housing in Rockland or Orange Counties, and who commute to work from Sullivan County. They finally ventured over what some people refer to as "The Mason-Dixon Line," or in other words, the Wurtsboro Hills.

While serving as the Town of Fallsburg Code Enforcement Officer/Building Inspector, I was often asked, "So, when's gambling coming to the Mountains?" I would give them my usual answer, "When I can go into a casino and roll the dice." Casinos have been coming here since the sixties. We were let down over and over, but finally the day has almost arrived for gambling at the Montreign/Adelaar. What a LONG journey that has been! The site is on part of the old Concord Hotel property and construction is running at full speed. The realities of a casino, because of the passage of the state referendum, are making the forty year old dream a reality.

"Tales" is written about the "good times" growing up in the mountains and what a magical place it was to live and visit. In that way, not much has changed. The attraction to the Borscht Belt is still alive and well. The difference between past generations and the current investors is that they have the money to spend.

Are the Catskill Mountains dead? Absolutely not. We're far from it. Now there are attractions such as Bethel Woods-the amazing new outdoor concert venue that was built at the original Woodstock site. There are some incredible performances at that venue throughout the summer season. The Monticello Racetrack has received an infusion with the construction of the Racino. Its Video Gaming has helped improve the attendance of the track. Kutchers Hotel, the last remaining Catskill behemoth was sold and almost completely removed as construction is well underway on what will become a world class health spa. There will always be new ventures brought into the Mountains since this is still a beautiful and diverse area that is only an hour and a half from the city. Just wait and see!

The Schematic

Adonalum .... A traditional Jewish song celebrating the arrival of Shabus.

Balabuster............. A hard working housewife who keeps her house immaculate. The Jewish answer to O.C.D. before the term became popular.

Batesum................. Balls, see chutzpah. They could vary in size depending on the situation.

Beshart................... It's meant to be.

Bimmie.................. Slang word for a guy who worked in a hotel or bungalow colony at the bottom of the food chain, as a clean-up guy, maintenance guy, or schleper like our band's bimmies. See schleper

Bloz............................ To blow, usually from your nose, "Give a little bloz in my tissue darling," or the annoying sound one would make when testing to see if a microphone is on, "phaff, phaff, Testing one two, phaff, phaff."

Bootkey.................. A shed or small garage.

Bookum................. Boys that have had their bar-mitzvah, and are now studying the Torah full time.

Boychick................. A young boy, also referred to as Boychickal, an even younger boy.

Braegus .... Hard or bad feelings. You try to avoid them at all costs, but if you weren't invited to your cousins wedding, Oy Yoy Yoy!

That could start a family crisis! "There's such a bragus between the two of you now, you shouldn't know from."

Brouch Ashem... "Tanks God" (that's with a little accent).

Bubamicea..............An old wives' tale, ie generally bullsh-t. Here's one: You should
never step over a small child, because it will stunt his growth.

Bumbas.................... . A very large Huckleberry. This word may not even be Yiddish,
but was used by my family when the kids went berry picking.
It sounds good doesn't it?

Chulant...................This is the Jewish answer to a good Irish stew or chili. It's
cooked with a good piece of flanken, lots of beans, and pota-
toes. It cooks overnight and when it's done, NASA could use
it for rocket fuel.

Chutzpah ....Gall, Balls

Clopped...........To bang away. Like when your neighbor's kid keeps clopping
on the toy drum his grandmother gave him, and it's giving you
a headache.

cuum, cuum.........Come, come

Faklempt ....Mixed up, dizzy, lost, like the way President Bush would speak
at a press conference.

Fatummeled.........See Faklempt, whichever one you like you can use and get the
same results.

Feh...................Something disagreeable, unpleasant, disgusting. "I had some
brisket at the dinner, feh. It was nothing like my Mom's."

Dovan   Pray, Jewish meditation without the incense.

Dreck ....Garbage, the dredges, Sh-t. It's what politicians always tell us.

Gay avek................Go away, get out of here, take a hike, get lost.

Gay cocken afen yum... Go sh-t in the ocean. I have no idea how that phrase
originated, and I don't know anybody who performed such an
act. I DO know that it's one hell of a derogatory statement to
say to someone.

Gelt...................Money, dough, cash

Gonif......................Thief, One who steals, a conniver. (If I had a picture of Mr. Kesten from "How We Got To Mountaindale", his face would be next to the word).

Goodtah.................The very best, usually referring to food or drink, like ordering Petrone tequila over Curveo, or eating a Mom's knish instead of one of those square imitations.

Goyium............These are non-Jews, Gentiles the non-chosen ones. Sorry guys, that's the facts.

Gribines.................This is rendered chicken fat and onions that made all our grandmothers' dishes taste so good. It has been outlawed, as if it was an illegal narcotic, but can still be purchased on the black market. They are considering making it available for medical purposes. If a patient NEEDS a spike in his cholesterol count, this can do wonders!

Hack.........................Not a Yiddish word, but used exclusively in the Catskills. It was the car service that brought you back and forth to the City. They were usually large limo-type vehicles or a station wagons (now there's a word you don't hear much anymore), with the suitcases always spilling out of the trunks, and strapped to the roofs.

Hain.........................Horseradish. Pronounced with the deep cha sound like when your clearing your throat, Ch- ain. When it's not cut with beet juice is sometimes referred to as "White Lightning". The stronger the better! If it doesn't make your eyes water it's not considered strong enough.

Hoching.............Always bugging or bothering someone
The act of being hochted but in the present moment. Sol's wife wouldn't stop telling him, " I told you not to buy that condo in Wisconsin." This is what kids do quite frequently to their parents!

Handl...............Horse trading, lets' make a deal, Okay, How much do you REALLY want to sell that for?"

Kadish......................Prayer for the dead

Kinderla......................Little kids, the ones that make you smile when you hear them laugh. Not the ones you pray are not going to sit next to you on an airplane!

Kichel........................They taste like dehydrated cream puffs, with nothing inside. Only worse.

Killa'........................Not really Yiddish, but a word used by Jews to describe a hernia. "Be careful when you move the couch. You could get a Killa. Oy Vey poo poo."

Kishka........................Real Jewish soul food. A delicacy made from farfel, carrots, a little chicken fat, and sautéed onions stuffed into the hechzal (throat of a cow). Now doesn't that sound tasty?

Kvetching......................The act of complaining, bitching, or whining. It's a hobby that has been perfected by some Jewish wives.

Kvel........................The envy of something. "I'm just kveling over the ring her husband bought her."

Kuchalaine ....Non-existent today. They were the shared kitchens where the women would have their own small counter space but would have to share the ice box (this is what was available before refrigerators), and the stoves. It really separated the "balabusters" from the slobs.

Launtsman............A fellow Jew who comes from the same district or town in Eastern Europe.

Machetzah.........A swimming pool privacy fence. They used to consist of large black plastic sheets attached to tall posts that became a very cheap method in obtaining the privacy needed at the Jewish colonies. Not long after they were installed, they looked like hell once the wind started ripping them apart. Today, local town laws govern their appearance because they were truly a Catskill eyesore.

Machaya ....A delightful experience, like a bowl of Ben and Jerry's ice cream on a hot day. Or the feeling you get when you walk into a "schvitz" on a cold day. (See schvitz).

Macha ....Big shot. The big kahuna! The Big Cheese!

Mensch . A very good man. The guy who pulls over to help you with a flat tire. (The guy who drives by and waves is NOT).

Menschlachite- ...Something very good, to live like a King, very respectable.

Minyan… ....10 Jewish men, number needed for a proper Jewish prayer ceremony. The only requirement is that they have to be breathing.

Micelas   ....Plural for mouse, and they always move in with their families, and never pay rent! Mice, the dreaded Catskill Mountain home wreckers.

Mikvah...................Religious bath house that has no regulation from the Department of Health, so can you imagine?

Moel........................His specialty is performing a circumcision. He works for tips. (Now that's an old Borscht Belt joke). Hopefully he's not that old so his hands don't shake too much! He learned his trade by slicing the Challah on Friday nights.

Nosh........................A little bit to eat, like a nibble. But it's usually a lot more like when your attending a bar-mitzvah and you say, "I'm just gonna have a nosh", which is impossible with all the free food that's in your face.

Oy.............................An exclamation usually said in a negative context like, "Oy, I can't believe they're not serving lox." A weary sigh sometimes made by older people when getting up from a chair. It may be followed by "Vey" to add emphasis. "Oy Vey, do my feet hurt!"

Plotz .... Fall over, not when you trip on the sidewalk, but more like when you got your kid's first cell phone bill and they used to much data, or falling on the floor from laughter. It could also mean drop dead!

Pesach .... Passover. The no bagel, no challah, no rye bread all matzo holiday.

Pish .... Urinate, as spoken in Yiddish dialect, "Go make a pish darling". You wouldn't use it to describe the bum you saw taking a leak in an alleyway.

Saltz .... Salt

Schlep .... A guy who dresses like a bum and drags himself as he walks. It's also the act of moving stuff.

Schlepper .... One who carries and moves stuff around. (I've been actually cursed my whole life with being a schlepper). A carrier, not like DHL, more like a Haitian carry a basket on their head or like Louie's Cadillac.

Schav .... Sour grass, cheap version of borscht, bitter to the taste, yuck!

Schlock .... Crap, garbage, something cheap, a step or two above dreck.

Schlocky .... A taste of schlock, Trashy. Not to be confused with dreck

Schtick .... Habits, routines. The Catskill comedians each had their own schtick.

Schmutz .... Dirt, filth, the stuff a kid gets on his face and his mom licks her finger to remove it.

Schmooze .... To have a conversation, what's done in Shul every Saturday after services, and sometimes, during!

Schpelkis .... While growing up, our parents would say, "That kid has ants in his pants." Today they gave it a fancy, schmancy name, A.D.D.

Schtockers .... Big shots, see Macha

Schvitz .... The steam bath in a hotel, or just sweating like after gulping down two bowls of hot matzah ball soup

Shabbos .... The holy Jewish Sabbath, Friday night thru Saturday night. No work and all pray.

Shonda.....................A sin that can vary in degree.

Shul..................Synagogue. The place where all Jews go to find out what they need to know about someone else. And boy do they want you to become a member.

SoftigAn ....abundantly proportioned woman.

Succa.......................Religious "hut" used on the holiday of Succot unregulated by the building code, so anything goes.

Tefilin ....Small black leather prayer boxes, one goes on the arm and the other on the head each containing scrolls with verses of the Torah. They are put on every day except Shabbos.

Ribeisen ....A dangerous kitchen tool used for slicing or grating. If you're not careful you could slice your finger off. Ok, maybe just a little skin. The original "Kitchen Magician" used by Jewish Mothers to grate a potato for latkis (a heavily fried pancake. Now there's a surprise?) Also used to finely slice an onion. The resulting tears remind her of how she always cries that her children never visit her.

Tzoris........................Problems, aggravation, like when you have a report due and your computer crashes.

Tuchas ....Ass, butt cheeks, similar too "Hey, check out that piece of ass!" Can also be used derogatorily, "He's such a pain in the tuchas."

Tummel   Lots of commotion, a lot of noise, activity. Like late summer afternoons at Levi Gumbo's bakery in South Fallsburg before Shabbos.

Voz is doos, bist fill mit dreck! ......"What is this? You're covered with sh-t! " (That's when you're having a really bad day).

Yalmaka A ....skull cap worn by Jewish males out of respect for God. Not like Spanky's of the Little Rascals. His had a propeller.

Zolsta voxum vee a zibala mit in cup in drear un feese a roof....... You should grow like an onion with your head in the ground and your feet in the air! Now that's one crazy Yiddish put down.

Accounts Recievable

I would like to thank all of the businesses, bungalow colonies, and hotel owners who hired Hy Frishman Plumbing & Heating, Frishman's Bottled Gas, Monticello Bendix Repair, Frishman Brothers Contracting, and of course all those who hired my rock & roll bands: The Predominant Four, The New Generation, Whale, Xanadu, and jug band, Chicken Lips, throughout the last 65 years. Without you, there'd be no tales to tell. I salute you all.

Abe Wand Butcher - Jefferson Street, Monticello
Andersons - Old Liberty Road, Monticello
April's Bungalows - Dillion Road, Monticello
The Bel-Air Resort - Glen Spey
Blocks Garage - Broadway and Park Avenue, Monticello
Bramble Brae - Glen Spey
Camelot Woods - Sacket Lake
Camp Hamilton - Hamilton Road, Monticello
Camp Kinnebrook - Camp Road, Monticello
Camp Pythian - Glen Spey
Capital Inn - Downs Road, Monticello
Charlou Restaurant - Broadway, Monticello
Clearview Country Club - Old Liberty Road, Monticello
Colony Club - Route 42, Monticello
Colony Park - Route 42, Monticello

The Columbia Hotel - Hurleyville

The Concord Hotel - Kiamesha

Country Meadows (Sunken Meadows) - Dillion Road, Monticello

Country Park Cottages (Forman's) - New Road, Mountaindale

The Country Squire Barber Shop - Broadway, Monticello

The Delano Hotel - Old Liberty Road, Monticello

Deutsch's Mountainview - Old Liberty Road, Monticello

Doctor Lockers - New Road, Mountaindale

Ehrenreich's Play Rest Hotel - Loch Sheldrake

Elm Shade - Route 42, South Fallsburg

Fialkoff's - Broadway and Waverly Avenue, Monticello

Feits, (Pardes) - Old Liberty Road, Monticello

Fountainlou – Broadway, Monticello

Furman's Corners - Route 55, Swan Lake

Friendship Cottages - LaVista Drive, South Fallsburg

Grand Park - Fraser Road, Monticello

Grand Mountain Hotel - Greenfield Park

Greenwood Park - Route 42, South Fallsburg

Greentree Village- Harris

Grossmans - Pleasant Valley Road, South Fallsburg

Hemlock Grove (Camp David) - Church Road, Mountaindale

Hollywood Bungalows - Cold Spring Road, Monticello

Homowack Hotel - Spring Glen

Ideal Bungalows - Route 42, Monticello

Irwin Seigel Agency- Lake Louise Marie Road, Rock Hill

Kasimows - Old Libety Road, Monticello

Kings - Otisville

Krauss (Har-Nof) - Route 42, Kiamesha

Kurts Cottages - Route 17 B, White Lake

Kirks Cottages - Lt. Brender Highway, Swan Lake.

Kutchers Country Club - Kutchers Road, Monticello

The Latern - Broadway, Monticello

Lashinsky's Butcher - Broadway, Monticello

Lefty's - Route 42, Monticello

Lewinters - Route 42, Monticello

Lorraine Bungalows - Mountaindale Road, Mountaindale

Moonlight Cottages - Rubin Road, Monticello

Nob Hill - Route 42, Kiamesha

Overlook - West Broadway, Monticello

Paramount Hotel - Cooley Road, Parksville

Pine Knoll - Route 42, Monticello

The Pines Hotel - Laurel Avenue, South Fallsburg

Pine Tree - Route 42, Monticello

Pussy Cat Lounge (across from the Concord Hotel) Kiamesha

Quickway Metals/Fountain Pools - Broadway, Monticello

Ralph Lauren, (Yes, the famous clothes designer. Okay it was his parents the Lipshitz's, but he paid the bill!), Pleasant View Avenue, Monticello

I&R Bungalows (Ruth's) - Thompsonville Road, Kiamesha

Ramat Gan - Ulster Heights

Ryke Inn - Concord Road, Monticello

Sadownicks (Rose Cottages) - Old Liberty Road, Monticello

Selkowitz - Old Liberty Road, Monticello

Silberts - Anawana Road, Monticello

Sims (Countryside Acres) - Old Liberty Road, Monticello

Slaters - Cold Spring Road, Monticello

Slatkins - Hamilton Road, Monticello

Spectors Pharmacy - Broadway, Monticello

Sun Valley - Route 42, Monticello

Sunny Oaks - River Road, Woodridge

Sun Ray - La Vista Drive, South Fallsburg

Tara Acres - Old Liberty Road, Monticello

Town & Country - Route 42 Monticello

Utopia Villa (Became part of Ideal) - Route 42, Monticello
Village Park (Community Cottages) - River Road, Woodridge
White Rock - South Woods Drive, Monticello

And there's probably a few more that my family and I can't remember any longer. Thanks again, kids!

The Plumber's, Apprentices, Journeymen & Mechanics

It took eleven years, ok, I'm up to twelve, of hard work and a great deal of help in writing this book. I wish I had kept up with my high school typing class, but because of my laziness I need to thank the following typists and of course several editors who struggled in reading all my chicken scratches, arrows and constant changes and corrections.

MECHANICS/ APPRENTICES:

Jean Catania	My first typist, I promised you Jean that your name would be listed in the book. I hope someone tells you it's finally finished.
Paige Bakken	Re-typed several stories in my old office in our down time.
Ginny Tolli	She produced my first real document from tons of scribbled notes and rough drafts. Now that was a real chore!
Susan Cioffi	My first editor many moon ago.
Eve Mauri Cropsey	Great typist and windows expert, at least in my eyes!

Denise Monforte	The last typist who helped me before I learned how to finally type.
Marilyn Laufer	Not only did she read, review and edit the entire book with me (before the final, final edit), as a result of her time and effort, I have become a better writer. What a great teacher and good friend. Okay, Marilyn, I still need a little help with punctuation. Those semicolons kill me.
Saraid Gonzalez	After a 1 year slump, she not only pushed me to get going again, she reformatted the book and kept telling me I had to finish. She is the most amazing document engineer, organizer (secretary), I have ever met. Hands down!
Shantal Riley	Being a newspaper journalist, she said," Let me work on a story or two for you." My final outside editor, fantastic belly dancer and good friend.
Lynn Neidorf	Thanks Lynn for taking a last minute look and helping me out.
Ellyane Hutchinson	My first photographer. We worked on some interesting concepts, but I'm saving those for the next book.
Jasmine Guara	Photographer of the cover photo and helped immensely with its design concept. www.ishotstudios.com
Lorrie Blank-Frishman	My incredibly, patient wife who endured so many hours of listening to me reading my stories over and over again

till I got them right. When I told her, "Honey it's ready to go," she said, "Let me take one last crack at it. You're a great story teller, but your English, eh." We spent every Saturday this past winter re-editing the book all day long, sitting by the wood stove and watching it snow. She truly helped by putting the icing on the cake, even though it's her mother who's the fantastic baker. I can't thank her enough. Alright, I'll clean the house a little bit more.

Best Buys | Thanks for giving me a great deal on my first laptop so I could finally have all the stories and notes in one place. What a major breakthrough THAT was.

JOURNEYMAN:

Raymond Eloza | Computer technical research department, and he just loves reading all my stories.

Richard (Ricky) Harris | Early inspirational input, and continuous support of the project. He just wouldn't die till the book was completely finished. He's a three time cancer survivor.

Beth Smile | She never gave up on me. Her memories of the Catskill Mountains helped push me along. Look for her book next year.

Louis Harrison | Thanks Louis for getting me to Home Plate. Without your knowledge this wouldn't have happened, period.

John Conway | Sullivan County Historian, friend and inspirational guru.

Irwin Richmond,
Phil Brown | Founders of the Catskill Institute, authors of Catskill Mountain books, and early motivators. "I told you, Irwin, it was a very early draft; you didn't have to do any editing. Phil, I bet you thought I'd never finish! Sometimes I didn't, either."

MASTER PLUMBERS:

These are friends & family members that helped to contribute some of the great tales and facts that are in the book.

Hy & Irene Frishman | My mom and dad, *Brouch Ashem*. God Bless them both for remembering so many family tales. There were both old classics and some that I had never heard until we sat down at the kitchen table for hours in Delray Beach.

Melvin Bailin | "Mad Cow"

Robert Bailin | Portions of "Mendels Mansion"

Paul Friedman | "The $400.00 Bathtub"

Steve Frishman | "Always On Empty"

Alvin Adler, Engineer | "Hey, Where'd That Bungalow go?" Part one

Jerry Weiss, Jack Degraw, Leon Lashinsky, Harold Gold | "Jerry Weiss and Other Characters of the Catskills"

Ted Drew, Florence Balch,   "To Day Camp…We're marching one by one"
David Herskowitz, Mike Gaswirth,
Sally Israel Masskarsky, & Eve Minson

Steve and Eddie Jacobs   "Hey, Where'd That Bungalow Go? " Part two.

Helen Harris   Family Historian and invaluable source of factual
                            context

So that's it. If I forgot someone, please, no *braegus*. I'll get you in my next book,
Catskill Chakiss & Schmalatz.

Biography

The author Allen Frishman, is 65 years old, and grew up in a family of plumbers with direct ties to the bungalow industry. As a child, Catskill life was going to day camp and much more. His family, on both sides owned two very different bungalow colonies, Hemlock Grove in Mountaindale and Sadownick's in Monticello. Allen lived in the Catskills for most of his life having witnessed the great times, the decline, and the new beginnings that are happening once again in the land of milk and honey. Okay forget the honey, make it Borscht. Performing in some of the big hotels like Kutchers, the Pines, and of course lots of bungalow colonies with his teen band "The New Generation" made for great times growing up Catskills. Allen has an extensive collection of Catskill memorabilia which has been displayed in various museum's around the country. The latest project he's co- partnered with is the creation of a Catskill Bungalow Museum where many of his rescued classic items would be displayed and enjoyed. His introduction to comedy came early in life having grown up listening to Mickey Katz, the Yiddish comedic singer and Spike Jones under his Dad's influence. When the extended family gathered it was always with fun, laughter, and great Jewish food. What else is there? Allen resides in Mountaindale, N.Y. in his museum-like home. You can reach Allen via e-mail: mtdaleboy@gmail.com. If you need to order a book or schedule a tour call him at 845-436-8945.

Made in the USA
Middletown, DE
15 July 2024

57359767R00149